Editing Historical Documents

Editing Historical Documents

A Handbook of Practice

Michael E. Stevens
Steven B. Burg

ALTAMIRA
P R E S S

A Division of Sage Publications, Inc.
Walnut Creek ■ London ■ New Delhi

Published in cooperation with the American Association for
State and Local History, the Association for Documentary Editing,
and the State Historical Society of Wisconsin.

For information contact:

AltaMira Press
A Division of Sage Publications, Inc.
1630 North Main Street, Suite 367
Walnut Creek, California 94596 U.S.A.

Sage Publications Ltd.
6 Bonhill Street
London EC2A 4PU United Kingdom

Sage Publications India Pvt. Ltd.
M-32 Market
Greater Kailash 1
New Delhi 110 04S India

Printed in the United States of America

Library of Congress Cataloging-in-Publication Data

Stevens, Michael E.
    Editing historical documents: a handbook of practice / by Michael E. Stevens
    and Steven B. Burg
        p. cm. — (American Association for State and Local History book series)
    Published in cooperation with the American Association for State
    and Local History, the Association for Documentary Editing, and the
    State Historical Society of Wisconsin.
    Includes bibliographical references and index.
    ISBN 0-7619-8959-5. — ISBN 0-7619-8960-9 (pbk.)
        1. Editing—Handbooks, manuals, etc. 2. Manuscripts—Editing—
    Handbooks, manuals, etc. 3. History—Sources—Publishing—Handbooks,
    manuals, etc. I. Stevens, Michael E. II. American Association for State and
    Local History. III. State Historical Society of Wisconsin. IV. Title. V. Series.
    PN162.B79 1997
    808'.027—dc21   97-21155
                                                                 CIP   .

97 98 99 10 9 8 7 6 5 4 3 2 1

Cover Design by Joanna Ebenstein
Interior Design and Production by Labrecque Publishing Services
Editorial Management by Erik Hanson

Contents

About the Authors

MICHAEL E. STEVENS is State Historian at the State Historical Society of Wisconsin and holds a Ph.D. in history from the University of Wisconsin–Madison. He is the former director of publications at the South Carolina Department of Archives and History and has edited ten volumes of historical documents, including *The State Records of South Carolina* series, the *Voices of the Wisconsin Past* series, *The Family Letters of Victor and Meta Berger, 1894–1929*, and *As If It Were Glory: Robert Beecham's Civil War, from the Iron Brigade to the Black Regiments*.

STEVEN B. BURG holds degrees from Colgate University and the University of Wisconsin–Madison, where he is a doctoral candidate in United States history. He currently is an editor at the State Historical Society of Wisconsin, where he is working on the *Voices of the Wisconsin Past* series.

Preface

The publication of historical documents has a long and venerable tradition in the United States. In 1792 the Massachusetts Historical Society became the first state historical organization to publish historical documents when it issued the initial volume of its venerable *Collections* series. Since that time, scholars, historical societies, and interested individuals have increasingly made the record of our past more accessible through their efforts. The past half century in particular has seen a flowering of historical editing in which some of the most essential records of our nation's past have become more widely accessible through the publication of modern editions. This handbook of practice draws on the work of the past two generations of documentary editors and provides guidance for anyone planning to publish historical documents in a book edition, magazine article, pamphlet, or microform, or on CD-ROM or the World Wide Web.

Although historical editors have produced a remarkable body of work, they have been reticent about codifying their practices. Prior to the early 1980s, prospective editors had relatively few sources to guide them as they began their work, although Samuel Eliot Morison provided ten pages on documentary editing in Oscar Handlin et al., Harvard Guide to American History (Cambridge, Mass.: Belknap Press of Harvard University Press, 1954), and Clarence Carter, in his 1952 Historical Editing (Bulletin of the National Archives, no. 7), offered a concise summary of the state of the art. With the formation of the Association for Documentary Editing (ADE) in November 1978, systematic literature on the methods of documentary editing began to appear in greater quantity.

In recent years, those who sought guidance on how to edit historical documents could follow one of several avenues. By 1984, the *Newsletter of the Association for Documentary Editing* had evolved into *Documentary Editing,* a quarterly that provided a venue for articles on editorial techniques as well as lengthy reviews of editions that examined methodological issues. Useful guidance could also be found in periodical literature outside of *Documentary Editing,* and the publication of Beth Luey's *Editing Documents and Texts: An Annotated Bibliography* (Madison, Wis.: Madison House, 1990) brought together abstracts of the growing body of literature. Although helpful, periodical literature, scattered in various locations, did not offer new editors a unified summary of the current state of practice. The publication of *A Guide to Documentary Editing,* by Mary-Jo Kline (Baltimore: Johns Hopkins University Press, 1987), helped remedy this problem by gathering together advice for editors. The *Guide* grew out of a proposal made in Arthur Link's 1979 ADE presidential address, in which he called for a manual for editors. Because of the varied approaches used, the manual evolved into a guide, summarizing current editorial theory and raising important questions for editors to consider. The Kline *Guide* helped editors steer clear of the shoals of bad practice and will appear in a revised second edition in 1997.

While the *Guide* provided a superstructure, editors still find themselves thumbing through already published documentary editions looking for models to emulate. Whereas the *Guide* provides both theory and the rationale for it, this handbook brings together samples of ways that editors have resolved different problems. By examining these solutions, editors can see both the range of choices and their practical implications. Some editors will undoubtedly still delve further into particular editions that match their concerns, but they can do so with the advantage of having seen various techniques compiled in a way that permits easy comparison.

At its heart, documentary editing is a form of translation, converting original documents into readable text. And like all good translation, it is part craft and part art. The art cannot be taught, but the examples provided here can teach the craft. Editors still must evaluate their documents, learn general principles of documentary editing, and consider the needs of their audience before beginning their projects, although they do not need to reinvent the wheel. By examining the choices made by other editors, beginners will be better informed and enabled to make their own decisions. This volume is aimed both at more experienced editors, who may wish to skip over the advice offered in the introduction, as well as at those who are new to the craft and want to know how to begin work on publishing historical documents of interest to them.

Compiling a work such as this one has forced us to make hundreds of choices, and we found ourselves frequently second-guessing ourselves. At the beginning, we set out several principles to which we tried to adhere. First, as indicated in the title, this handbook deals with the publication of historical documents. While we have drawn some of our examples from the works of literary figures such as Thoreau and Twain, most of the examples are chosen from what are conventionally known as historical editions, since literary editors have developed many of their own conventions.

We also agreed that this handbook should be descriptive rather than prescriptive, although we have tried to be firm on issues where a professional consensus exists. For instance, there are many ways to present the text of a document, ranging from heavily emended to absolutely literal. No matter what editorial method editors use, however, we believe that they have an obligation to explain how they have treated the text. We have stated these requirements clearly and presented samples of how editors have met them.

We also noted that the nature of new editorial projects has changed considerably since the formation of the ADE, the publication of the first edition of the Kline *Guide,* and the establishment in 1972 of the National Historical Publications and Records Commission's Institute for the Editing of Historical Documents. Many new editors plan to work on short-term projects, often a one-volume or even article-length work. Thus, we have consciously tried to meet the needs of those for whom documentary editing will be a brief part of their professional lives as well as of editors who work on long-term projects. We hope that individuals who work in local and state historical societies and museums as well as staff at colleges and universities will find this guide useful in their efforts. We have consciously selected a large proportion of our examples from book editions and multivolume series that are likely to have national distribution on the theory that readers who find these examples particularly helpful will be able to consult the complete works in a library in their region. Although the examples come from larger editions, the techniques developed by editors of these projects can be applied to smaller undertakings with equal success.

In a work of this sort, endless debate could occur (and at times it did) over the choice of examples. We chose the examples reproduced here because they illustrate a particular decision in a clear and concise fashion. They do not represent an anthology of preferred practice (something that would have been impossible to do, in any case, because of the diversity of methods), although we have also tried not to select examples that seemed to represent dubious practice. We reviewed our choices with the project's advisory committee; however, we assume the ultimate responsibility for what is included.

Does the handbook make judgments about what to include? Of course it does. Editors make hundreds of choices, and it would have been impossible to include an illustration of every possible option. We have tried to identify the most significant problems and show how editors have resolved them. Will the examples we have chosen stand the test of time? We hope not. As documentary editors develop new ways of handling texts, especially with electronic publishing, new editorial conventions and models will evolve. The publication of historical documents is nearly as old as civilization itself, yet editors continue to struggle to prepare better and more accurate texts. We hope we have contributed to that tradition.

* * *

As every practicing editor knows, decisions about an edition are not necessarily made in the order in which the reader encounters the finished product. Problems have a way of forcing choices at any time, especially when dealing with idiosyncratic documents. Nonetheless, this handbook divides the examples into chapters, each dealing with different questions in the order in which one normally encounters them. The book opens with an introduction, offering general advice on how to begin the work of editing historical documents. We have organized the main body of the text into chapters subdivided into topical sections and numbered subsections. While those planning an edition or learning the practice of documentary editing may want to read this handbook cover to cover, others may wish to use the handbook as a reference guide to examine how editors have dealt with a particular issue of interest.

Chapter 1 discusses the fundamental questions of purpose and audience faced by any editor. It covers questions of comprehensiveness and how far an editor will search for documents, as well as issues related to the form of publication. With these fundamental issues settled, Chapter 2 deals with questions about selection and arrangement. It includes examples in which the rationale for inclusion of documents is spelled out, a discussion of the order in which documents are printed, and examples of alternatives to the full printing of all documents.

The longest section of the book, Chapters 3 through 5, examines transcription, or how editors present documents to their readers. Some of the thorniest issues relating to preparing editions are found in these chapters. Chapter 3 looks at different modes of transcription in general, Chapter 4 deals with the kinds of sources used by editors and the challenges they pose, and Chapter 5 discusses some of the specific problems that editors encounter.

Once the presentation of the text is fixed, editors still need to explain and provide access to the documents. Chapters 6 and 7 show how editors have used annotations to explain the provenance of the documents and help readers better understand the text. Chapter 6 introduces some of the general categories of annotation, while Chapter 7 provides examples of typical forms. Chapter 8 deals with systems of access and indexing. Chapter 9 covers the various kinds of front and back matter, illustrations, and addenda that have helped make editions more accessible.

We have included examples from both book- and article-length editions in our discussion. Where pertinent, we have also brought in examples from microform editions. Electronic editions are so new that we have used only a few examples, although we expect that these editions will soon modify some of the print-based conventions and that their creators will help develop standards suitable for that medium. When we have omitted a passage in the middle of an example, we have marked the deletion with four asterisks. The facsimiles usually do not reproduce full documents, but only present the portion necessary to explain the matter under discussion. A complete listing of works cited, together with their short titles (used to identify the excerpts reproduced herein), appears at the back of the volume.

*   *   *

We greatly appreciate the efforts of many individuals who helped with this project. Nancy Sahli, formerly program director at the National Historical Publications and Records Commission, helped develop the idea for this volume in a series of conversations. An advisory committee helped plan the project and reviewed successive drafts. Their thoughts and sound judgments proved essential to our work. The members include Jeffrey J. Crow, director of the North Carolina Division of Archives and History; Ann D. Gordon, editor of the *Papers of Elizabeth Cady Stanton and Susan B. Anthony* at Rutgers University; John P. Kaminski, editor of the *Documentary History of the Ratification of the Constitution* at the University of Wisconsin–Madison; Martha J. King, assistant editor of the *Nathanael Greene Papers* at the Rhode Island Historical Society; and Leslie S. Rowland, editor of *Freedom: A Documentary History of Emancipation, 1861–1867* at the University of Maryland. Beth Luey of Arizona State University also provided suggestions in a number of conversations about this book. Ellen Goldlust-Gingrich did some of the initial conceptual research for the project as well as initial copyediting of the manuscript. Kari Benson, Eric Daniels, Kristen Foster, and Ted Frantz provided research assistance. Judy Patenaude, with the aid of Bobbi Couillard and Phoebe Hefko, prepared the scans used to produce this volume. The authors are grateful to the National Historical Publications and Records Commission for its financial assistance for this project. Finally, we appreciate the generosity of the various publishers and copyright holders who granted permission to reproduce the examples found here. A complete list of the sources we used appears at the rear of this volume.

Introduction

At a recent gathering, a historian spoke about the continued appeal of the Smithsonian's National Air and Space Museum. Although decidedly low-tech in contrast to recreational theme parks, it continues to draw immense crowds. The museum features no rides and has no costumed interpreters to entertain visitors, yet its collections seem to enthrall both children and adults. His explanation of the museum's appeal was brief and to the point: "People want the real thing."

As presented in textbooks, history can range from the interesting to the dull, but in every case the story has been already digested and presented by an all-knowing narrator. Events and movements have beginning and ending points. Textbooks serve an important function: They provide a valuable road map to the subject, but they are no substitute for a trip down the road itself.

The authentic words of men and women from the past offer a way to experience the real thing. Historical documents, carefully selected, clearly explained, and presented in a readable format, provide an immediacy not otherwise found in conventional narratives. Reading the words of men and women who do not know how their own particular lives will play out helps avoid the sense of inevitability found in many history books. First-person historical accounts are equally powerful when ordinary men and women tell their own stories—versions that do not usually make it into the history books. They reinforce the idea that history belongs not just to politicians, generals, or doers of great deeds. The publication of historical documents, or documentary editing, is an effective way of making history vivid.

Documentary editing is practiced in diverse settings and fashions. It can range from the publication of a multivolume edition of a president's papers prepared by a staff of a half dozen scholars to documents that appear in a newsletter produced on a personal computer by an all-volunteer historical society. The usefulness of published historical documents depends not on the format or the budget but rather on the care with which the documents are presented to the potential audience.

Historical documents have been published for many reasons. Prior to the development of microfilm and microfiche, they were printed as a means of preservation. Thomas Jefferson urged the publication of documents, calling on citizens to save the historical record, "not by vaults and locks which fence them from the public eye and use, in consigning them to the waste of time, but by such multiplication of copies, as shall place them beyond the reach of accident." The development of micrographics and improved archival storage conditions have reduced the need to publish documents for their preservation, although publication still may be the only means to ensure the preservation of some documents in private hands. Jefferson's call for a "multiplication of copies" still is a valid goal for those who wish to make historical records accessible. Documents no longer may be fenced "from the public eye and use" in modern archives, yet only the few who have the time and funds to travel can view these materials. Publishing documents in a book, magazine, or newsletter can make these pieces of living history easily available to the general public who may enjoy history, but are unable to use the originals themselves. Printed collections of historical documents also can bring together in a single volume material that has been dispersed in different manuscript collections around the world. Published documents can further serve as an effective means of telling a story without the intervention of a historian's narrative.

So how do you as a prospective editor go about editing and publishing historical documents? Any editing project, no matter the size, begins with an idea. Often someone encounters documents that are simply too good to leave hidden in an archive. Whether this initial enthusiasm turns into a publication usually depends on how well the effort is planned, a theme that will be emphasized repeatedly in this handbook. Whether you find the documents at a state or local historical society, in a university research library, or in private hands, you still have to decide what portion of the documents will be published, for what reason, how they will appear, and who you think will want to read them. Documentary editing requires consistent and careful execution that offers the reader confidence in the reliability of the printed text. Planning the enterprise, stating the plan clearly, and then implementing the plan with consistency are the fundamentals of documentary editing, regardless of whether the project is a multivolume book edition or a 500-word article for a weekly newspaper.

Planning your project's scope, even in an informal way, helps ensure that you complete it in a timely fashion. For instance, suppose you find a set of letters from a community's founder covering the era 1850 to 1890. Will you publish the letters from this entire time period in order to document the development of the region? Or perhaps the Civil War letters are the most interesting; maybe you should publish just those. On further searching, you find that there are surviving Civil War letters from others who lived in the same township. Maybe grouping the letters together will offer a more interesting perspective. Will you publish letters written to your subjects? What if some of your letter writers kept diaries; will you publish them with the letters? Thinking carefully about your project will help avoid defining its scope too narrowly or too broadly.

You should also consider where you will find the documents for your project. Are they all located in a single collection, or will you have to check other archives and libraries to see whether they hold similar materials? If you want to publish both sides of correspondence, you may have to look in several locations, unless the heirs of each letter writer donated their ancestors' correspondence to the same institution. From the start, you will need to decide how hard you are willing to look for documents for your publication.

Before proceeding too far, you should determine whether the documents are protected by copyright and who holds it. Copyright of unpublished documents is a complex issue, and legislation governing it continues to be revised. As a general rule, it is good to remember that copyright does not reside in the owner of the document but rather in the writer and the writer's heirs. Thus, if Mary sends John a letter and his heirs donate it to a local historical society, Mary's heirs still own the copyright to the words written on the document. It is the editor's responsibility to obtain permission to publish the materials.

You should also identify your audience. Who will find your publication most useful? Will the documents appeal primarily to specialist historians or to a more general audience of history enthusiasts? Will it be of greatest use as classroom supplemental material? Or will the primary audience be the members of an organization, for instance a church that is celebrating its anniversary? What format works best for your audience? Even in this electronic era, books still remain an effective method of presenting information and serve multiple audiences. If book publication is not feasible, there are other ways of presenting historical texts that may be more within the means of an individual or a small historical society. A single letter, a few related documents, or excerpts from a diary may be best suited for publication in a magazine, a journal, or an organization's newsletter. A pamphlet could also be an excellent way to produce a small group of documents. For instance, a collection of letters related to a historic structure might be gathered in a pamphlet or printed on a poster and sold in a site's gift shop. Publication of documents in a newspaper can reach a wide audience and publicize a collection or organization. Microforms might be the preferred method for large collections of material aimed at specialists. Electronic technologies, such as CD-ROM and the World Wide Web, offer additional possibilities for publication of documents that have not yet been fully explored. Chapter 1 offers suggestions for planning your project.

You will also need to decide very early in your project how many documents you want to publish. There are very few historical figures whose every word ought to be put in print. If you have a ten-year run of correspondence, do you need to publish every letter? While your role as editor is not to censor the past, you will also need to make sure that your readers are not bored or fatigued by it. At the same time, you should determine in what order the documents to be published will be arranged. Many editions publish documents in chronological order because it allows readers to see an unfolding story, but there are other equally valid approaches. Perhaps a story can be told better by arranging the documents topically or by geographic location. Perhaps it would be better to separate documents by their form; for instance, you might publish an individual's diary separately from her letters even though the dates overlap. Chapter 2 illustrates how other editors have dealt with problems of selection and arrangement of documents.

You should put in writing the initial decisions you make about selecting, arranging, and presenting your documents. As you begin your work, you may find yourself changing your mind. New documents, suggestions from a prospective publisher, and insights from working with the documents themselves may lead you to revise your original ideas. Your written plan, which can be very informal for small projects, should be updated and revised as you make changes. When you write the preface or introduction to the documents (which is often the last thing that is written), tell your readers what you have done and why. You will find that your notes about your decisions along the way will ease the process, since you will not have to reconstruct them from memory.

Whether you are working on a large or a small project, you probably will want to make photocopies of the original documents. Although ideally you would like to consult the original manuscripts, photocopies permit you to mark up the manuscript and eliminate concern over the security of the original. If you do make copies, you will need to identify each of them with the source of the original so that you could locate it again, and also to include it in your citations. For larger projects you will have to identify collections to be searched, copy the materials within scope, and set up filing and retrieval systems. A small project with only a few documents does not require a complex filing system. Whatever system you use should be suited for the material at hand.

After gathering the documents and making preliminary decisions about what will be published, you finally can get down to the business of preparing the text. Your initial step is to accurately record the text or to transcribe it. Some might suggest, "just copy it down right," yet establishing an accurate text is not as simple and straightforward as it might seem. Mistakes in transcription will cast doubts on the reliability of the publication. Many early editions have been redone because of inaccurate transcriptions, and careers of some distinguished historians have been tarnished or destroyed as a result of transcription problems. Jared Sparks's mid-nineteenth-century edition of the writings of George Washington received public criticism during his own lifetime because of the unreliability of the texts. Worthington Ford's career at the Massachusetts Historical Society came to an end in 1928 when the Society decided that it had to recall and republish the first volume of the *Winthrop Papers* because of the severity of transcription errors.

Transcription is akin to translation, for no editor can take a document and convert it into another form without somehow changing it. Chapters 3, 4, and 5 outline the many decisions you will face in presenting the text. Just as you planned what you will publish, you will make many decisions about how you will present the text, and you should record these in writing. You will have to decide if and how you want to standardize the form of the document. For example, where will you place datelines, how will you indent irregularly spaced paragraphs, how will you represent signatures? Will you standardize the placement of salutations or complimentary closings? By making the presentation of documents consistent within your work, you can help the reader locate important information and can avoid the difficulty and expense of reproducing the irregular physical layout of many documents.

You will also be faced with decisions concerning what changes or "emendations" you will make in translating a handwritten or typed document into print. Some editors make few changes, presenting a near-literal transcription of the text, while others modernize the text to make it easier to read. Most editors make choices that place them on a spectrum between these two options. For instance, should the first word of each sentence be capitalized? How do you represent forms of punctuation such as the thorn (a letter that looks like a "y" but is pronounced "th" as in "ye" for "the") that are no longer in use? Should you correct obvious slips of the pen (for instance an author who writes "slips of the the pen")? Should you supply missing punctuation at the end of sentences, spell out unusual abbreviations, or correct misspellings? How will you handle superscripts, subscripts, canceled passages, interlineations, marginalia, drawings, and other marks that are very clear in a handwritten document, but that require decisions on your part as editor?

As you adopt a set of editorial principles, you will need to consider how those changes may affect the information contained in the documents and how best to present them to your primary audience. There is no single agreed-on method of transcription. Editors use different methods, often choosing from among five major forms presented in Chapter 3, to find a style that best suits the needs of their audiences, the purposes of their editions, and their personal preferences.

After entering the text of the document in your word processor and checking to make sure that it conforms to the style you have selected, you will want to verify the accuracy of your transcription through careful proofreading. (Spelling checkers and grammar checkers are of limited use to documentary editors who want to present an accurate text.) In proofreading you will—alone or with an assistant—compare your typescript against the original document or a photocopy for accuracy of all textual details, such as correct wording, phrasing, spelling, punctuation, capitalization, paragraphing, and consistent emendation. After making the corrections, you should repeat the process several times until you are sure that the text is absolutely correct. Techniques for proofreading are outlined in Chapter 3.

In addition to presenting an accurate text, you will want to help your readers understand the documents by adding explanatory notes or annotation. Your explanatory material will answer three fundamental questions: What is this document? (provenance notes); what does it say? (textual notes); and what does it mean? (contextual or informational notes). Provenance notes tell a reader where the original document is located, a basic obligation of any editor. A provenance note can also give the reader additional information about the document. For example, while a reader can easily tell that a document is a letter by its form (the salutation, closing, and so on), once a document appears in print, one can no longer determine if the source is the recipient's copy, a copy retained by the writer, or a draft that was never sent. Provenance notes let readers know what they are seeing on the page.

Textual notes help readers see elements of documents that you cannot or choose not to render in type. Unless you offer explanation, the reader cannot tell if the document is torn or missing a paragraph. Are there words struck out or inserted? Does the handwriting give evidence that there are multiple authors? Is there important evidence written in the margins?

Informational or contextual notes will help your reader understand the documents. Here you can clarify the information in a document by identifying persons named, describing mentioned events, or clarifying ambiguous passages. For instance, phrases such as "I met with our mutual friend" or "The events of yesterday horrified me" cry out for explanation. The reader deserves to know who is the "mutual friend" or what were the horrifying "events." These kinds of notes allow you to share your expertise with the readers and help them more fully appreciate the meaning, background, and content of a document. The writing of informational annotation, while satisfying for the editor, requires a good deal of judgment and restraint. It is easy to get drawn into a research project to explain a reference in the text and end up writing notes that dwarf the documents. Good historical editing will offer readers only what they need to know, and will not use the edition as an opportunity to offer interpretive essays on subjects of the editor's interest.

You may wish to provide annotation either as footnotes or endnotes, or in many other forms. Headnotes and introductory essays may be a more appropriate means for adding annotation for a popular audience. Sometimes information that appears frequently throughout a book can be better explained in specialized biographical or geographical directories. Glossaries that explain the meaning of archaic or technical language may be better and more concise than presenting the information in footnotes or endnotes. Maps, illustrations, drawings, genealogical tables, and chronologies can also effectively explain the documents. Chapters 6 and 7 offer examples of how editors have dealt with annotation.

Editors who publish their work in books or on microform also need to think about how they can provide access to the published documents. Usually this is done through an index. Although freelance indexers can be hired, as the editor you probably know the material in your book better than anyone else. You should consult some of the standard works on indexing, such as those listed in Chapter 8, and perhaps have a professional indexer review the index you have prepared. Specialized issues can sometimes face those who index historical documents; these, too, are addressed in Chapter 8. The index to a documentary volume is usually longer than that of a conventional history because of the large number of names and topics it contains.

Editors who publish documents in books also need to make decisions about the front matter, or preliminaries, and back matter. Although the reader encounters the front matter of a book first, it is among the final things to be produced. You should write an introduction in which you explain the value of the project and justify the various editorial decisions made in presenting the text. (The same is true for works that appear in other formats.) You will also acknowledge those whose skills and financial support helped you with the project, and you may want to provide tools, such as a chronology or other tables that will help the reader understand the documents. There are some other items that need to be included (e.g. a title page, copyright page, table of contents, dedication, and the like) that either are created to aid cataloging or are long-standing publishing conventions. It is important to review these to make sure that they meet the needs of your book. Chapter 9 discusses these details.

As the editor of the documents, your work is not completed when you finish the manuscript. If you are publishing a book, you will have to deal with a publisher and should enter the relationship with some understanding of book publishing. There are a number of books to consult on the subject. Two excellent works are Judith Appelbaum, *How to Get Happily Published,* 4th ed. (New York: HarperPerennial, 1992), and Beth Luey, *Handbook for Academic Authors,* 3rd ed. (Cambridge and New York: Cambridge University Press, 1995).

If you are publishing the documents in a format other than a book, you will want to make sure that the documents appear as you desire. For instance, if you intend to publish your documents in a magazine, newspaper, or journal, you need to find out prior to publication if the publisher is willing to print the text as you prepared it. It would be frustrating to prepare your documents in a fashion that preserved original spelling only to discover that a copyeditor corrected all the spelling or ran it through a spelling checker.

The various modes of publication will require you to become familiar with the technical details, at least to make the appropriate arrangements with vendors. If you choose to self-publish the documents in a book or pamphlet, you need to plan the manufacturing details, distribution, and marketing of the work. Publication of transcribed documents on the World Wide Web requires an understanding of SGML (Standard Generalized Markup Language), while publication on microfilm will call for meeting national technical standards in the production of the film. Each of these subjects is beyond the scope of this volume and can be explored in the literature of the respective fields. The sources cited in the introduction to this volume and the Association for Documentary Editing (ADE) can serve as a good place to start for information on these changing subjects.

The editing of historical documents requires a great deal of care and consistency. The pages that follow illustrate some of the choices that other editors have made in producing their volumes. While serving as a guide, they should *not* be viewed as the definitive answer to every editorial problem. Your colleagues in documentary editing serve as another resource, and you should feel free to call on them. The ADE maintains a directory of its membership, which is useful in identifying editors you might wish to consult. Their generous advice has helped many new editors. The quality of your work ultimately will depend on the care and consistency with which you apply the principles and precedents that have been worked out over the years. While the work can be tedious at times, when it is done, you will have the satisfaction of knowing that you have made history more powerful and immediate to the current and future generations.

Chapter One

What, Why, How, and for Whom?

Why Edit Historical Documents?

1.1 People edit and publish historical documents because they believe these materials have enough significance to merit the time, energy, and money needed to make them accessible to a wider audience. Whether intended as research tools, study aids, or simply pleasurable reading, the basic mission of historical editions is to provide easy access to the unique information contained in original documents. Editors reproduce documents through the creation of facsimiles or transcriptions, make them understandable by providing annotation, facilitate access to them through devices such as indexes, and publish these documents via microforms, computer networks, CD-ROMs, or the printed page. Historical editors do not simply reproduce texts; they also provide readers with the information needed to understand the content of historical documents.

Scope

1.2 However small or grand a project, from a single document in a historical journal to a multivolume book edition or a multireel microform edition, documentary editors begin by defining the scope of the project. Whatever the topic, the editor should articulate a clear and well-defined statement of scope that includes a definition of who or what is being documented, the dates under consideration, and the reasons for undertaking the project. By clearly specifying a project's scope, editors use resources more efficiently and bring coherence to the work of collecting, editing, and publishing documents.

1.3   A project may use an individual as its subject. For example, the editors of the *Papers of Woodrow Wilson* document the thought, character, and career of Wilson in their edition:

> The editors hope to publish a comprehensive edition that will include all important letters, articles, speeches, interviews, and public papers by Woodrow Wilson. These volumes, when complete, should make available to readers all the materials essential to understanding Wilson's personality, his intellectual, religious, and political development, and his careers as educator, writer, orator, and statesman. The editors also hope that these volumes will be useful to scholars and others in various fields of history between the 1870's and the 1920's.

Fig. 1.3a Link, Wilson, 1:xiv

Many editors define the project's scope more narrowly. For example, the editors of the *Papers of George Washington: Revolutionary War Series* set chronological and topical guidelines for winnowing the huge number of documents associated with the Continental Army under Washington's command:

> Fortunately the task immediately at hand is not to collect and print every surviving document relating to the Continental army. Rather, it is to identify and print those surviving documents written by and to George Washington between 1775 and 1783 that deal directly with Washington as commander in chief of the Continental army or simply as a man.

Fig. 1.3b Chase, Washington: Revolutionary, 1:xx

An editor may use aspects of individuals' lives, such as their professional careers, to illustrate a broader historical topic. The editors of the *Papers of Daniel Webster: Legal Papers* used Webster's legal career to explore the nineteenth-century legal profession:

> It is the purpose of these two volumes to provide a sense of the texture of the practice of law in early nineteenth-century America. Webster presents a rare occasion for shaping that portrait because his practice evolved from a struggling rural environment to an elite urban setting. As Webster moved, he touched various strands and aspects of the profession. In order to provide a view of the actual practice, in part to fill what we have perceived as a gap in the historical literature for this period, we have included several variables that constitute practice, such as clients, legal doctrine, statutes, social environment, and economic

conditions. In the process, we have hoped not only to examine legal history and the legal profession, but also to illuminate social history and its relationship to law through the vehicles of formal and informal legal documents. There is information in these volumes as varied as the conduct of everyday business affairs, housing construction practices, and mental illness.

Fig. 1.3c Konefsky, *Webster: Legal*, 1:xix

The editors of the *Booker T. Washington Papers* sought to document both the man and an era of United States race relations:

Unlike the subjects of most earlier enterprises in historical editing, Washington was neither a founding father nor a national political leader. Yet his importance in American history is firmly established, and his significance as a subject for an editing project stands securely on the wealth of social history revealed in his papers as well as the fact that Washington was a leading black American.

The Washington Papers project does not seek to build a monument to this controversial figure or his social philosophy but to reveal black culture in all its complexity and rich human interest and the story of American race relations, black and white, in the late nineteenth and early twentieth centuries. This critical approach to the central figure is not adopted because he was black or because he was Booker T. Washington, but because of the editors' belief that history should serve the cause of social criticism instead of exalting a people or an individual hero. Because Washington was a middleman between the white and black America of his day, his papers also shed light on interracial relations in the "age of accommodation." But the reader should be warned that there is an imbalance in the Washington Papers, for with the exception of occasional mention of the crop-lien system or lynching or discrimination, Washington rarely admitted that there were deep racial problems in America. He generally took the hopeful view on the ground that it was more constructive, an approach that soothed white southerners and loosened the purse strings of philanthropists. By including incoming correspondence the editors hope to broaden the focus of the papers beyond Washington's restricted perspective. This wealth of sources transcends Washington's private and public life, and the editors seek in the selection of documents to portray not only Washington's life but as far as possible his age as well.

Fig. 1.3d Harlan, *Washington*, 2:xxxi

1.4   The papers of two or more individuals or correspondents may be edited together if their personal interaction or the nature of existing documents makes such a compilation logical. The editors of the microfilm edition of the *Papers of Elizabeth Cady Stanton and Susan B. Anthony* chose to publish the two women's papers together because their work was so interconnected:

> The edition presents the papers of both women as a single, interfiled collection. Their good friend Theodore Tilton once described how difficult it could be to separate the individuals from the remarkable partnership between Stanton and Anthony.

> Elizabeth Cady Stanton, or, as she is sometimes called, Susan B. Anthony, is a celebrated lady with snow-white and auburn hair, plump and slender figure, Grecian and Roman nose, and lives simultaneously in two houses—one at Tenafly, N.J., and the other at Rochester, N.Y. Indeed, Mrs. Stanton, or, to call her by her maiden name, Miss Anthony, is a ubiquitous personage, and not only attends all the woman's meetings wherever they are held, but also has been known on certain occasions to be writing the resolutions, and at the self-same moment to be delivering the speech, in their support. It has been sometimes suspected that Mrs. Stanton and Miss Anthony are two distinct persons, united by a cartilege like the Siamese twins, but in the absence of any medical or other scientific proof of this hypothesis, I remain of the opinion that, like Liberty and Union, they are "one and inseparable."[2]

> Two distinct personalities emerge from this edition, but Tilton put his finger on a problem for the researcher or editor who tries to treat one woman independently of the other. Through half a century apiece of activism, they worked within the same realms of public life toward closely interconnected goals. To separate their stories is, in a sense, to distort how they themselves regarded the relationships between different reforms.

> By combining their papers in a single edition, the papers of each woman are enriched by association, by being available within a broader context of related reform. In terms of editorial work, the search for documents for each woman independently would lead to endless redundancy. The richest lodes of documentation produced the papers of both women. When they worked in tandem, the problem is more practical. Whose papers are those that were written together over the dining-room table at the Stanton household? When Stanton accepted invitations to speak at events she had no intention of attending and Anthony faithfully delivered Stanton's address in her stead, whose papers should document the meeting?

> Had either woman retained a large corpus of papers about her private life, the editorial decisions might have differed. That which distinguished the two women would have competed with that which they shared, rendering use of the edition somewhat awkward. Because most of the papers in this edition treat political activity and issues arising in public life, that outer world of agitation dominates the narrative. Two characters and all their co-workers move across a common stage, growing older, adapting their schedules and their domestic habits, but fighting to the last for acceptance of woman's self-sovereignty.

Fig. 1.4a Holland, *Stanton–Anthony*, 2

The editors of the *Adams Family Correspondence* combined all personal correspondence among family members, an arrangement that highlights their interaction but also separates an individual's private and public papers:

Since the record of these constants and these changes is so extended and so detailed, and since the letters that the Adamses wrote each other have been so carefully preserved, the editor in chief decided at an early stage in his planning to present the family correspondence as a unit by itself. A disadvantage of this arrangement is that it adds another chronology to a pattern already complicated enough. But its advantages seem much greater. For one thing, it will present the letters and replies of the Adams statesmen *to each other* in the same sequence, rather than widely separated in the volumes devoted to each statesman's general correspondence and other writings. For another thing, it enables the women of the family, both those born into it and those who married into it, to take their places beside the Adams men instead of being obscured by them. Finally, and, as the editors believe, most significantly, certain kinds of evidence furnished by the family correspondence are not too abundant in print elsewhere and are better recognized today than formerly by historians as peculiarly precious.

Fig. 1.4b Butterfield, *Adams Family*, 1:xxiv

1.5 The significance of some individuals is so closely tied to a particular institution or organization that it may make sense to edit the documents of the individual and the organization together. The editors of the *Marcus Garvey and Universal Negro Improvement Association Papers* created their project with the intent of studying both the man and the organization:

> The Marcus Garvey and Universal Negro Improvement Association Papers are based on a comprehensive survey of all the presently available historical manuscripts and records pertaining to the life and work of Marcus Mosiah Garvey as well as to the popular worldwide organization that he founded and led from its inception in 1914 until his death in 1940. As the record of the only organized international mass movement of persons of African descent and as the history of a mass social phenomenon, these Papers go beyond a preoccupation with the fortunes of a single, even if major, historical figure. Their focus is as much on the participation of members and supporters as on Garvey's activities as the political leader of the movement.

Fig. 1.5a Hill, *Garvey*, 1:xci

The editors of the microfilm edition of the *Papers of the Women's Trade Union League and Principal Leaders* found it necessary to collect the papers of the organization's leaders to fully document the organization's activities:

> With the cooperation of seven different repositories, it has assembled in one edition the principal manuscript collections pertaining to the League.

The collections vary in size and in scope. Two represent the surviving files of the National WTUL. When the League disbanded in 1950, the main portion of its files went to the Library of Congress and a smaller segment to the Schlesinger Library. The edition also includes the only other substantial body of official records still extant, those of the New York WTUL.

Fortunately for the history of the WTUL, these institutional records could be supplemented and fleshed out by substantial collections of personal papers. Foremost among them is the large and comprehensive collection of the papers of Margaret Dreier Robins, the guiding force of the League during its formative and peak years. Of considerable depth and richness also are the papers of Leonora O'Reilly, which illuminate both the League's New York activities and O'Reilly's own special intensity and inspiration. The Rose Schneiderman Papers, though relatively sparse, further document the New York scene; the Agnes Nestor Papers do the same for League activities in Chicago. Mary Anderson's papers, although confined to her years as head of the federal Women's Bureau, thus omitting her earlier experience as an organizer for the Chicago and National WTUL, record her continuing participation in the League and some of its inner concerns. Smaller collections give glimpses into the history of the Boston and Chicago Leagues and into the life of Mary Kenney O'Sullivan, co-founder of the National WTUL.

Fig. 1.5b James, *WTUL*, 13

1.6   An organization or institution may be the subject of an editing project. The editors of the *Documentary History of the Supreme Court of the United States* deal with the court's first ten years:

This multi-volume documentary history will provide scholars and lawyers with the first accurate record of all cases heard by the Supreme Court between 1790 and 1800. It will also present an ample selection of contemporary comment about the justices and their duties, the business of the Court, and the function of the Court in the constitutional framework. A compilation of official records, private papers, and other primary sources, this series will bring together and make readily available hitherto unpublished materials. They will document the Court's important role in creating administrative procedures for the American judicial system and establishing the legal precedents that enabled the new government to prosper.

Fig. 1.6 Marcus, *Supreme Court*, vol.1,1:xlii

1.7   Editors may collect documents illustrating a particular topic, theme, or event. A topic may be concrete or abstract as long as it is defined well enough to guide the collecting and editing of documents. For example, the editors of *Freedom: A Documentary History of Emancipation* delineated specific topics that they would and would not include in their work on the transition from slavery to freedom in the southern United States:

The editors found it imperative from the outset to be selective. They have focused their attention upon the wartime and postwar experiences of slaves and ex-slaves, but have also sought to illuminate the social, economic, and political setting of the emancipation process. The formation of federal policy, for example, is not central to the project's concerns, except insofar as the preconceptions and actions of policy makers influenced the shape that freedom assumed. Therefore, the volumes published by the Freedmen and Southern Society Project will not undertake a history of the Freedmen's Bureau, the U.S. Army, the Bureau of Colored Troops, or any other governmental agency; nonetheless, documents about the operations of these agencies will be prominent when they describe activities of freedpeople and shed light upon the context in which former slaves struggled to construct their own lives. Throughout the selection process, the editors have labored to reconstruct the history of the freedpeople rather than the institutions that surrounded them.

Above all, the editors have sought to delineate the central elements of the process by which men and women moved from the utter dependence slaveholders demanded but never fully received, to the independence freedpeople desired but seldom attained.

Fig. 1.7 Berlin, *Freedom*, ser.1,1:xx–xxi

Form of Publication

1.8   Each editor decides the form of publication most appropriate for the selected materials, including both the medium in which the documents will be published and whether the documents will be presented as facsimiles, as transcriptions, or in both forms.

1.9   Edited documents can be distributed through several different media. Printing documents in a historical magazine or another type of periodical makes them accessible to a wide audience, although the number of publications willing to print historical documents is limited, and they must of necessity limit the quantity of documentary materials. Self-publishing one or more documents in a pamphlet is a fairly easy and affordable way to reach an audience, especially for an institution like a library or a historical society that has a gift shop.

Editors of larger projects may want to publish the results of their work in a book edition, be it a single volume or multivolume set. Book editions are easy to read, compact, and portable and may be read without expensive viewers or computer hardware. When produced on acid-free paper they can have a shelf life of hundreds of years. Yet books are expensive to produce and require a publishing house willing to take on the costs of printing and distributing the work. The potential market for the edition or the availability of a subvention or endowment will affect both the number of volumes and the size of the press run.

Microform editions provide a compact and less costly means of reproducing and preserving large numbers of documents, but viewing microforms can be hard on the eyes, can produce images that are difficult to read and copy, and furthermore, requires the use of machines. Editors may also consider using computer and scanning technology to put their documents onto computer disks, CD-ROMs, or the World Wide Web (the Internet). The immediate appeal of electronic media is their ability to store vast amounts of information that can be disseminated at a low cost. However, electronic media have an uncertain shelf life, with carefully stored disks and electronic tapes holding data for ten or fewer years and CD-ROMs predicted to last from fifty to 100 years. Furthermore, the fast rate of change in computer technology threatens all electronic media with rapid obsolescence. Purchasers of electronic editions must adapt them to new systems, preserve the machines and software needed to use the existing format, or lose access to the information contained in the editions.

1.10   Whether publishing documents on the printed page, on microform, or via electronic media, editors must decide whether documents should be presented as facsimiles, as transcribed texts, or in both forms. While many microform and electronic editions present only facsimiles—thus saving the time, labor, and expense of transcribing and annotating documents—these editions can be hard to read, difficult to understand, and impossible to search unless the editors mark the texts or provide thorough indexes. Each user, in essence, approaches the documents afresh, without any of the expertise of the editor. In editing documents, the greatest service editors can provide readers is a clean, readable, transcribed text, followed closely by a convenient method for gaining access to the information in the documents and explanatory annotation.

Audience

1.11   Editors should identify their intended readers and consider the knowledge and expectations they are likely to bring to the work. Accounting for the specific needs of different kinds of readers affects decisions editors make about the selection, annotation, and presentation of documents.

1.12   Editions aimed at scholars and professional communities will often be tailored toward a knowledgeable audience well versed in the language and background of the subject. Scholarly and professional audiences use documentary editions as research tools and therefore require full and authenticated texts, notes that provide information beyond common historical knowledge, and exhaustive indexes. For scholars, the narrative flow and readability of an edition are secondary to the information contained in the documents.

1.13 Editions aimed at audiences of students and general readers are characterized by brevity, readability, and a preference for using narrative rather than academic forms of annotation. Editors of documents aimed at students and general
readers strive to make their works readable without sacrificing the accuracy of
their content. In place of footnotes, an editor may, for example, use introductions
and headnotes to provide a basic historical context and to define unfamiliar words
or phrases. Editors also frequently abstract or excerpt documents to maintain the
flow of the narrative and to keep readers interested.

1.14 Editions intended for different audiences present documents on the
page in different ways. In *Benjamin Franklin: Writings*, an edition intended for
general readers, Franklin's autobiography is presented without editorial markings (*top*), while the *Autobiography of Benjamin Franklin: A Genetic Text* created
a scholarly edition that used editorial symbols extensively to mark textual
details (*bottom*):

> My Time for these Exercises & for Reading, was at Night
> after Work, or before Work began in the Morning; or on
> Sundays, when I contrived to be in the Printing House alone,
> evading as much as I could the common Attendance on pub-
> lick Worship, which my Father used to exact of me when I
> was under his Care:—And which indeed I still thought a
> Duty; tho' I could not, as it seemed to me, afford the Time
> to practise it.

Fig. 1.14a(1) Franklin, *Writings*, 1320

> My Time for these Exercises ↑↑& for Reading,↓↓ was <after
> Work at Night> ↑at Night after Work,↓ or before <it>
> ↑↑Work↓↓ began in the Morning; or on Sundays, when I con-
> trived to be in the Printing House alone, evading as much as I
> could the <usual> ↑common↓ Attendance on publick Worship,
> which my Father used to exact of m{y}e when I was under his
> Care:— And which indeed I still thought a Duty; tho' I could
> not, ↑as↓ it seemed ↑to me,↓ afford the Time to practise it.

Fig. 1.14a(2) Lemay, *Franklin: Genetic Text*, 14

The editors of *Freedom: A Documentary History of Emancipation* (*top*) republished many of the same documents in a volume they created for students and
general readers entitled *Free at Last: A Documentary History of Slavery, Freedom,
and the Civil War* (*bottom*). The editors adapted their documents for general

readers by writing introductory headnotes, presenting the documents in larger type, and limiting or eliminating the scholarly annotation at the end of the documents:

73: Officers of a Black Union Association to the Commander of the Department of the Gulf

> New orleans Dec 22th 1862
> In obedience To Th High chift an Command of Th Head quarters Department of Th Gulf Maggor Gen N P Bank We Th members of Th union association Desir Th & Respectfully ask of you Th privirliges of Salabrating Th first Day of January th 1863 by a Large procesion on that Day & We Wish to pass th Head quarters of th union officers High in a authority that is if it Suit your approbation & We also Wish to Give a Grand union Dinner on th Second Day of Januay that is if it so pleas you & th profit of th Dinner Will Go To th poor people in th Camp th Colour Woman & childeren   Your Most Homble obedien servant
> J M Marshall th president of th union association
> HISr   Henry clay th Superintender of th Dinner

J. M. Marshall and Henry Clay to Gen. N. P. Bank, 22 Dec. 1862, M-62 1862, Letters Received, ser. 1956, Field Records – Banks' Expedition, Dept. of the Gulf, RG 393 Pt. 1 [C-824]. The letter and both signatures are in the same handwriting. A search of the copies of letters sent in the records of the Department of the Gulf revealed no reply to the Union Association.

Fig. 1.14b(1) Berlin, Freedom, ser.1,1:235

> While planters trembled at the prospect of the Emancipation Procla-
> mation, slaves and free people of color prepared to celebrate the
> Day of Jubilee. In New Orleans, the officers of a "union association"
> asked General Banks to allow its members to observe the day in a
> manner befitting an event their people had awaited more than two
> hundred years.

> New orleans [*La.*] Dec 22th 1862
> In obedience To Th High chift an Command of Th Head quarters Department of Th Gulf Maggor Gen N P Bank We Th members of Th union association Desir Th & Respectfully ask of you Th privirliges of Salabrating Th first Day of January th 1863 by a Large procesion on that Day & We Wish to pass th Head quarters of th union officers High

in a authority that is if it Suit your approbation & We also Wish to Give
a Grand union Dinner on th Second Day of Januay that is if it so pleas
you & th profit of th Dinner Will Go To th poor people in th Camp th
Colour Woman & childeren   Your Most Homble obedien servant

J M Marshall   th president of th union association

HLSr   Henry clay   th Superintender of th Dinner[65]

Fig. 1.14b(2) Berlin, *Free*, 85

Sources

1.15   Editors decide which genres of documents (e.g. letters, diaries, etc.) will be included in their editions as well as the sources from which those documents will be obtained. Establishing clear guidelines regarding the types of documents that will be used and identifying the locations of relevant groups of documents early in the planning process allow an editor to search for documents in a systematic, thorough fashion.

1.16   When deciding which types of documents to include in an edition, an editor takes into account both the scope of the project and the nature of available sources. Editors may choose to edit only a single genre of documents (such as an individual's letters or diary) or to compile a much larger selection of genres (such as speeches, memos, professional papers, telegrams, or published works). In addition, editors may want to specify the authorial origin of the documents that will be collected, deciding whether to limit collection to documents produced by the subject, received by the subject, written about the subject, or some combination thereof. A precisely defined scope and a familiarity with the content of major collections of documents will help editors make these decisions.

1.17   Editors should consider how many documents a project will collect, how thoroughly the editor or project staff will be able to search appropriate manuscript repositories and archives for relevant documents, and how many documents will be published. In all cases, the editors' aspirations should be matched by financial resources sufficient to see the project through to completion.

1.18   One document can stand alone as the focus of an editing project. A particularly interesting letter, a vivid diary, or an important published work may warrant editing and publication on its own. For example, see the short diary edited by John Hammond Moore and published as *A Plantation Mistress on the Eve of the Civil War: The Diary of Keziah Goodwyn Hopkins Brevard* (Columbia: University of South Carolina Press, 1993). A single document also may be suitable for publication in a newspaper, historical magazine, journal, or newsletter. The following letter occupied a half page in the Rock County Historical Society's newsletter, *The Recorder*:

> *Charles Spencer of Janesville was in the Civil War with the Twelfth Wisconsin Battery, Light Artillery . He wrote home Thursday, October 6, 1864, at age 18, describing a battle for the fort at Allatoona, Georgia. (The original letter was 8 pages.) Spencer returned to Janesville after the war and died here of consumption June 28, 1870.*
>
> Dear Mother
> I suppose you have heared before this that we have hade a terrble battle here yesterday. Aboute one oclock wedendsay the pickets

Fig. 1.18 Rock County, *Recorder*, April 1997:10

1.19 Documents drawn from a single manuscript collection or a solitary repository can provide sufficient sources for an editing project. Whether editors want to publish only a few documents or a great many, using the holdings of a single repository eases the collecting process, reduces the work of acquiring permission to publish documents, and may bring a sense of unity to the project, especially if the documents share a common history. Because many institutions have created or actively collected documents on particular subjects, a single library, historical society, or archive often may have a rich collection of documents on a given topic. For example, the editorial staff of *Freedom: A Documentary History of Emancipation* conducted all its research in the holdings of the National Archives:

> In the fall of 1976, with a grant from the National Historical Publications and Records Commission, and under the sponsorship of the University of Maryland, the Freedmen and Southern Society Project launched a systematic search of those records at the National Archives that promised to yield material for a documentary history of emancipation. Over the course of the next three years, the editors selected more than 40,000 items, which represented perhaps 2 percent of the documents they examined. Indexed and cross-referenced topically, chronologically, and geographically, this preliminary selection constitutes the universe from which the documents published as *Freedom: A Documentary History of Emancipation* are selected and annotated, and from which the editors' introductory essays are written.

Fig. 1.19 Berlin, *Freedom*, ser.1,1:xx

1.20 A documentary editing project may collect documents from multiple institutions. Many of the largest projects have completed worldwide searches spanning several decades that took the editors from historical archives to the holdings of collectors and manuscript dealers to the recesses of family barns and attics. Editors of smaller projects may also find themselves culling multiple collections at different institutions to acquire a larger or more diverse selection of documents. Rarely are both sides of a mutual correspondence located at a single institution. Likewise, some of the extant correspondence produced by a subject probably resides in the hands of recipients, their heirs, or various repositories. A thorough search in multiple archives may provide the only means of assembling a comprehensive collection of documents. Even though electronic cataloging, photocopying, and microfilming have made access easier than in the past, the cost of travel and lodging or of hiring researchers makes multiple-institution searches time-consuming and costly. Consider, for example, the difficulties incurred by the editors of the *Papers of Benjamin Franklin* in conducting their extraordinarily thorough worldwide search to gather the documents for their edition:

> The editors' first task was to locate and photocopy Franklin manuscripts and printed works in the scores of institutions and private collections where they are preserved. The major bodies of Franklin materials are well known to historians: the American Philosophical Society, the Library of Congress, the National Archives, the Historical Society of Pennsylvania, the University of Pennsylvania, Yale University, the Massachusetts Historical Society, and the French Foreign Office each owns more than 500 manuscripts. Scholars have long been acquainted with the Franklin papers in Harvard College Library, the William L. Clements Library, the New York Public Library, the New-York Historical Society, the Pierpont Morgan Library, the Henry E. Huntington Library, the Library Company of Philadelphia, the Pennsylvania State Records Office, and, abroad, in the British Museum, Public Record Office, Royal Society, and Bibliothèque Nationale. These twenty libraries and about a score more composed the first list of probable owners which the editors prepared when they began their work in 1954.
>
> Obtaining photostats or microfilms from the larger libraries was, for the editors, relatively easy. (In a very few cases, for some special reason, manuscript transcripts had to be made.) By correspondence and personal visits single letters were located in smaller libraries and collections. University libraries, state and municipal libraries, and state and local historical societies were routinely

canvassed. The indexes prepared by the Federal Historical Records Survey of the Works Progress Administration provided helpful information, as did, in Great Britain, the *Reports* of the Historical Manuscripts Commission. The *Catalogue Général des Manuscrits des Bibliothèques Publiques de France* led to a dozen or more provincial libraries, and the admirable centralization of library facilities in France enabled us to examine and copy these manuscripts in the Bibliothèque Nationale in Paris. The director of the National Historical Publications Commission had a search made of the Continental Congress Papers and other promising collections in the National Archives at Washington and provided microfilms. Institutions which Franklin served, like the Pennsylvania Hospital and the Associates of the late Reverend Dr. Bray, almost always had a letter or two. Colleagues and strangers reported the existence of Franklin letters in their friends' libraries or in places to which we would probably never have addressed an inquiry, like the Riverdale Country Day School. Sometimes, as in the Salem County, N.J., Historical Society and in Christ Church in Philadelphia, while searching for a manuscript we believed to be there, we found others we had not known about. No place, it turned out, was too improbable to hold a Franklin letter: there are eight at Windsor Castle (seven of them presented to the Prince of Wales, later Edward VII, during his American tour in 1860), and two (each to a president of Yale College) in the Karl Marx University at Leipzig. We began as scholars, but have become sleuths and venturesome serendipitists as well.

Descendants of Franklin and his principal correspondents, especially in Philadelphia, without exception took a lively interest in the work, as their parents and grandparents did in the work of Smyth and Sparks, and allowed copies of their manuscripts to be made, or, if they had no manuscripts themselves, sent us to aunts and cousins who did. Autograph collectors, many of them members of the Manuscript Society, also responded to our requests and cordially and promptly allowed copies to be made of their treasures. As the first volume goes to press, about 220 institutions and some 110 private owners have given permission to print their manuscripts in this edition. All seem to regard *The Papers of Benjamin Franklin*, in words J. Francis Fisher of Philadelphia used to Jared Sparks, as "a national work," which they wish to promote as they can. Nor is this cooperation limited to owners in the United States. Photocopies have reached us not only from thirty-one states from Maine to Hawaii, and the District of Columbia, but also from twelve foreign countries extending from Canada to the Soviet Union. This response suggests that an edition of Franklin's writings may now be regarded as an international work.

Carrying the search to yet another level, the editors examined the published correspondence of Franklin's contemporaries, printed archival collections, the periodicals of historical societies and associations; and found other letters, from now lost manuscripts, printed in whole or in part in the book and autograph sales catalogues of Goodspeed, Henkels, Maggs, Parke-Bernet, and others.

Even this exhaustive search is, of course, not ended. It will continue throughout the preparation of this edition, and even then manuscripts will continue to turn up. Just as Sparks, for some reason, did not or could not see the Franklin-Mecom correspondence that was preserved in Boston at the time he was working; and Smyth could find no trace of Franklin's letters to Ingenhousz, which had been sold only a few years before; so we have been unable to verify in any way a report that Franklin letters are in possession of descendants of Joseph Galloway in Eire. So the search continues, and with it an appeal to those who read these pages to inform the editors (in care of the publishers) of any Franklin manuscripts of whose existence they know.

Fig. 1.20 Labaree, *Franklin*, 1:xxviii–xxx

1.21 Because many interesting and important documents reside outside the collections of repositories, editors should consider other locations where documents might be found. Newspapers and magazines can provide texts of speeches, news accounts, public announcements, advertisements, and letters. Collectors, local historical societies, or individuals may own important documents or family papers that have escaped public attention. The files of businesses, newspapers, and organizations may also hold rare clippings or documents. While it may be beyond the means of documentary editors to locate all documents within a project's scope, editors should think creatively when searching for documents and should seek advice from other editors and scholars who have already completed similar searches.

Comprehensiveness

1.22 A comprehensive edition includes all known documents within a project's scope. A project with a narrowly defined scope and few pertinent documents may produce a short but exhaustive article or edition, while a project with a broad scope and many relevant documents may produce a very large although not necessarily comprehensive edition. While some comprehensive editions whose scopes encompass thousands of documents have been published as book editions spanning dozens of volumes, few topics are important enough to warrant the expense of reproducing routine papers, variant drafts, or form letters in such a format. More common are book editions that print the most informative letters in full but provide a comprehensive overview of other documents (including information about where a reader could obtain those documents in the original) through devices such as extracts, abstracts, and calendars. (For examples of extracts, abstracts, and calendars, see Chapter 2.) When the reproduction of a large number of routine documents is essential to the scope of a project, it is common to produce comprehensive microform editions in which all documents are reproduced in facsimile form but not transcribed. Such an edition can stand alone or serve as a companion to a selective book edition.

1.23   A selective edition does not publish all in-scope documents discovered in the course of the document search. Most documentary editions are selective because editors will deem some documents unworthy of publication. Editors may omit documents to increase readability, to save time, to reduce printing costs, to meet space limitations, or because certain documents are inaccessible because of privacy or copyright considerations. Editors of selective editions should develop explicit criteria for selecting documents and then describe them clearly for their readers. (For a discussion of selection criteria, see Chapter 2.)

Chapter Two

Selection and Arrangement of Documents

Selecting Documents for Publication

2.1   Editors decide which documents collected by their projects will be published and should consider a number of criteria in doing so. On some occasions, the choice may be obvious—for example, a short, well-written diary or an autobiography; but for many topics a decision must be made between publishing all the collected documents or only a selection. Comprehensive editions provide an invaluable historical resource capable of presenting important documents as well as details of day-to-day life that are seldom available in selective editions. However, not all editors will want or be able to produce comprehensive editions. Editors may produce selective editions as a result of time and financial constraints, space limitations, copyright restrictions that prevent use of certain documents, preexisting high-quality collections of published documents, or a desire to present only the most interesting or historically significant documents. In deciding whether to produce a comprehensive edition or a selective one, editors should remember that most topics receive treatment in documentary editions only once. Some important figures or topics might have more than one documentary edition, but usually no more than one in any single generation. The existence of an edition may preclude others from securing the requisite financial backing or publishing support and thus may prevent revisitation of the topic for decades. Whenever feasible, editors should seek to produce editions that are as comprehensive as possible and that will make the greatest contribution to modern scholarship. Whether a project publishes all the documents it collects or only a small portion, editors should clearly explain to readers how the documents that appear in the final work were selected.

2.2   Editors may choose to publish all known documents within their project's scope, a decision that requires careful consideration of the quantity of documents that will be published and the resources available to do so. The

Correspondence of Roger Williams is an example of a project that published all documents within its scope, a task made manageable by the small number of extant letters:

> The present edition includes all letters to and from Roger Williams that could be found. Because the entire collection of correspondence is relatively small, all documents—including some routine letters—have been printed in full.

Fig. 2.2a LaFantasie, Williams, 1:lxix

Projects that have gathered much larger quantities of documents have also aspired to comprehensiveness, such as the *Papers of Benjamin Franklin*:

PRINCIPLES OF SELECTION

This edition will present the full text of every document of Franklin's career, signed or unsigned, that we can locate and establish to our satisfaction to have been written by Franklin or by Franklin with others. There are essays in the contemporary press which he may have written, and when the weight of the evidence supports the idea of his authorship, we shall print them, indicating that evidence, but also making clear its limits and our uncertainty. Writings which previous editors have assigned to Franklin but which subsequent research has proved not to be his, or which our own study leads us to judge are not by him, will be presented only by title and location, in their chronological order, with our reasons for rejecting them.

The important state papers in which Franklin participated and which he signed will be printed in full, with annotation indicating the nature and extent of his contribution. Where his part in the drafting was substantial, we shall include such preliminary versions as will show the evolution of the document into its final form.

There are some very large volumes of records of Franklin's printing business, and of official, post office, and personal affairs. Printing these in full would take a great deal of space and would serve the purposes of none but a very few scholars of limited and highly specialized interests. We shall give the description and location of each such record book in its proper chronological place, that is, according to the date of the earliest entry. We shall indicate its nature and, when warranted, reproduce sample entries. Like treatment will be accorded groups of miscellaneous business papers, invoices, bills of exchange, and calling cards. Many legal documents will appear only in the form of abstracts.

We shall normally exclude two other categories of documents actually written by Franklin. The first consists of documents of bodies which he served as secretary or clerk, such as the Pennsylvania Assembly and, occasionally, the Library Company of Philadelphia. The journals, minutes, and addresses of such institutions, though in his autograph, are not properly parts of the Franklin Papers; and they are useful mainly in annotation. The same is true of the hundreds of routine official documents which he signed or which came to him as minister to France and as president of the Supreme Executive Council of Pennsylvania—passports, commissions, orders on the state treasurer, bankruptcy petitions, and the like. We shall print an example of each of these forms, perhaps in facsimile, and we shall present such individual pieces as derive significance from other documents in the Franklin Papers or are of general historical importance. But to include all this sort of thing would add nothing either to the interest or to the usefulness of this edition.

The ultimate test to be applied in determining whether to print any document or part of a Franklin document is whether the contents are in any sense the product of his mind.

Fig. 2.2b Labaree, *Franklin*, 1:xxxiv–xxxv

Although the editors of the *Papers of Benjamin Franklin* used some abstracts and eliminated several categories of routine documents to reduce the size of their publication, the large quantity of remaining materials later made it necessary to reduce further the number of documents reproduced in full:

> The initial policy of including in this edition the full text of everything to or by Franklin has been modified. Résumés, first introduced in Volume 15 for reasons explained there in an editorial note, are more frequent in the current volume than in any of its predecessors; we have summarized three petitions, for example, which Franklin did not write but of which he was one among many signers, and the proceedings in the Chancery suit that William Whately brought against him. We have also omitted, but noted, an open letter to him in a newspaper because it is routine rhetoric without significance. The number of such summaries and omissions will increase in future volumes. Franklin became more active as he aged, not less; the bulk of his papers grew accordingly, and to many of them he could have given only the most cursory attention. Until further notice all documents within our rubric will be noted in one way or another, but those that have only a peripheral bearing upon Franklin's activities will not

be published in full. This decision is necessary, in the opinion of the editors and the Administrative Board, if the edition is to be completed within a reasonable time.

Fig. 2.2c Labaree, *Franklin*, 21:xxxiv

2.3 Editors wishing to publish comprehensive editions may choose to publish both selective book editions and exhaustive microform editions. For example, the selective book edition and comprehensive microfilm edition of the *Papers of Daniel Webster* were produced together to satisfy the needs of scholars and general readers while controlling the cost of publication:

> From its inception the Papers of Daniel Webster was planned as an integrated project, using both microfilm and letterpress publication. The persistent pressure of time and the steadily rising cost of book publication were important factors in the choice of the dual media, but the overriding consideration was the desire to bring all of Webster together, without abridgment or gloss, for those who were equipped to use it that way, while providing the less dedicated scholar and the general reader with the essential Webster in convenient annotated form. The microfilm edition, in four different groupings, is as complete as the surviving records permit.
>
> * * * *
>
> The value of this film, including as it does virtually all known Webster papers, cannot be overstated; but its very magnitude makes it unmanageable. It is relatively expensive, requires special equipment to use, is hard on the eyes, and effectively buries the grains of wheat by mixing them unevenly with an enormous amount of chaff. The user of the film, moreover, must decipher for himself often difficult or faded handwriting. He must search out the identity of persons and the nature of events alluded to, and finally he must rely upon his own judgment as to the significance of the given document. In the letterpress edition all this has been done for him, even to the selection of documents in terms of their significance, by editors totally immersed in the time and place and almost as familiar with the central characters as was Webster himself.
>
> The letterpress edition in effect complements and renders more useful these various microfilm collections, whose very existence has made it possible to select more rigorously the documents important enough to be offered to the larger audience reached by the printed book. Each volume of correspondence, moreover, includes a calendar of letters written in the same time period but not selected for publication. For each of these the microfilm frame number is cited, as is volume and page citation for any document now available only in a printed version. Footnote references are also made to the film wherever appropriate. For the general reader and for the student of the period rather than of the man, the editors believe the selection of items printed will be ample. The biographer, and the

scholar pursuing an in-depth study of some segment of the times, will need the film, to which he will find the printed volumes an indispensable annotated guide.

Fig. 2.3a Wiltse, Webster: Correspondence, 1:xiv–xv

Two comprehensive microfilm collections were created before the editors of the *Samuel Gompers Papers* produced a selective book edition that served as an introduction to the microfilm collections and as a more accessible, readable text:

> The project's selective, annotated, printed edition, of which this volume is the first, complements our microfilm publications. In the process of searching for Gompers materials, evaluating and organizing them, and preparing them for filming, the editors are in an excellent position to identify the documents that illuminate the rich themes, important insights, and defining contours of this vast collection. Gompers' immense energy, his longevity, and his volubility served to create an enormous body of manuscripts in which middle- and lower-level labor and ethnic leaders, a wide range of working-class people, and those interested in or associated with them play the supporting roles. The printed edition should serve as one key for scholars interested in probing the larger body of Gompers documents, give students, teachers, and writers ready access to a distilled and annotated research collection of the first importance, and provide the large number of serious readers within the labor movement and among the general public with a more intimate sense of the history of organized labor and the working-class experience.

Fig. 2.3b Kaufman, Gompers, 1:xxii

2.4   Publishing selective editions requires editors to exclude some in-scope documents. To guide this process, editors should establish clear selection criteria. The development of these criteria is a subjective matter based on professional expertise, a familiarity with the collected documents, and the judgment of the project staff. Editors should develop a procedure for selecting documents that best fulfills the mission of their projects.

2.5   Editors may select the documents that best illustrate the historical significance of a project's subject. For example, the editors of the *Papers of Martin Luther King, Jr.* selected those documents that they felt best documented King's life and work, and those that had the greatest public impact:

> We examined thousands of King-related documents and recordings and selected those that were biographically or historically significant to King's life, thought, and leadership. Because only a small proportion of all the available documents could be published, we developed certain principles and priorities to guide our selection process.

King's writings were assigned highest priority for inclusion. Because of their impact on the public, all of King's published writings were included. Although many of these writings are already accessible, few have been annotated and some exist only in obscure periodicals. King's public statements—his sermons, speeches, interviews, and recorded comments—were given the next highest priority for selection. King's unpublished manuscripts, such as his student papers, were included when they provided information about the development of his ideas. Letters to and from King reveal much about his life and thought. Preference was given to correspondence that influenced King or revealed his impact on others. Routine correspondence and office-generated replies to unsolicited letters were excluded.

Documents produced by others were selected in cases of clear biographical or historical significance to King. This category included confidential academic evaluations, published and unpublished interviews, transcripts or reports of meetings in which King participated, documents from legal proceedings involving King, and FBI transcripts of King's conversations. Correspondence not directly involving King and time-specific printed matter concerning King's activities (such as church programs or political leaflets) were transcribed only if they had special historical value.

Fig. 2.5a Carson, *King*, 1:91

The editors of the *Family Letters of Victor and Meta Berger* selected documents that illustrated many different aspects of the Bergers' lives but gave special weight to documents produced between 1914 and 1920 because of the importance of events of that period in the subjects' lives and in history:

> The letters in this volume were chosen to illustrate Victor and Meta's political activities; Victor's congressional career and his newspaper publishing business; Meta's involvement in the suffrage movement; the Bergers' views on the major political and social issues of the era; and their association with key figures in the labor, socialist, suffrage, peace, and civil liberties movements. In addition, the selected correspondence depicts Meta and Victor's evolving relationship and their family life. Because World War I and the Red Scare that followed are crucial to understanding the couple's lives, more than a third of the letters printed here are from the period 1914–1920, providing a comprehensive account of the Bergers' views on the war, Victor's trial and conviction under the Espionage Act, and his subsequent exclusion from the U.S. House of Representatives in 1919 and 1920.

Fig. 2.5b Stevens, *Berger*, 29

2.6   One way that editors reduce the quantity of in-scope documents under consideration is by limiting the publication of routine documents. The editors of the *Papers of Chief John Ross* used abstracts and excluded several forms of routine documents:

The aim of the editor in gathering materials for *The Papers of Chief John Ross* was to discover all correspondence to and from Ross and all documents bearing his signature or intent. It soon became apparent, however, that a policy of selection would have to be established for publication purposes to resolve the dilemma of limiting documents without diminishing the contribution of the project. Therefore, most letters addressed to Ross have been presented in abstracted form, while many routine items by Ross have been excluded. The latter include Cherokee warrants, laws, resolutions, and receipts bearing Ross's signature and Cherokee documents (such as claims against the federal government) with Ross's certification. Policies of selection were also established for further exclusion of documents since this was not to be a comprehensive edition of Ross's papers. The following types of items have been omitted: Ross's letters written in behalf of other persons; documents to which Ross was a secondary signer; receipts, due bills, invoices, and the like signed by Ross; documents printed in other readily accessible sources; and letters to Ross that were considered less worthy of inclusion. The final category was the largest area of exclusion, and within that area are a great number of letters that Ross answered; those answers are included and fill an apparent gap. It is believed that nothing of enduring historical value has been omitted.

Fig. 2.6a Moulton, *Ross*, 1:xxiii

The editors of the *Papers of Woodrow Wilson* established selection criteria for each of the five major genres of Wilson documents they collected:

1. To publish all letters by Wilson that are essential to understanding his thought and activity. These, they think, have the highest priority. This first volume includes all of Wilson's letters thus far discovered for the period that it covers. Selection of letters for future volumes will obviously depend upon their quality and significance. The editors, when necessary, will also publish incoming letters or extracts from or digests of such letters, particularly when they provide the only indications concerning Wilson's missing replies or furnish the only information about events in Wilson's life. The first two or three volumes, which cover a hitherto sparsely documented period, will include a substantial proportion of incoming letters.

2. To print a selection of Wilson's speeches. Public speaking was for Woodrow Wilson a very important form of communication, and the editors will not neglect it. But Wilson made hundreds of speeches during his lifetime, and publication of all of them would consume disproportionate space. It seems advisable, therefore, to publish in full only the most important speeches, and to edit others by eliminating inordinate repetition.

3. To print as much as seems wise of a wide variety of Wilson manuscripts. Diaries will be published in full, but only samples of Wilson's voluminous classroom and lecture notes will be included. Additional items, such as commonplace books, memoranda, lists, accounts, records of organizations in which Wilson participated, and marginal notes in books, will be printed in whole or in part depending upon importance. However, the editors will describe the contents of all important Wilson documents (e.g., scrapbooks, notebooks, and copybooks) that they do not print in full.

4. To publish all of Wilson's important articles, because the journals in which they appeared are in many cases unavailable even in good libraries.

5. To publish from among Wilson's books only *Congressional Government* and *Constitutional Government in the United States*, on the ground that they are so central in the development of his political thought that they cannot be omitted from a comprehensive edition of his papers.

Fig. 2.6b Link, *Wilson*, 1:xiv–xv

The editors of the *Microform Edition of the John Muir Papers* did not include Muir's published works or certain types of drafts:

Because the Muir family papers at the University of the Pacific contain some 7,000 published items, including a large clipping file and many papers added after Muir died, some selectivity was necessary in appraising material to be filmed. From Series III (Manuscripts and Published Works) only two kinds of material were included: holograph or typescript articles that have not been published previously, and holographs of draft manuscripts that differ significantly from published versions. Excluded from this series are published works, typescripts of published works, and revised holograph versions of published works. In the latter category are author's copies of published articles, most of which contain holograph corrections and revisions in soft pencil. These tear copies have been badly treated over the years; most of the holograph information cannot be deciphered without painstaking care and infinite patience. Transcribing these problematic documents did not seem warranted under the circumstances; hence the decision was made reluctantly to exclude them.

Fig. 2.6c Limbaugh, *Muir*, 5

2.7   Editors may select documents that provide new or varied insights into their subjects. For example, the editors of the *Papers of William Penn* gave preference to documents that contained new perspectives and information about Penn:

Our selection process is necessarily subjective, but we have been guided by the following principles. In deciding which letters and papers to exclude, we omit documents which survive only as abstracts or brief extracts. We also omit routine correspondence of minimal content, and form letters. In deciding which documents to include, we look for letters and papers which are clearly the product of WP's own mind, or which received his close attention. We look for documents which add in some way to the reader's understanding of WP's beliefs and actions. We print correspondence with a cross-section of persons significant to WP, people of the "lower sort" as well as historically important figures. In choosing between two letters which have much the same character and content, we prefer the letter which introduces a new correspondent, or which contributes new information or fuller argument. In selecting representative examples from a sizable group of letters and papers (in the present volume, for example, WP's correspondence with his Anglican, Presbyterian, and Baptist adversaries during the 1670s), we look for interesting variations in presentation and content. And we bring attention to previously neglected categories of documentation, such as WP's business records.

Fig. 2.7a Dunn, *Penn*, 1:9

The editors of the *Papers of Andrew Jackson* published a greater proportion of documents from Jackson's lesser-known early years than from his better-documented later years:

In the interest of presenting a full and balanced picture of Jackson's life, the editors have adopted for this volume a broad definition of "papers" to include outgoing and incoming correspondence, agreements, powers of attorney, commissions, accounts and other records of financial transactions, petitions, legislative reports and resolutions, and even second party reports of speeches and reminiscences. Most of the volumes in this series will include only a selection from the entire body of papers, but, because Jackson's early life is so little known, the editors have chosen a more comprehensive treatment for this volume.

Fig. 2.7b Smith, *Jackson*, 1:xxxi

The editors of *John Jay* included only documents that had not been previously published, documents that had been previously published with substantial errors, or significant documents that had been published previously but had insufficient annotation:

This volume, as well as the others to come, has as its objective the publication of the significant papers to and from John Jay which have never before been published or, if printed elsewhere, to reproduce only those previously printed with substantial errors of omission or transliteration. Exception has been made in the case of a few state papers of immense significance, documents which have not hitherto been adequately annotated. Thus, the editorial guidelines, notes, and annotations seek to furnish the reader with the background needed to identify the persons and subjects treated in the correspondence and such other data essential to an understanding of its contents or to clarifying the relationship to previously published correspondence of the unpublished items herein printed for the first time.

Fig. 2.7c Morris, *Jay,* 1:10

The editors of the supplemental microfilm edition of the *Papers of Andrew Jackson* published only documents not included in earlier print or microfilm editions:

> This Microfilm Supplement to the Library of Congress Andrew Jackson Papers and the National Archives microfilm series comprises <u>all</u> Jackson documents found in the project's search <u>not</u> included on those two publications. It includes all additional copies of Jackson documents; variant copies or drafts; a typewritten or printed copy in the absence of a manuscript; documents from the Library of Congress Andrew Jackson Papers, Series 10 and 12, which have not been filmed; documents from the National Archives not available on film; documents from the Library of Congress and National Archives films incorrectly dated or identified; and all Jackson documents in collections other than the Jackson Papers in the Library of Congress, whether previously filmed or not.

Fig. 2.7d Moser, *Jackson,* xliii

2.8   Selecting items for an edition of legal papers can pose special problems because of the large quantity of documents associated with legal practices, the frequent use of routine forms, and the delegation of work to clerks. The editors of the *Papers of John Marshall* selected legal cases that were significant, cases that illustrated legal practices of the time, and cases in which Marshall played a direct role:

> Selecting cases proved less difficult than originally anticipated. The essential requirements were that the case had to contain at least one Marshall document and had to illuminate some area of his practice. This eliminated many routine cases and those for which the evidence of Marshall's participation was scanty. Further winnowing was achieved by applying other criteria: Was the case broadly representative of a particular type of legal action common in Marshall's Virginia? Was it significant from the perspective of social and economic history as well as that of legal history? If possessing only modest legal and historical significance, did it at least yield an interesting story?
> Each of the cases presents one or more Marshall documents, here defined as any manuscript or printed item that he wrote or that derives from his written or spoken words. This definition embraces documents either in Marshall's hand or signed by him, those known

to have been produced by him though not in his hand or signed, and those by others reporting Marshall's words spoken in court. Selection of other documents depended on their capacity to elucidate the dispute and their suitability for illustrating various stages of pleading and procedure. Stereotyped writs and pleadings have been restricted in most instances to one example of each kind. One declaration in debt on a bond or one in indebitatus assumpsit for goods sold and delivered can easily stand for all such declarations. The same is true of a writ for commencing a suit or for executing a judgment. The cumulative intent is to draw from the surviving records a composite picture of the kinds of legal documents and cases prepared by Marshall in the Virginia and federal courts.

Fig. 2.8a Johnson, *Marshall*, 5:xxvii–xxviii

The editors of the *Legal Papers of Andrew Jackson* used several different criteria for determining whether to include the documents relating to a particular case:

SELECTION OF CASES AND DOCUMENTS

Of necessity, this edition of Jackson's legal papers is a selective one. Because the great majority of the documents that have been collected relate either to litigation in which Jackson participated as counsel or to matters that he heard as a member of the Superior Court, the editors concluded that arrangement of the documents by cases provided the most efficient method of presentation.

The selection process included two steps. First, the editors made an initial selection of the cases that were to be published. The editors chose to follow criteria similar to those set forth by L. Kinvin Wroth and Hiller B. Zobel in the *Legal Papers of John Adams* in making this initial determination:

(1) whether the case in question illuminates a particular legal issue;
(2) whether the case contained an unusual document;
(3) whether the case, when considered with others, accurately illustrated the development of Jackson's legal career;
(4) whether the case was of interest for historical, social, or cultural reasons if not from a purely legal point of view; and
(5) whether there was any justifiable reason for not including the case.

Second, once each case had been selected for inclusion, two additional principles were applied:

(1) any Jackson document relating to the case—*i.e.*, any manuscript in Jackson's hand or addressed to Jackson and any document about Jackson—would be printed, except for the most perfunctory of items, and
(2) any other document would be printed if it explained or illuminated the case or was of interest for any other reason and was not merely cumulative of other documents.

Fig. 2.8b Ely, *Jackson*, xi

2.9   Editors may omit documents that are within their project's scope because of concerns for copyright, confidentiality, or personal privacy. They must determine if the documents to be published are protected by copyright and, if so, obtain the permission of the copyright holder. The editors of the *Collected Papers of Albert Einstein* sought to include the full text of all significant letters written by Einstein and the full text of many letters written to him. In some cases, however, the editors could not obtain permission to publish particular documents; therefore, they presented abstracts of materials they could not legally publish:

> All available letters written by Einstein will be published in this edition. Letters addressed to more than one recipient are printed only once, and all known addressees are noted. Letters to Einstein are handled more selectively, however. All significant letters to him, for which we are able to obtain permission to publish, are printed in whole or in excerpt. In case such permission cannot be obtained, a summary is provided. Authors and dates of known letters not published here are listed in the chronological sequence, and the letters are summarized where necessary.

Fig. 2.9 Stachel, Einstein, 1:xxx

2.10   Government classification systems, closed records, and censorship may limit the ability of editors to publish documents. For example, the editors of *Foreign Relations of the United States* consider the effects of the publication of government documents on current diplomatic affairs and national security when they select documents:

> The publication *Foreign Relations of the United States* constitutes the official record of the foreign policy of the United States. The volumes in the series include, subject to necessary security considerations, all documents needed to give a comprehensive record of the major foreign policy decisions of the United States together with appropriate materials concerning the facts that contributed to the formulation of policies. Documents in the files of the Department of State are supplemented by papers from other government agencies involved in the formulation of foreign policy.
>
> The basic documentary diplomatic record printed in the volumes of the series *Foreign Relations of the United States* is edited by the Office of the Historian, Bureau of Public Affairs, Department of State. The editing is guided by the principles of historical objectivity and in accordance with the following official guidance first promulgated by Secretary of State Frank B. Kellogg on March 26, 1925.
>
> There may be no alteration of the text, no deletions without indicating where in the text the deletion is made, and no omission of facts which were of major importance in reaching a decision. Nothing may be omitted for the purpose of concealing or glossing over what might be regarded by some as a defect of policy. However,

certain omissions of documents are permissible for the following reasons:

> a. To avoid publication of matters which would tend to impede current diplomatic negotiations or other business.
> b. To condense the record and avoid repetition of needless details.
> c. To preserve the confidence reposed in the Department by individuals and by foreign governments.
> d. To avoid giving needless offense to other nationalities or individuals.
> e. To eliminate personal opinions presented in despatches and not acted upon by the Department. To this consideration there is one qualification—in connection with major decisions it is desirable, where possible, to show the alternative presented to the Department before the decision was made.
>
> Documents selected for publication in the *Foreign Relations* volumes are referred to the Department of State Classification/Declassification Center for declassification clearance. The Center reviews the documents, makes declassification decisions, and obtains the clearance of geographic and functional bureaus of the Department of State, as well as of other appropriate agencies of the government.

Fig. 2.10 Glennon, Foreign Relations, 1:iii–iv

2.11   Editors working on recent topics face a particular challenge because of the enormous quantity of documents produced by modern bureaucracies and issued under the name of public officials. For instance, General Dwight D. Eisenhower's name appeared on numerous documents emanating from his office. The editors of his papers developed the following criteria to address this situation:

> After working some time with the Eisenhower papers, we came upon one relatively simple and objective standard for selection. We discovered that the mechanized and bureaucratic nature of communications in a large modern organization forces a similar problem of selection on the men who head them. The leader at the top of a huge enterprise carrying out complex operations must decide with care and precision what matters he will handle personally. He must be able to recall what papers he prepared and who prepared others that he reviewed and signed. In the Army, as in most modern organizations, the writer or the dictator of a letter or message is indicated on at least one copy kept for the files. These initials indicated how we might solve our problem of selection.
>
> In a sense, we could let General Eisenhower do the choosing: that is, we decided to select and annotate only those documents which he himself had written or dictated or which he had taken a direct part in preparing. In fact, to use any other criterion would be to publish the papers of an office not a man. If all the significant papers of the War Plans Divisions (WPD), Allied Force Headquarters (AFHQ), and Supreme Headquarters Allied

Expeditionary Force (SHAEF) that went out over Eisenhower's signature were printed, shelves of volumes would have to be published. Even the number of messages prepared by Eisenhower's personal staff often ran to over a thousand a week. If all of these were included, the activities of the man would be totally lost in those of the organization.

* * * *

Because the initials of the person dictating a letter or cable rarely appear on the ribbon copy and only occasionally on the outgoing messages, we have had to search for and work from file copies. The disadvantage of not using the ribbon copy is that we did not have Eisenhower's signature and often, in the case of letters to Britishers, the salutation. We could also have missed handwritten insertions. Fortunately, Eisenhower's secretaries appear to have typed most of the handwritten comments on the file copy. A thorough search of the ribbon copies in the papers of George Catlett Marshall, Walter Bedell Smith, Winston Spencer Churchill, and others indicates that Eisenhower did not regularly add handwritten remarks and that the secretaries did record on the file copy nearly all those he wrote. In using the file copies we have considered all those initialed "DDE" and all radio or cable messages where the originator was listed as the Commander in Chief or Supreme Comander as having been dictated by Eisenhower.

We have not published the more routine letters and messages that Eisenhower wrote or dictated. These include many perfunctory messages of congratulations, condolences, and thanks for gifts and congratulations received; messages that merely acknowledged the receipt of a letter or reported that he was busy; and those where Eisenhower forwarded information to others without some comment on or addition to it. Nor did we usually print requests for transfers or jobs when Eisenhower merely acknowledged the letter and forwarded it to the proper authority. Where he sent much the same letter or message to different people, we printed one but indicated who else received it and what minor modifications were made in the other copies.

Where the file copy indicated that an Eisenhower-signed document was dictated by another person, we printed the document if we knew Eisenhower was personally involved in its preparation. This was determined in several ways. Often Eisenhower would write on the incoming document directions to his Chief of Staff, planning officers, or aides on the preparation of the reply. As often, too, he gave similar verbal instructions. Where the office diaries indicate such instructions, we included the document. In headquarters files, we occasionally found references to Eisenhower's involvement in the writing or preparing of a document.

Fig. 2.11 Chandler, *Eisenhower*, 1:xiv–xvi

Organizing the Documents for Publication

2.12   Once documents have been selected for publication, editors decide the order in which these materials will be presented. Ideally, the form of presentation should reflect the purpose of the work and the nature of the documents.

2.13   Chronology is an organizing principle used by most editions. This principle can be used by editors in different ways and may be applied within an article or a volume or throughout a multivolume series. The editors of the *Papers of Thomas Edison* explained why they used chronology as their dominant organizing principle:

> The documents in this edition are organized in chronological order. The editors chose chronological rather than subject or document-type organization in order to maximize the historical understanding of Edison's work and to eliminate the need for multiple publication of the same document. Edison generally pursued several projects at one time, and often they were technologically interrelated. With chronological organization the juxtaposition of documents from different projects reveals the interconnectedness of the technical work and the significance of its historical context. A subject approach would have isolated Edison's developmental thinking and in some cases would have placed later labels on work originally conceived quite differently. Organization by document type—that is, personal, business, or technical materials—would have ripped activities from their historical fabric and would have isolated related ideas and events. The chronological approach presents Edison's work in the richness of its personal, technical, financial, and social interrelationships.

Fig. 2.13 Jenkins, Edison, 1:liii

2.14   If many documents are to be printed, editors may consider dividing them at the chapter, volume, or series level into groups united by a similar purpose, theme, or genre. The editors of the *Adams Papers* organized their documents into three series, reflecting both the authors and the genres of documents collected by the project:

> *Series I* will embrace the Adams Diaries and will be divided into at least three parts of disparate length: one for each of the Adams statesmen and possibly a fourth for the diary fragments and autobiographical writings of Louisa Catherine Adams.

* * * *

> *Series II* will be devoted to the Adams Family Correspondence. It will extend in a single chronological sequence from the courtship letters exchanged by John and Abigail Adams beginning in 1762,

through three generations and part of a fourth, to the death of Abigail Brooks Adams in 1889.

* * * *

Series III will have the over-all title General Correspondence and Other Papers and, like Series I, will be divided into three parts: The Papers of John Adams, The Papers of John Quincy Adams, and The Papers of Charles Francis Adams. Each part will contain a comprehensive selection from the letters written by and to the statesman concerned (excluding letters exchanged between him and members of his family) and from his other writings, such as committee reports, diplomatic dispatches, newspaper communications, speeches and messages, literary productions, and the like.

Fig. 2.14a Butterfield, *Diary,* 1:xxxviii–xl

The editors of the *Emma Goldman Papers: A Microfilm Edition* decided to establish three different series because of the major differences between the chronology and content of three major types of documents—correspondence, writings, and government documents:

The microfilm edition of the *Emma Goldman Papers* consists of three series: Correspondence (reels 1-46), Goldman Writings (reels 47-55), and Government Documents (reels 56-66). The documents in each series are organized chronologically with the exception of reels 54-55 in the Goldman Writings series, which are devoted exclusively to drafts of essays and lectures and are organized thematically. Three supplementary reels, consisting of material that arrived too late for the editors to incorporate at the appropriate place in the microfilm, complete the collection: reel 67 (Government Documents and Goldman Writings supplement) and reels 68-69 (Correspondence supplement).

The editors rejected the possibility of one chronologically organized series because of the diverse nature of the documents. First, the dates of correspondence and of published material relate very differently to the point of intellectual origin. Dates of correspondence are immediate, whereas the publication of a Goldman manuscript could occur months or even years after authorship. Hence, combining correspondence and publications would misrepresent the flow of Goldman's life. Second, by placing the writings in a separate series, the editors have tried to highlight the difference between the private unfolding of Goldman's life and he more formal published personae.

Similarly, combining government documents with correspondence would mislead readers. The government documents present an interpretation of Goldman's life from the perspective of various governments' interest in her as a dangerous or suspicious person. Naturally, such a view colors the material and creates distortions. Agents' reports on Goldman, even transcriptions of her speeches or letters contain many inaccuracies, and much time could pass between the occurrence of an event and its report. Many of the records also went through several versions, in the course of which different government agencies reproduced them in whole or in part, increasing the chances for distortion. In short, as scholarly evidence, the different characteristics of correspondence and government documents demanded they be filed separately.

Fig. 2.14b Falk, *Goldman*, reel 1:5–6

The editors of *Freedom: A Documentary History of Emancipation* divided their edition into five thematically defined series, with each volume arranged into thematic chapters:

> Reflecting editorial interest in a *social* history of emancipation, *Freedom* is organized thematically, following the process of emancipation. At each step the editors have selected documents that illustrate processes they believe are central to the transition from slavery to freedom. The first two series concentrate primarily on the years of the Civil War. Series 1 documents the destruction of slavery, the diverse circumstances under which slaves claimed their freedom, and the wartime labor arrangements developed as slavery collapsed. Series 2 examines the recruitment of black men into the Union army and the experiences of black soldiers under arms. The remaining series, while drawing in part upon evidence from the war years, explore most fully the transformation of black life that followed the conclusion of armed conflict. They document the struggle for land, the evolution of new labor arrangements, relations with former masters and other whites, law and justice, violence and other extralegal repression, geographical mobility, family relationships, education, religion, the structure and activities of the black community, and black politics in the early years of Reconstruction. The series are organized as follows:
>
> Series 1   The Destruction of Slavery and the Wartime Genesis of Free Labor
> Series 2   The Black Military Experience
> Series 3   Land, Capital, and Labor
> Series 4   Race Relations, Violence, Law, and Justice
> Series 5   The Black Community: Family, Church, School, and Society
>
> Each series comprises one or more volumes, and topical arrangement continues within the volumes. Each chapter is introduced by an essay that provides background information, outlines government policy, and elaborates the larger themes. The chapters are further subdivided, when relevant, to reflect distinctive historical, economic, and demographic circumstances.

Fig. 2.14c Berlin, *Freedom*, ser.1,1:xxi–xxii

The *Documentary History of the Supreme Court of the United States* divided its projected seven-volume edition into four separate subject areas focusing on different aspects of the origin and function of the court as well as on specific cases:

> We do not intend to publish all the documents we have collected. Our series of seven volumes will contain only those documents we believe to be most useful and of most interest to scholars, lawyers, and the reading public. (The criteria for selecting items will be explained in each volume.) Volume 1 presents documents that establish the structure of the Supreme Court and recount the official record of the Court's activity during its first decade. It will serve as an introduction and reference tool for the subsequent volumes. The second volume will consist of items bearing on the origins of the federal judiciary. These documents will provide a framework for understanding the development of Article III of the Constitution and legislation dealing with the judicial system during the first ten years of its existence. The special focus of the volume will be references to the structure and role of the Supreme Court. Volume 3 will treat the justices on circuit and include, among other things, a circuit court calendar for each of the three circuits from 1790 to 1800 and a collection of all grand jury charges that we have found, both in print and in draft form. The four volumes that follow will concentrate on the specific cases that came before the Supreme Court and, if space permits, miscellaneous documents dealing with a variety of topics such as the extrajudicial activities of the justices and plans for where the Court was to sit in New York, Philadelphia, and Washington.

Fig. 2.14d Marcus, *Supreme Court,* vol.1,1:xliii–xliv

2.15 Legal cases pose special problems for editors arranging legal editions as a result of the long duration of many cases, the existence of multiple simultaneous cases, the large numbers of routine documents, the different jurisdictions of courts where cases might be heard, and the disparate nature of cases. The editors of the *Papers of John Marshall* used the jurisdiction of cases as their primary criteria for arrangement, with cases ordered chronologically within each section. The front matter of volume 5 described how the documents were arranged:

> It consists of forty-three cases, which in turn are divided into six sections corresponding to the court in which they were heard. Within each case and section chronology prevails, though between one section and another there may be a considerable overlap in time.
>
> In a broader sense the volume divides itself into two parts. The first (Case Numbers 1–18, Sections I–IV) embraces suits brought in a court of original jurisdiction and presents numerous documents drawn principally from the case files. The second (Case Numbers 19–43, Sections V–VI) is a selection of reported cases and appellate arguments in the General Court and the Court of Appeals. In three

cases (Numbers 3, 5, and 7) Marshall also argued the appeal, and his reported argument has been included with the documents in the original action rather than presented separately in the Court of Appeals section.

Fig. 2.15a Johnson, *Marshall*, 5:xxiv–xxv

The editors of the *Legal Papers of John Adams* divided their edition into topical sections corresponding to different types of legal cases:

> The plan of these volumes is topical. With the exception of the first two sections, which deal with law study and pleading, the materials published have been grouped under the time-honored divisions of the law—torts, contracts, property, and the rest. The headings chosen are very broad. For example, the section labeled "Property" treats numerous variants of the topic, including real estate, probate matters, and water rights. Many cases, of course, defy categorization; the ultimate location depends on what seemed to be the dominant theme. Each of the eighteen topics has been given a different alphabetical designation.
>
> Since the Adams Legal Papers are primarily case-oriented, the documents published under each topical subdivision (again excepting the first two topics) have been grouped into sixty-four numbered principal cases. Within each topic the cases are usually in chronological order according to the date on which the litigation commenced.[7] The dates affixed to each case represent the inclusive dates for the litigation—the years of commencement and final disposition.

Fig. 2.15b Wroth, *Adams*, 1:xxxv–xxxvi

2.16   Some editors, especially those filming archival collections, will retain the archival arrangement of the documents when creating their editions. For example, the editors of the microfilm edition of *American Federation of Labor Records* maintained the documents as they were originally arranged by the AFL:

> This microfilm edition of the William Green Papers consists of ten separate files: Historical File, Convention File, Relations with the CIO, Political Collaboration with the CIO, Papers Favoring AFL-CIO Unity, National and International Union Correspondence, State Federations of Labor Correspondence, Central Labor Union Correspondence, Local Union Correspondence, and Miscellaneous Correspondence. These files, with the exception of the Historical File and part of the Convention File, are made up of folders that were arranged topically by the AFL; these files are further divided into subject classifications within each folder. For those files that are arranged topically, this Reel Index reproduces the AFL's filing system: i.e., the files are referenced by means of folder title as well as subject classification within each folder. For the files that were not arranged topically, i.e., the Historical File and Box #4 of the Convention File, this Reel Index indicates the major subjects, reports, and policy formulations appearing in each folder, as well as the principal correspondents.

Fig. 2.16a Boehm, *AFL Records*, part 2, ser.A:1

The editors of the *Henry Knox Papers* made few modifications in the arrangement of the original manuscripts when creating their microfilm edition:

> **No attempt has been made to re-edit the papers; they are presented as they were originally catalogued and bound, with few exceptions. In some cases scholars working the papers have suggested that individual letters be transferred to their proper chronological position in the collection; but little else has been changed.**

Fig. 2.16b Massachusetts Historical Society, *Knox*, 56:4

Challenges of Chronology

2.17   Even editors choosing to order their documents chronologically will face problems—multiple documents of the same date, documents that are partially or completely undated, and documents with uncertain dates. Editors should clearly state how they have addressed such problems and announce when they have made exceptions to the stated policies.

2.18   Editors need to establish policies for ordering multiple documents written on the same date. The editors of the *Papers of James Madison* used alphabetical and sequential organization for multiple documents written on the same date:

> Several letters written on one day, as increasingly was the case as Madison gained in prestige, are alphabetized by the last names of his correspondents. If he wrote to a person on the same day that person wrote to him, the letters are arranged, if possible, in their exact time sequence; if this is unknown, Madison's letter precedes the other. Documents of the Continental Congress are placed among the "C's" and those of the Virginia General Assembly among the "V's."

Fig. 2.18a Hutchinson, *Madison*, 1:xxxv–xxxvi

The editors of the *Papers of General Nathanael Greene* ordered documents by genre and then alphabetically thereunder:

> Letters and documents are arranged chronologically. If two or more related items are dated the same day they are arranged in sequence; if unrelated to each other, they are arranged as follows:
> 1. Military orders and documents (as opposed to letters)
> 2. Letters from NG, alphabetically by recipient
> 3. Letters to NG, alphabetically by sender

Fig. 2.18b Showman, *Greene*, 1:xxxv

The editors of the chronologically arranged *Papers of Robert Morris* developed policies for ordering documents that were partially dated, supplied with a date by the editors, or undated:

> **The editors have placed the dateline at the head of each document, regardless of its place in the manuscript, and have supplied dates for documents in which they are partially or wholly missing. Such documents are placed according to the following rules:**
>
> **1. When no day within a month can be assigned, the document is placed after all others in that month.**
>
> **2. When no month is given, the document is placed at the end of the year.**
>
> **3. When the year is missing and a probable one can be supplied, it is inserted in square brackets with a question mark and the document placed at the end of that year.**
>
> **4. When a single year cannot be assigned, inclusive dates are conjectured within square brackets, and the document is placed following all others at the end of the first year.**
>
> **5. Documents for which no date can be conjectured will be arranged under the heading "n.d." in the final volume of the series.**

Fig. 2.18c Ferguson, Morris, 1:xxxiii–xxxiv

The editors of the *Papers of Martin Luther King, Jr.* developed policies for dating undated documents such as school essays and for dating published or publicly released works:

> **Date.** In those cases where the original bears no date, the editors have assigned one. Range dates that correspond to the dates of a school term are given to some undated papers such as school essays. Those documents bearing range dates are arranged after precisely dated documents, unless logic dictates another order. The date of photographs is presented without brackets if the donor provided a date. The date of published or printed papers is the date of publication or public release rather than the date of composition.

Fig. 2.18d Carson, King, 1:444

2.19   When editors develop rules to address the particular needs of their editions or alter established policies for special cases, these instances should be clearly stated. For example, the editors of the *Papers of Benjamin Franklin* chose to place their documents in chronological sequence but noted exceptions when chronological order would not suffice:

> One exception to this system of dating will be *Poor Richard's Almanack,* which Franklin prepared for the years 1733 through 1758. He might announce publication of his almanac at any time between early October and mid-December of the preceding year.

But since the almanacs covered particular calendar years, it seems appropriate to print the material drawn from them as the first documents of the years for which Franklin prepared them, rather than on the earlier dates when he first announced their publication.

Another exception to strict chronological arrangement has to do with miscellaneous brief news reports, notes, and advertisements in *The Pennsylvania Gazette*. These record or reflect Franklin's interests, his activities, or his sense of humor; as such they deserve to be included in this edition, but are too short or too inconsequential to justify printing as separate documents in regular chronological order. We have made selections of such items from each year of the *Gazette* from 1729 through 1747, when Franklin took a partner into his printing office; and we shall print a group of them, under the heading "Extracts from the *Gazette*," at the end of each year to which they belong. The issue in which each individual item appeared will be noted with it.

Franklin began to write his Memoirs, as he called his autobiography, in 1771. He continued them in 1784, 1788, and 1789. In this edition the Memoirs will be printed in four parts, under the four dates when Franklin wrote them.

When two or more documents have the same date, they will be arranged in the following order:

1. Those by a group of which Franklin was a member (e.g., the American Commissioners in Paris)
2. Those by Franklin individually
3. Those to a group of which Franklin was a member
4. Those to Franklin individually
5. "Third-party" and unaddressed miscellaneous writings by others than Franklin.

In the first two categories letters will be arranged alphabetically by the name of the addressee; and in the last three, by the name of the signatory. An exception to this practice will occur on the rare occasions when a letter to Franklin and his answer were written on the same day: in such cases the first letter must precede the reply. The same rules will apply to documents lacking precise dates printed together at the end of any month or year.

Fig. 2.19 Labaree, *Franklin*, 1:xxxvi–xxxvii

2.20 The placement of diary entries is a matter of editorial judgment. The editors of the *Diaries of George Washington* chose to print his diaries independent of his other papers for reasons that were both practical and designed to present the diary in the best manner:

Although in a generic sense the diaries in this edition are part of Washington's "papers," they are published separately from the forthcoming series, *The Papers of George Washington*. This decision seems fitting because the diaries span Washington's entire career in relatively few volumes and are thus a complete work in themselves. There are lamentable gaps, but the reader may savor the man's words and works as they evolved from the day he set out as a boy of sixteen, to survey for Lord Fairfax, until that day before his death when, always conscious of the weather, he wrote a final entry: "Mer[cury] at 28 at Night."

Another persuasive reason to issue the diaries before the *Papers* has been the time required to assemble, from repositories and private owners all over the world, the letters and documents that will comprise the main series. While these thousands of manuscripts were being located, catalogued, and transcribed by some members of our staff, others proceeded with the editorial work on the diaries. The fact that as these diaries go to press we are still receiving substantial numbers of manuscripts for inclusion in the *Papers* provides further justification for our decision.

Fig. 2.20a Jackson, Washington, 1:li–lii

The editors of the *Papers of Dwight David Eisenhower* treated each dated diary entry as a separate document and placed it in chronological order, interspersed among other documents:

2   *Eisenhower Mss., Diaries*

D<small>IARY</small>   *January 3, 1951*

So far as my new job is concerned—the "staff mind" is working in typical channels in Washington.[1] Instead of everybody concerning himself with the substance of the problem (Nat'l Attitudes; industrial capacities; military programs and present strength) the principal subject of discussion is the one so dear to the hearts of academic soldiers & sailors—"command systems." Principally this stems from the primary failure to see that command in Allied ventures implies & imposes a great national responsibility upon the nation assuming it. Since staff think of command in terms of kudos & glory (arising out of the erroneous thinking that such command is comparable to that exercised by the individual over his own service).[2]

Fig. 2.20b Chandler, Eisenhower, 12:6

The editors of the *Documentary History of the Ratification of the Constitution* presented pertinent excerpts from multiple diaries in chronological order:

Noah Webster Diary, Philadelphia, Tuesday, 18 September[4]

General Washington leaves town. Dr. Franklin presents the Speaker of the House of Assembly in Pennsylvania with the federal system which is read. Bells ring. All America waits anxiously for the plan of government.

Philadelphia Pennsylvania Packet, 18 September

We have the heartfelt pleasure to inform our fellow citizens that the Federal Convention adjourned yesterday, having completed the object of their deliberations. And we hear that Major W[illiam] Jackson, the Secretary of that honorable body, leaves this city for New York this morning in order to lay the great result of their proceedings before the United States in Congress.

William Samuel Johnson Diary, 18, 19 September (excerpts)[5]

18th. Set out at 10 o'clock in the stage, Governor [William] Livingston, [William] Few, [Abraham] Baldwin, [William] Jackson, etc. in company came to [New] Brunswick. Cold.

Fig. 2.20c Jensen, *Ratification*, 1:319

The editors of the *Papers of Woodrow Wilson* placed excerpts from the diary of Colonel House amid the papers of Wilson because of House's close relationship to Wilson, his insider's vantage on events in Washington, and the high quality of his diary entries:

From the Diary of Colonel House

October 2, 1914.

Cleveland Dodge came by appointment early this morning. I wished to discuss with him the State Chairmanship, in reference to his brother-in-law, William Church Osborn. I also showed him Walter Pager's [Page's] recent letter giving a statement of his income and outgo for the past year, and asked him for a check in compliance with his understanding with the President. It was agreed that he should give me a check for $10,000. to start with made payable to Arthur W. Page, and that Arthur was to send

Fig. 2.20d Link, *Wilson*, 31:122

Excerpts, Abstracts, and Calendars

2.21 Editions may present documents without publishing them in full in a number of ways. The most interesting or relevant portions may be printed as excerpts. If many documents are similar in form and content, editions can publish examples. Editors may use abstracts to avoid publishing routine documents or form letters, to save space, to provide reference to a more complete edition, to publish short quotations from long documents, or to provide information about documents that are no longer extant. Calendars are even more concise, providing a chronological list of documents with only minimal descriptive information.

2.22 Editors may choose to excerpt portions of documents in order to present only the most interesting or pertinent sections. Excerpts may be brief or long, eliminating a few irrelevant sentences or extracting a single line from a several-page document. The extent to which editors use excerpts will depend on the desire or need to publish only the most pertinent passages of documents. Editors should use great care in excerpting to avoid altering the meaning of passages removed from their context. An excerpt should be indicated through the use of ellipsis points (...). The following document occupied seven full pages in the *Documentary History of the Ratification of the Constitution*, but the editor of *A Necessary Evil?: Slavery and the Debate over the Constitution* published a three-line excerpt containing the only lines in the document that concerned slavery:

AN OFFICER OF THE LATE CONTINENTAL ARMY (WILLIAM FINDLEY)
Philadelphia *Independent Gazetteer*, November 6, 1787[9]

The objections that have been made to the new constitution, are these: . . .
    20. The importation of slaves is not to be prohibited until the year 1808, and SLAVERY will probably resume its empire in Pennsylvania.

Fig. 2.22a Kaminski, *Necessary Evil*, 125

The editor of "On Convoy Duty during World War I: The Diary of Hoosier Guy Connor" excerpted from Connor's diary entries, omitting less interesting passages and technical information such as detailed map coordinates:

October 24—1918
Made 15 knots all night and caught up with the convoy about 8 am. The captain figures on ten days going over and ten coming back. I only hope we pull into New York instead of Yorktown. Copied Bermuda this morning . . . Was on watch today from 7:45 am until 3:15 pm on account of Belmar starting to send a reply to Nanen on one of the peace notes. It was history in radio because it

was the first time we have communicated with Germany direct since war was declared.[31] Now I have the eight to twelve pm watch making fifteen hours and thirty minutes on watch today. We are making fifteen knots all the time now and this will be a quick trip if we have no bad luck. . . .

Fig. 2.22b Patrick, *Indiana*, 89:347

2.23   Abstracts may be used to convey the information found in a document without printing its text. The *Papers of Jefferson Davis* used abstracts, complete with explanatory footnotes, in place of routine documents:

ABSTRACT

Thomas P. Gwynn to Thomas S. Jesup

Fort Winnebago,[1] [Michigan Territory][2]
April 10, 1830

Gwynn[3] transmits a number of reports to the quartermaster general,[4] apologizes for the way in which post reports were made out, and states that he has "been relieved from the duties of A[cting] A[ssistant] Q. m. for the present by Lt. Davis . . . ."[5]

LS (NA, RG 92 Records of the Office of the Quartermaster General, Consolidated Correspondence File, Fort Winnebago, G–97, 1830), 3. Addressed: "Gen. T. S. Jessup Q M Gen U. S. A. Washington City D. C." Signed: "T P Gwynn Lt act[ing] ass[istant] Q M." Endorsed: "Recd June 8th. 1830." Enclosures missing.

1 See 1:144, *n.* 1.
2 See 1:149, *n.* 2.
3 Thomas P. Gwynn (sketch, 1:148, *n.* 1) left on furlough April 28 (Post Return, April 1830 [NA, RG 94, Fort Winnebago, 1828–45]).
4 Thomas S. Jesup (1788–1860), a Virginian, was quartermaster general for forty-two years (1818–60), having been first commissioned a second lieutenant in 1808. Jesup served as General William Hull's brigade major and ad-

jutant general in the War of 1812 and was brevetted lieutenant colonel and colonel in 1814 for his conduct in the battles of Chippewa and Lundy's Lane. Even though the army was greatly reduced after the war, he was retained as an infantry major and was major general by 1828. In the Seminole War (1836–38) Jesup commanded the army in Florida. He is credited with a massive and efficient reorganization of the Quartermaster Department, and was honored by having two army posts named for him. He died in Washington and was succeeded by Lieutenant Colonel Joseph E. Johnston (*DAB*; Heitman, *Historical Register*, I, 573; Risch, *Quartermaster Support of the Army, passim*).
5 Davis also relieved Gwynn in the office of assistant commissary of subsistence (1:175).

Fig. 2.23a Monroe, *Davis*, 1:133

The editors of the *Papers of Henry Laurens* used abstracts as a substitute for printing routine documents:

TO ROGERS & DYSON

[Charles Town] 12th May 1748

[Encloses bill of exchange.]

SOURCE: Letterbook copy, HL Papers, S. C. Hist. Soc.

Fig. 2.23b Hamer, *Laurens*, 1:136

Abstracts may be used to provide information from documents that once existed but can no longer be found, as in the following example from the *Papers of Robert Morris*:

To Le Couteulx and Company

[Philadelphia, July 31, 1781. RM made the following note in his Diary of this date: "Wrote a Letter to Messrs. Le Couteulx & Co. advising of Bills Drawn." *Letter not found.]*

Fig. 2.23c Ferguson, *Morris*, 1:419

2.24   Calendars may be used to provide readers with a dated, descriptive list of correspondence. The editors of the *Correspondence of James K. Polk* provided a complete calendar listing all known Polk correspondence, including short content descriptions:

CALENDAR

N.B. Items entered in *italic* type have been published or briefed in the Correspondence Series.

1816

14 July   From William Leetch. ALS. Pvt. Ms. of W. R. Ewing, Cleveland, Tennessee. Sends personal and family news to Polk, who attends the University of North Carolina.

1817

8 July   *From Samuel Thomas Hauser.*

Fig. 2.24a Weaver, *Polk*, 6:405

The editors of the *Papers of Josiah Bartlett* calendared documents not printed in the book edition and included the frame numbers of those that had appeared in the microfilm edition:

Calendar of Correspondence Not Printed

[1751]

25 July   From Hannah Kent. RC (Mr. & Mrs. Rodney M. Wilson, Kingston, N. H.). Sends price list of medical supplies. MJB, 21.

1756

18 March   From Daniel Rogers. RC (Mr. & Mrs. Rodney M. Wilson, Kingston, N. H.). Note, with invoice for medical supplies. MJB, 53.

1759

26 April   From Daniel Rogers. RC (Mr. & Mrs. Rodney M. Wilson, Kingston. N. H.). Encloses invoice for medical supplies. MJB

Fig. 2.24b Mevers, *Bartlett*, 413

The editors of the *Papers of John C. Calhoun* explained the information contained in their calendar and the types of documents noted therein:

> This Calendar summarizes Calhoun papers not printed in this volume and lists others not so printed to which reference is made in the editorial notes. (Compare pages xv and xxxiv-xxxviii.) Unless otherwise stated, any action noted was by Calhoun.
>
> The location or source of each paper is cited within brackets at the beginning of the Calendar entry. The symbol *als* (autograph letter signed) indicates a letter written and signed by the same person; *ls* (letter signed) indicates a letter written by one person and signed by another; and *fc* (file copy) indicates a document preserved in the form of a letter-book or clerk's copy. Other abbreviations and symbols used in this Calendar correspond with those used elsewhere in this volume (see pages xxxix-xl).

Fig. 2.24c Meriwether, *Calhoun*, 1:421

The editors of the *Papers of Zebulon Baird Vance* provided in columnar form the date, subject, and location of each unpublished document:

PAPERS NOT PRINTED IN THIS VOLUME

Correspondents	Date	Subject	Repository
W.H. Croom to ZBV	May 28	bridge	A&H:GP
Archy Brown to ZBV	May 28	appointment	A&H:GP
John W. Brock to ZBV	May 28	furlough	A&H:GP
John M. Worth to ZBV	May 28	salt workers	A&H:GP
D.T. Towles to ZBV	May 28	transfer	A&H:GP
Alexander Walker to ZBV	May 28	slaves	A&H:GP
G.W. Walker to ZBV	May 28	furlough	A&H:GP
H. Cabarriss et al. to ZBV	May 28	conscription	A&H:GP
Robert Strange to Richard H. Battle	May 29	commission	A&H:GP

Fig. 2.24d Johnston, *Vance*, 2:386

Chapter Three

General Principles of Transcription and Proofreading

Introduction to Transcription

3.1　　Transcription is the process of converting textual and nontextual elements of original documents into readable, publishable, typescript form. In so doing, editors strive to represent original documents faithfully. All transcription, however, is a form of translation and requires editors to make innumerable decisions about how to present documents. Editors make choices about standardization of the form of the documents (placement of datelines, uniform indentation of paragraphs, etc.) as well as about how to emend the text (capitalization, punctuation, etc.). In the past, the typesetting of textual features such as superscripts, subscripts, canceled passages, interlineations, marginalia, drawings, and other marks was costly, and these features were reproduced for only the most important texts or were represented through editorial symbols. Modern typesetting and printing techniques have reduced the difficulty and expense of reproducing unusual textual characteristics, and, as a result, cost is no longer the primary consideration. Instead, editors evaluate the types of documents they will be transcribing, consider the needs of the audience, and then select the form or forms of presentation that best convey the information contained in the document. Transcription methods should be presented in an introductory statement and then consistently implemented.

Principles of Emendation

3.2   Emendations are textual changes made by editors when transcribing original documents. The most common forms of emendation include capitalizing proper nouns and first letters of sentences and supplying terminal punctuation, but editors might also supply or delete other types of punctuation, convert archaic forms into modern usage, spell out abbreviations, standardize accidentals, supply letters or words missing from damaged manuscripts, and correct spelling. Editors should carefully consider whether to alter textual characteristics and, if so, which ones. Most important, they must consider how those changes may affect the information contained in the documents.

3.3   Silent emendation modifies the text of a document during transcription without alerting the reader at the point that the text has been altered. Editors may inform their readers in the edition's introduction that certain standard emendations will occur throughout the volume, or they may list textual changes at the back of the edition. If editors employ silent emendation, it is incumbent on them to explain how the texts presented in their editions deviate from the original documents. Exceptions to these general emendation rules are usually indicated in editorial notes.

3.4   Overt emendation is the process of modifying the text of a document during transcription in a way that alerts the reader that a change has been made. Editors may use symbols such as arrows, lines, brackets, italics, small capital letters, or footnotes to indicate where and how a text has been altered.

Methods of Transcription

3.5   There is no single agreed-on method of transcription. Rather, editors use different types of editorial apparatus and different degrees of emendation depending on the nature of the documents and the intended audience. Editors choose among five major forms of document presentation (photographic facsimile, typographical facsimile, diplomatic transcription, expanded transcription, or clear text transcription) to find a style that best suits the needs of their audiences, the purposes of their editions, and their personal preferences. Expanded transcription is used most frequently by editors of historical editions, but all editors must evaluate the advantages and disadvantages each form of presentation might bring to their editions.

3.6   Photographic facsimile editions reproduce original documents and present them on the page, screen, or microform frame free from alterations caused by converting manuscripts or original print into modern type. For typed or clearly written documents, photographic facsimile offers an effective method of presentation that is quicker to execute and less expensive than transcription. Hard-to-read documents will remain hard to read as photographic facsimiles, although documents photographed for a book or microform edition may have better contrast than the originals, and electronic editions may allow readers to adjust the size, contrast, brightness, and resolution of the images. The editors of the book edition of the *Johns Hopkins University Seminary of History and Politics: The Records of an American Educational Institution* published their documents as photographic facsimiles:

Fig. 3.6a Gettleman, *Hopkins*, 1:105

The editors of the microfilm edition of the *Benjamin Harrison Papers* published their documents as photographic facsimiles:

Fig. 3.6b LOC, *Harrison*, ser.1, reel 12

The editors of the *Emma Goldman Papers* published several documents on the project's World Wide Web home page as photographic facsimiles:

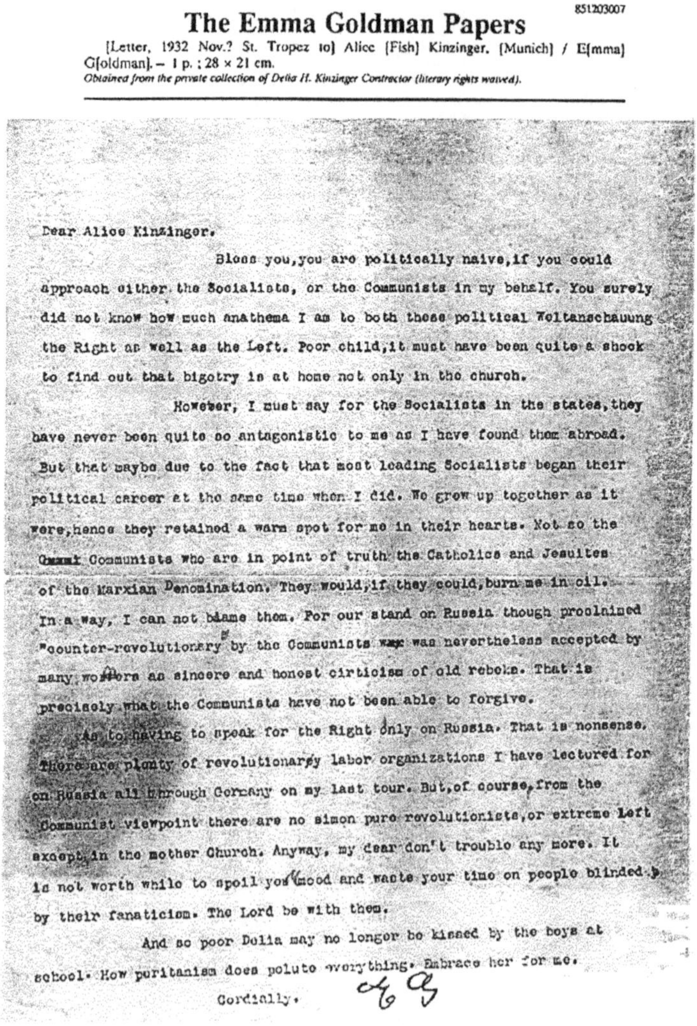

The Emma Goldman Papers 851203007

[Letter, 1932 Nov.? St. Tropez to] Alice [Fish] Kinzinger. [Munich] / E[mma] G[oldman]. – 1 p. ; 28 × 21 cm.
Obtained from the private collection of Delia H. Kinzinger Contractor (literary rights waived).

Fig. 3.6c Goldman, WWW

3.7   Editors who use typographical facsimile as a method of transcription transfer original documents into type so that the appearance and physical arrangement of words on the typescript page mimic that of the original. The *Documentary History of the Supreme Court of the United States* used typographical facsimile to put a page of original minutes (*top*) into type (*bottom*) but did not render the linebreaks of the original:

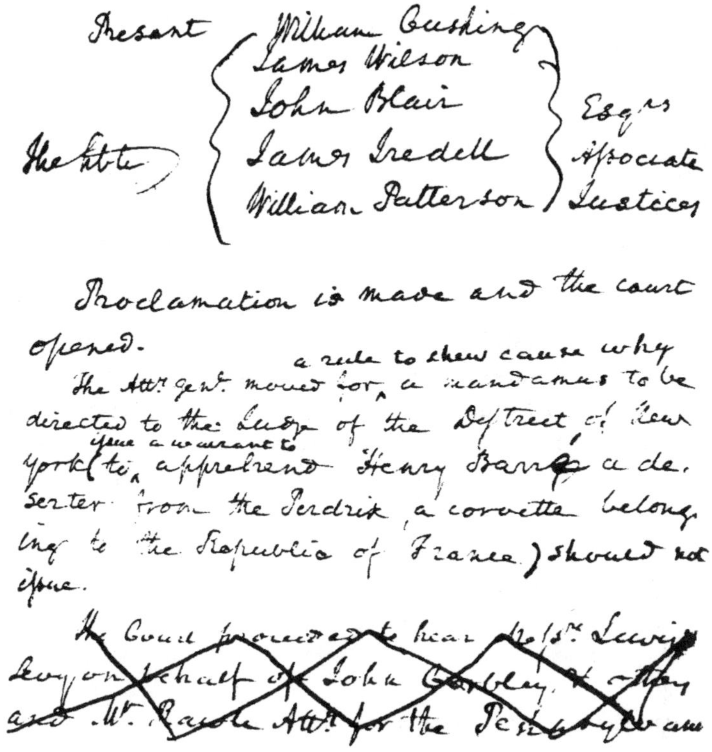

Fig. 3.7a Marcus, *Supreme Court*, vol.1,1:387

Present

	William Cushing	
	James Wilson	Esqⁿ
The hble	John Blair	Associate
	James Iredell	Justices
	William Patterson	

Proclamation is made and the court opened _

a rule to shew cause why

The Att.ʸ Gen! moved for ˄ a mandamus to be directed to the Judge of the

issue a warrant to

District of New York (to ˄ apprehend Henry Barré[104] a deserter from the Perdrix, a corvette belonging to the Republic of France) should not issue.

The Court proceeded to hear Messⁿ Lewis & Levy on behalf of John Corbley & others and M.ʳ Rawle Att.ʸ for the Pennsylvania District on behalf of the United States on the subject of the petition of said Corbley & others & on a motion made by their council

Fig. 3.7b Marcus, *Supreme Court*, vol.1,1:386

3.8   Editors using diplomatic transcription transfer the text of a document into modern type but use symbols such as arrows, carets, and brackets to indicate the document's stylistic details and appearance, a system dubbed "barbed wire" by the author and critic Lewis Mumford. This method is often used for documents for which the reader may be interested in the composition process. The editors of the *Papers of Henry Laurens* began using diplomatic transcription in volume 10, marking insertions with up and down arrows (↑ inserted ↓) and canceled passages with strikethrough type (~~canceled~~):

[1ˢᵗ][2] Your Letter of the 25ᵗʰ· November ~~which inclosed~~ [2ᵈ] The Treaty, between Major Robinson ~~on the part of the Enemies of American Liberty and~~ Yourself & Major Mayson[3] ~~on our part, together with~~ [3] A Return of Troops under Your Command ~~in the Fortified Camp~~ at Ninety-Six_[4] [4] Another Letter ~~of the same date.~~ ↑dated as above_↓ ~~*illegible*~~ [5ᵗʰ] Richᵈ· Pearis's affidavit_ &

Fig. 3.8a Hamer, *Laurens,* 10:524

The editor of the *Complete Works of Washington Irving: Journals and Notebooks* also employed diplomatic transcription, using arrows to mark insertions (↑ inserted ↓) and angled brackets (<canceled>) to mark canceled passages:

lasting impressions. A Frenchman is all life, gaiety & spirit – his feelings are acute and ↑as↓ easily ↑<as>↓ wounded <but> as delighted yet they do not retain long any sentiment either of anger or pleasure. Though <his courage is> no one is more sensible of an insult or more prompt to resent it – yet he is easily pacified the least concession restores him to good humour.

Fig. 3.8b Wright, *Irving,* 1:329

3.9   Expanded transcription encompasses a wide spectrum of editing styles, all of which standardize accidentals, datelines, and signatures; mark paragraphs with indentations; and do not attempt to reproduce the excessive spacing and physical layout of the text of documents. Editors who employ expanded transcription announce the ways they will emend the text and use those methods unless otherwise indicated. Editors have the greatest leeway for making decisions about the appearance of their text with the expanded method of transcription. Choices range from a near-literal rendering to significant emendation. Editors who opt to use expanded transcription will face difficult decisions about how to best convey the substance of historical texts without distorting them or cluttering the page with editorial devices. (For more information on the execution of expanded transcription, see Chapter 5.)

3.10   Editors who use a more conservative style of expanded transcription alter the text as noted in Section 3.9 but otherwise try to convert the text of the document into type as literally as possible. The editors of *Freedom: A Documentary History of Emancipation* employed a conservative style of expanded transcription, maintaining the original manuscripts' syntax, spelling, punctuation, wording, capitalization, paragraph breaks, superscripts, contractions, and abbreviations. The editors limited intervention to indenting the beginning of new paragraphs, incorporating interlineations into the body of the text, providing extra space in the place of missing terminal punctuation, making ambiguous characters and punctuation conform with modern practice, and indenting and printing in small type extended quotations within documents:

> Hdq^{rs} U.S. Forces. East^{n} Shore Va Eastville Feb^{ry} 15
> /65
>   Resp^{ly} returned. The Statements of B. L. Parish are entirely
> false. My employees are more loyal than the party making the
> charges, and are entirely worthy of the trust placed in them.
>   The Statements made concerning the hiring of colored persons by
> force is also false. These Statements are based upon an order issued
> from my office requiring all colored persons to labor for a
> livelihood.[1] This order in all it's details has been approved by Major
> Carney Supt. of Negro affairs Dept: Va, by Brig: Genl Shepley Com^{g}
> the Dist: of East^{n} Va, by Major Genl Ord Com^{g} this Dept: and was
> approved by Major Genl Butler when in Command of the Dept of Va
> & N.C.
>   For a more complete answer to within letter I would resp^{ly} refer to
> my Communication of the 6th inst: addressed to the Major Genl:
> Com^{g} this Dept: forwarded through Hdq^{rs} Dist: East^{n} Va.[2] Frank J.
> White Lt Col Com^{g} U.S. Forces East^{n} Shore Va.

Fig. 3.10a Berlin, *Freedom*, ser.1,2:220

The editors of the *Papers of Ulysses S. Grant* used a conservative form of expanded transcription that entailed lowering superscripts to the line, marking canceled passages with strikethrough type, and reconstructing or noting torn, mutilated, illegible, and lost materials:

GEN.

I have just recieved yours of the 23d inst. informing me that I have given Lt. P. Andrews 2d Art.y credit for 100$ on my accounts for 2d quarter 1848. The name should read 1st Lieut. Geo. P. Andrews 3d Artillery.

> I am Gen
> Very Respectfully
> Yr. Obt. Svt.
> U. S. GRANT
> 1st Lt. 4th Inf.y
> A. A. C. S.

To Gen Geo. Gibson
Com.y Gen. Sub.

Fig. 3.10b Simon, *Grant*, 1:182

3.11 Editors who employ a more liberal style of expanded transcription standardize the text as noted in Section 3.9, but then make significant additional interventions. In the first volume of the *Documentary History of the Ratification of the Constitution*, the editors employed a liberal style of expanded transcription that heavily emended the text, as described in the volume's editorial methods statement:

Capitalization, Punctuation, and Italics in Manuscript Materials

Capital letters are used to begin each sentence. Random capitals and italics are removed except when they are evidently used by the author for emphasis. Periods are placed at the ends of sentences instead of dashes, colons, or no punctuation at all. Punctuation is altered within sentences if needed to clarify meaning.

Spelling

With one exception, spelling is made to conform to present-day practice. For example, "labour" and "foederal" are spelled "labor" and "federal." The exception to this rule is the spelling of names of individuals. While it is easy enough to correct the spelling of the names of a "Madison" or a "Washington," there are hundreds of legislators and other men whose names are spelled in various ways in document after document, and sometimes in the same document.

The editors therefore follow the practice of the editors of such modern publications as the papers of Thomas Jefferson, John Adams, and Benjamin Franklin, who print the names as they are spelled in each document.

Abbreviations, Contractions, Superscripts, Numbers, Crossed-out Words, and Blank Spaces

Abbreviations such as those for place names ("Phila." for Philadelphia, for example) and military titles are spelled out. Contractions such as "can't," "tis," and "altho" are retained. Superscripts are lowered to the line. Archaic forms such as "yt" and "ye" are spelled out, "&c." is printed "etc.," and "&" is printed "and." Numbers are printed as they appear in the documents. Crossed-out words in documents, if they are significant, are placed in editorial notes. Otherwise they are not reproduced. Spaces intentionally left blank in documents are indicated by an underline.

Fig. 3.11a Jensen, *Ratification*, 1:44–45

The style of expanded transcription employed by the editors of volume 1 of the *Documentary History of the Ratification of the Constitution* produced a text that replaced many of the abbreviations and unusual textual features of the manuscript with fully spelled-out abbreviations and modernized punctuation, capitalization, and spelling—as can be seen by comparing this volume's transcription of a letter (*top*) to the version provided by the *Papers of James Madison* (*bottom*), which used a more literal form of expanded transcription:

When the plan came before Congress for their sanction, a very serious effort was made by R [ichard] H [enry] Lee and Mr. [Nathan] Dane from Massachusetts to embarrass it.

Fig. 3.11b Jensen, *Ratification*, 1:347

When the plan came before Congs. for their sanction, a very serious effort was made by R. H. Lee & Mr. Dane from Masts. to embarrass it.

Fig. 3.11c Hutchinson, *Madison*, 10:217

3.12 Clear text editions use silent emendation and limited editorial apparatus to produce clean typescript transcriptions of documents. Clear text editions offer a page of text that is free of editorial apparatus or commentary. Emendations and notes to clear text editions, if provided, are usually placed at the back of those editions, with page and line references to the text. Clear text transcription is most often used for editions of literary works so that they might be easily read. The editors of *Henry D. Thoreau: Journal* presented Thoreau's journals in clear text, with all annotation and textual emendation noted in the back of the edition:

142   JUNE 24, 1840

dust which day has raised– A column of smoke is rising
from the woods yonder to uphold heaven's roof till
the light comes again. The landscape, by its patient
resting there, teaches me that all good remains with
him that waiteth–and that I shall sooner overtake the
dawn by remaining here, than by hurrying over the hills
of the west.

"Morning and evening are as like as brother and
sister. The sparrow and thrush sing, and the frogs
peep–for both.

"The woods breathe louder and louder behind me
–with what hurry-skurry night takes place! The wagon
rattling over yonder bridge is the messenger which

Fig. 3.12a Broderick, *Thoreau*, 1:142

662   TABLE OF EMENDATIONS

142.5   waiteth] *possibly* waileth
142.8   and evening] an evening *in MS*
142.12   hurry-skurry] *possibly* hurry skurry

Fig. 3.12b Broderick, *Thoreau*, 1:662

3.13 An excerpt from Thomas Jefferson's draft of the Declaration of Independence is rendered below in each of the five forms of documentary presentation. This photographic facsimile is from the *Works of Thomas Jefferson*:

Fig. 3.13a Ford, *Jefferson*, 2:facing 200

This typographical facsimile example was created for this handbook:

one
When in the course of human events it becomes necessary for a people to
~~other~~
dissolve the political bands which have connected them with another, and to
~~advance from that subordination in which they have hitherto remained, & to~~ as
separate and equal
-sume among the powers of the earth the ^ ~~equal and independant~~ station to
which the laws of nature & of nature's god entitle them, a decent respect
to the opinions of mankind requires that they should declare the causes
the
which impel them to ~~the change~~ separation.

Fig. 3.13b

This diplomatic transcription example was also created for this handbook, whose authors marked insertions with arrows (↑ insertion ↓) and canceled words with strikethrough type (~~canceled~~):

When in the course of human events it becomes necessary for a ↑one↓ people to ~~advance from that subordination in which they have hitherto remained, & to~~ ↑dissolve the political bands which have connected them with another ↑other↓, and to↓ assume among the powers of the earth the ↑separate and equal↓ ~~equal and independant~~ station to which the laws of nature & of nature's god entitle them, a decent respect to the opinions of mankind requires that they should declare the causes which impel them to ~~the change~~ ↑the separation. ↓

Fig. 3.13c

The editors of the *Papers of Thomas Jefferson* used expanded transcription to present the text as it read before it was edited and then noted the later deletions and insertions in the document's footnotes:

When in the course of human events it becomes necessary for a people to advance from that subordination in which they have hitherto remained, & to assume among the powers of the earth the equal & independant station to which the laws of nature & of nature's god entitle them, a decent respect to the opinions of mankind requires that they should declare the causes which impel them to the change.

Fig. 3.13d Boyd, *Jefferson,* 1:423

This clear text transcription is from *Thomas Jefferson: Word for Word*:

> **When, in the course of human events, it becomes necessary for a people to advance from that subordination in which they have hitherto remained and to assume among the powers of the earth the equal and independent station to which the laws of nature and of nature's God entitle them, a decent respect to the opinions of mankind requires that they should declare the causes which impel them to the change.**

Fig. 3.13e Harrison, *Jefferson,* 39

Verifying the Text

3.14   Proofreading is the process of comparing a transcript of a document against the original text for accuracy of all textual details, such as correct wording, phrasing, spelling, punctuation, capitalization, paragraphing, and consistent emendation. Proofreading is an essential step in the editing process. Editors must ensure that all parts of the edition, including documents, notes, quotations, headings, and titles, have been accurately presented. The text must be rechecked for accuracy whenever errors might be introduced into the final text. For a list of proofreading symbols and an example of a marked-up proof, see the *Chicago Manual of Style*, 14th ed., figs. 3.1 and 3.2.

3.15   The most effective method of verifying a text employs a two-person team: a document holder who reads aloud from the original document or a clear photocopy, noting every capital letter, punctuation mark, or irregular spelling; and a reader who follows along, inspecting the typescript copy of the document. When a difference is discovered, the original document and the typescript version are compared to determine the correct form, and any changes are marked onto the typescript draft. After the entire document has been read, the typescript version is corrected. If time and resources allow, this process is repeated, with the two people exchanging roles or with two different people. This method may also be employed by a single editor who reads the original documents into a tape recorder and then listens to the tape while proofreading the typescript text. Proofreaders should be equipped with a style sheet explaining the rules of presentation and emendation that will be used in the volume.

3.16 Computers currently play a limited role in verifying historical texts because of their inability to accurately compare an original document and a typescript text. Spelling-check and grammar-check programs may detect flagrant misspellings or improper grammatical usage in modern documents, but they cannot verify that a typescript text accurately represents the spelling, wording, and punctuation of an original document, especially if the document was written by an author using nonstandard English. In addition, spelling checkers do not catch incorrectly spelled words that happen by chance to spell another word (e.g. "two" transcribed as "too"). Double-keying, a process whereby two different typists transcribe the same documents and a computer compares the typescript versions for dissimilarities, can be used to verify texts, but it is extremely labor-intensive and moreover does not guarantee an accurate text, which depends on the skill of the two transcribers and their familiarity with the original texts. As editors develop ways to use computers to check the accuracy of their texts, these new techniques must be judged by the standards used to evaluate other proofreading methods: their capacity to accurately detect inconsistencies between original documents and typescript texts.

Chapter Four

Transcription: Types of Sources

Sources

4.1   Different types of sources present editors with different transcription problems. Before establishing a transcription policy, editors should evaluate the texts to be published and consider which methods will accommodate differences in form, function, writing style, and content. Editors should strive to follow a consistent method of transcription from the initiation to the conclusion of a project, so any policy decisions should reflect the full range of sources that will be transcribed over the life of the project.

4.2   Editors seldom publish multiple versions of a document. Instead, they select as their source text the fullest or most reliable version or the one most consistent with the aims and principles of the edition. Editors choose between early and final drafts, published and unpublished versions, and retained copies and recipients' copies of letters. Editors establish criteria for selecting the source text and then meticulously follow these guidelines. The editors of the *Papers of Andrew Jackson* provided readers with a ranking of their preferred genre for source texts:

> In cases where several copies of a document have been available, the recipient's copy has been preferred. Second choice has been a letterbook copy; third, a retained draft. Generally, printed copies have been used only in the absence of manuscript versions, but in cases where the document was intended for publication the contemporary newspaper copy has been used.

Fig. 4.2a Smith, *Jackson,* 1:xxxii

The editors of the *Papers of William Livingston* offered their system of prioritizing variant drafts from different sources:

SELECTION AMONG MULTIPLE VERSIONS

When multiple copies of a manuscript exist, the following priority system determines which version is to be published: (1) autograph letters or other documents, (2) broadsides, (3) contemporary newspapers, (4) drafts, (5) letterbook copies, (6) later printed copies. Significant deviations among the versions are noted, but minor variations are not.

Fig. 4.2b Prince, *Livingston,* 1:xix

If significant variations between drafts of a text exist, they may be noted in footnotes, as was done by the editors of the *Papers of Chief John Ross:*

[1] In the draft copy of this letter are extra lines not in the autograph copy. These lines read:

for example—when the white People first landed at these shores and placed their feet upon this Continent—they were but few in numbers and were consequently weak in physical strength but in knowledge they were strong for their minds were cultivated—and the red people were then numerous and strong, but in knowledge they were comparatively weak for their minds were uncultivated. The whites readily perceived this, and by artifice soon courted the friendship of the Indians and secured their hospitality & were kindly treated. For their own preservation the whites contrived & succeed[ed] in creating quarrels and wars between neighbouring tribes, while they themselves sought refuge under the protection of their neutrality, until their numbers in process of time by emigrations from europe became numerous & strong. They then were bold enough in conjunction with

Fig. 4.2c Moulton, *Ross,* 1:287

Handwritten Sources

4.3   Documents written by hand pose a number of challenges for transcribers. Individual authors introduce peculiarities into their manuscript documents, influenced by circumstances such as background, education, health, emotional state, and the physical conditions under which the document was written. Authors produce documents that contain indecipherable handwriting, nonstandard spelling, faulty grammar, obscure abbreviations, and inconsistent punctuation. Other peculiarities can be attributed to the writing conventions of particular eras. Documents written before the standardization of American English in the mid–nineteenth century contain irregular spelling, archaic usages, and nonstandard punctuation, while handwritten documents from the sixteenth century through the early twentieth century frequently used superscripts, subscripts, contractions, and abbreviations. Editors must clearly state the editorial conventions they use.

4.4   Editors transcribing handwritten documents from the seventeenth century encounter forms of capitalization, spelling, abbreviation, and usage that are unfamiliar to most modern readers. The editors of the *Papers of William Penn* retained many of these now-unusual features, changing only those that would cause confusion:

     5. The text of each document is rendered as follows:
       a. Spelling is retained as written. Misspelled words are not marked with an editorial [sic]. If the sense of a word is obscured through misspelling, its meaning is clarified in a footnote.
       b. Capitalization is retained as written. In seventeenth-century manuscripts, the capitalization of such letters as "c," "k," "p," "s," and "w" is often a matter of judgment, and we cannot claim that our readings are definitive. Whenever it is clear to us that the initial letter in a sentence has not been capitalized, it is left lower case.
       c. Punctuation and paragraphing are retained as written. When a sentence is not closed with a period, we have inserted an extra space.
       d. Words or phrases inserted into the text are placed {within braces}.
       e. Words or phrases deleted from the text are ~~crossed through~~.
       f. Slips of the pen are retained as written, and are not marked by [sic].
       g. Contractions, abbreviations, superscript letters, and ampersands are retained as written. When a contraction is marked by a tilde, it is expanded.
       h. The thorn is rendered as "th," and superscript contractions attached to the thorn are brought down to the line and expanded: as "the," "them," or "that." Our justification for this procedure is that we no longer have a thorn, and modern readers mistake it for "y." Likewise, since modern readers do not recognize that "u" and "v" were used interchangeably in the seventeenth century, we have rendered "u" as "v," or "v" as "u," whenever appropriate.
       i. The £ sign in superscript is rendered as "l."
       j. The tailed "p" is expanded into "per," "pro," or "pre," as indicated by the rest of the word.
       k. The long "s" is presented as a short "s." The double "ff" is presented as a capital "F."

Fig. 4.4a Dunn, Penn, 1:17–18

In contrast to the fairly literal style employed by the editors of the *Papers of William Penn*, the editor of the *Correspondence of Roger Williams* modernized and standardized many of the peculiar features of seventeenth-century prose:

Spelling

Spelling is preserved as found in the manuscripts or printed sources, except for regularization, in accordance with modern practice, of the interchangeable letters *u* and *v*; *i* and *j*; *vv* and *w*; and, less frequently, for initial letters *i* and *y*. Obvious slips of the pen or false starts are silently corrected.

Capitalization

Capitalization is retained as found in the original manuscripts, except in the following instances. Personal names and geographical names have been capitalized. When it is not certain whether Williams or other writers intended to use a capital or lowercase letter, modern usage is followed.

Punctuation

Punctuation is retained as found in the manuscripts and printed sources, except for the following conventionalizations. Williams's ubiquitous colons, when used as terminal punctuation, have been replaced by periods; colons used for medial punctuation, however, have been retained. In cases where it has been difficult to determine whether Williams intended a colon to serve as medial or terminal punctuation, the colon has been retained. Virgules have been replaced by commas or periods. Williams frequently used parentheses but commonly forgot to close parenthetical statements with a final mark. Because his style precludes most attempts to determine where a closing parenthesis should be placed, the opening parenthesis has been treated in such cases as a slip of the pen, and thus has been silently omitted. Sometimes Williams used parentheses within parentheses to such a degree as to cause complete confusion in his syntax; in those instances, the confusion has been silently remedied by replacing his interior parentheses with commas or dashes. Square brackets, used by Williams to set off quoted matter, have been replaced by modern quotation marks. Every sentence ends with a period unless it is not clear where a sentence ends, in which case the original punctuation—or lack of it—is retained. Bracketed punctuation is occasionally emended for clarification.

Abbreviations, Contractions, and Symbols

Abbreviations and contractions are preserved as found in the manuscripts, but those that are not recognizable to modern readers are expanded in square brackets after the first appearance in the text of each letter (e.g., Matie [Majesty]). Some abbreviations, however, are treated as follows: "yor" is expanded silently to "your"; "o^r" is expanded silently to "our"; "S^r" is expanded silently to "Sir." Ampersands are converted to read "and," though the abbreviation for *et cetera* (&c) is converted to read "etc." with a period added even if not found in the original. However, ampersands used in foreign phrases, such as "viis & modis," are retained. The thorn is always printed as *th*. The tilde is replaced by the letter or letters it represents. The tailed ẞ is expanded silently and replaced by the letters it represents (i.e., *per*, *pre*, *pro*, and less often, *pur*). Symbols, such as monetary signs, are printed as closely as possible to the original representation, given the limitations of modern typography. Thus, Williams's symbol for pounds (money and weight), which essentially served as an abbreviation for *livres*, is printed 8o li.

*　*　*　*

Other Textual Procedures

Superscript letters and interlineations have been brought down to the line. Words and phrases struck out by the writer are generally omitted without editorial comment. In some cases, however, when canceled matter is deemed important, deleted words have been restored in the text and explained in a note.

    Obsolete words and usages are clarified for the reader by means of a definition (usually a synonym) placed in square brackets immediately following the obscure word or words, or when necessary a longer definition or explanation is supplied in a note. Definitions of obsolete words or archaic terms taken from the *Oxford English Dictionary* have not been given a citation.

Fig. 4.4b LaFantasie, *Williams,* 1:lxxi–lxxiii

4.5   Eighteenth-century documents raise many of the same transcription issues as those dating from the seventeenth century, including irregular spelling, obscure abbreviations, superscripts, the tilde, the thorn, and other now-vanished symbols. The editors of the *Papers of General Nathanael Greene* outlined the basic issues presented by eighteenth-century handwriting and their methods of addressing them:

Spelling

Spelling is retained as written. If a misspelled word or name is not readily recognizable, the correct spelling follows in brackets. Names are correctly spelled in notes and index.

Inadvertent repetitions of words are corrected silently.

Capitalization

The author's capitalization is followed, including the eighteenth-century practice of capitalizing words within sentences, except where necessary to conform to the following rules:

1. All sentences begin with initial capitals.

2. Personal names and titles used with them, honorifics (such as "His Excellency"), geographical names, and days of the week and months are capitalized.

Abbreviations and Contractions

1. Shortened word forms still in use or those that can easily be understood (as "t'was" or "twixt") are rendered as written.

2. Those no longer readily understood are treated thus: "cmsy [commissary]" or "warr[an]t."

3. Abbreviations of names or places—forms known only to the correspondents or their contemporaries—are also expanded in brackets, as in S[amuel] A[dams] or Chsn [Charleston].

Symbols Representing Letters and Words

When any of the following symbols are expanded they are done so silently:

1. The thorn, which by 1750 had been debased to "y" as in "ye," is expanded to "th." Such abbreviations as "ye," "yᵗ," or "yᵐ" are rendered as "the," "that," or "them."

2. The macron is replaced by the letter(s) it represents—as in comission, which becomes commission, or hapen, which becomes happen.

3. The 𝔭 sign is expanded to the appropriate letters it represents (e.g., per, pre, or pro).

Punctuation

Where necessary, punctuation is changed to conform to the following rules:

1. A period or question mark is placed at the end of every sentence.

2. Dashes used in place of commas, semicolons, periods, or question marks are replaced with appropriate punctuation; dashes are retained when used to mark a suspension of the sense or to set off a change of thought.

3. No punctuation is used after a salutation.

Fig. 4.5a Showman, *Greene,* 8:xxii–xxiii

The editors of the *Papers of James Madison* noted many of these same stylistic forms and described their edition's method of transcription:

The editors have sought to follow the original texts of documents with scrupulous fidelity, but several exceptions should be noted. Superior letters have been brought down, thorns ("ye," "yt," "yn,") as well as words with a tilde ("comĩssrs" and "comĩtee.") have been expanded, and confusing punctuation has been eliminated. The first letter of a sentence is invariably capitalized, regardless of the writer's eccentricities. Inconsequential decoding errors made by Madison, Jefferson, or Monroe in their ciphered correspondence have been ignored, but substantial mistakes have been corrected (with brackets) or annotated. Obvious slips of the pen, usually repeated words, are silently corrected. Long dashes or gaps have been interpreted to indicate a new paragraph. Beyond these exceptions, alterations are noted in textual footnotes.

Fig. 4.5b Hutchinson, *Madison,* 8:xxiii

4.6   Nineteenth-century writers discontinued many of the habits of seventeenth- and eighteenth-century writing, particularly the use of the thorn and the tilde, resulting in a style that is more familiar to modern readers. But other differences persisted, such as greater use of superscripts and abbreviations, multiple ways of ending sentences and indicating paragraphs, and greater freedom regarding capitalization. The editors of the *Letters of Henry Adams* addressed the nineteenth-century stylistic conventions of their letters:

Textual editing has been relatively simple since there are but few instances where we were not able to work from the surviving letters. Between the autograph manuscript and any previously published version, the auto-

graph text has the authority of being the author's intention. We have ad-
hered to that text as closely as common sense allows. We have kept Adams'
misspellings and special usages. Readers may note his difficulty with *Ten-
nesee* and *McLellan* and his omission of the first *a* from the name of his friend
MacVeagh. They may also observe that he follows a common nineteenth-
century practice and often puts apostrophes in *your's* and *it's* (as his father
did before him).

Inscription errors (for example, *the* for *that*), which are by definition not
what the author intended, are categorically different from misspellings.
Such mechanical errors have been silently corrected unless they are possible psychological slips. In those cases we preserve the manuscript text or,
when correction is called for in order to avoid confusion of meaning, we
note the change. Corrected errors in dating, since they might make a letter
hard for someone to find in the microfilm edition of Adams' letters, have
been noted. As to inscription changes which Adams himself made, we do
not note them. He wrote fluently and made relatively few false starts or
running corrections. A detailed record of changes, Adams' own and the
editors', has been kept for the use of future scholars.

Simple procedures have sufficed for the making of copy text. Thanks
to the clarity of Adams' handwriting, the number of cruxes is remarkably
small. The original letters are in a state of excellent preservation, and the
rare cases of defective manuscript have been noted. Where Adams' autograph contractions abridge words and add superscript letters, we preserve
those which are immediately readable when superscript letters are brought
down to the line (*Dr Mr &c* and leave-taking phrases like *Yr obt servt* or *Af-
fecly yrs*); where such transcription might not be immediately readable and
a standard abbreviation exists, we substitute the latter (*Dec.* for *Dec'*);
where Adams points his superscript contraction (*2ᵈ* or *obᵗ*) and modern
usage does not, we again follow usage (*2d* or *obt*); where there is no equiva-
lent, we expand autograph contractions (*which* for *whᶜʰ*). We have not followed Adams' inconsistent practice, but have normally put commas and
periods within quotation marks.

Fig. 4.6a Levenson, *Adams,* 1:xlii–xliii

The editors of *Freedom: A Documentary History of Emancipation* outlined the
basic stylistic issues and how they handled them:

THE RENDITION of nineteenth-century manuscripts into print pro-
ceeds at best along a tortuous path. Transcribing handwritten documents into a standardized, more accessible form inevitably sacrifices
some of their evocative power. The scrawl penciled by a hard-pressed
army commander, the letters painstakingly formed by an ex-slave new
to the alphabet, and the practiced script of a professional clerk all
reduce to the same uncompromising print. At the same time, simply
reading, much less transcribing, idiosyncratic handwriting poses enormous difficulties. The records left by barely literate writers offer special

problems, although these are often no more serious than the obstacles created by better-educated but careless clerks, slovenly and hurried military officers, or even the ravages of time upon fragile paper.

The editors have approached the question of transcription with the conviction that readability need not require extensive editorial intervention and, indeed, that modernization (beyond that already imposed by conversion into type) can compromise the historical value of a document. The practical dilemmas of setting precise limits to editorial intervention, once initiated, also suggest the wisdom of restraint. In short, the editors believe that even when documents were written by near illiterates, the desiderata of preserving immediacy and conveying the struggle of ordinary men and women to communicate intensely felt emotions outweigh any inconveniences inflicted by allowing the documents to stand as they were written. Fortunately for the modern reader, a mere passing acquaintance with the primer usually led uneducated writers to spell as they spoke; the resulting documents may appear impenetrable to the eye but are perfectly understandable when read phonetically. In fact, reproduced verbatim, such documents offer intriguing evidence about the spoken language. Other writers, presumably better educated, frequently demonstrated such haphazard adherence to rules of grammar, spelling, and punctuation that their productions rival those of the semiliterate. And careless copyists or telegraph operators further garbled many documents. Both equity and convenience demand, nonetheless, that all writings by the schooled – however incoherent – be transcribed according to the same principles as those applied to the documents of the unschooled. Indeed, a verbatim rendition permits interesting observations about American literacy in the mid-nineteenth century, as well as about the talents or personalities of particular individuals.

Therefore, the textual body of each document in this volume is reproduced – to the extent permitted by modern typography – *exactly* as it appears in the original manuscript. (The few exceptions to this general principle will be noted hereafter.) The editorial *sic* is never employed: All peculiarities of syntax, spelling, capitalization, and punctuation appear in the original manuscript. The same is true of paragraph breaks, missing or incomplete words, words run together, quotation marks or parentheses that are not closed, characters raised above the line, contractions, and abbreviations. When the correct reading of a character is ambiguous (as, for example, a letter "C" written halfway between upper- and lower-case, or a nondescript blotch of punctuation that could be either a comma or a period), modern practice is followed. Illegible or obscured words that can be inferred with confidence from textual evidence are printed in ordinary roman type, enclosed in brackets. If the editors' reading is conjectural or doubtful, a question mark is added. When the editors cannot decipher a word by either inference or conjecture, it is represented by a three-dot ellipsis enclosed in brackets. An undecipherable passage of more than one word is represented in the same way, but a footnote reports the extent of the illegible material. (See p. xxxiii for a summary of editorial symbols.)

Handwritten letters display many characteristics that cannot be exactly reproduced on the printed page or can be printed only at considerable expense. Some adaptations are, therefore, conventional. Words underlined once in the manuscript appear in italics. Words underlined more than once are printed in small capitals. As for printed forms with blanks filled in by hand, the words originally in print are set in small capitals and the handwritten insertions appear in lower-case, with spaces before and after to suggest the blanks in the form. Internally quoted documents that are set off in the manuscript by such devices as extra space or quotation marks on every line are indented and printed in smaller type. Interlineations are simply incorporated into the text at the point marked by the author, without special notation by the editors unless the interlineation represents a substantial alteration. Finally, the beginning of a new paragraph is indicated by indentation, regardless of how the author set apart paragraphs.

Fig. 4.6b Berlin, *Freedom*, ser.1,1:xxv–xxvii

4.7 In the nineteenth and twentieth centuries, as grammar, spelling, and punctuation have become standardized through the development of style guides and dictionaries, transcribing handwritten documents has become less a matter of addressing archaic stylistic conventions and more one of deciding how to handle violations of accepted standard practice. Common difficulties encountered in twentieth-century manuscripts include missing or inappropriate terminal punctuation, irregular paragraphing or sentence breaks, nonstandard spelling and grammar, and use of obscure abbreviations. Editors of modern documents evaluate whether to alter these irregular forms to make them more comprehensible or to make them conform to standard written English, and then consider how these changes might affect readers' appreciation of the historical documents. The editors of the *Letters of Eugene V. Debs* noted the issues presented by Debs's manuscript documents and their methods for addressing them:

As a general principle we have tried to reproduce the original text of each letter as accurately as possible. All the letters are transcribed in full, and idiosyncratic spelling, punctuation, and usage have been preserved.

* * * *

Errors in spelling, punctuation, etc. have been left in the text except in cases where it is judged that they are the result of a typographical error or a slip of a pen. In cases where a word has obviously been left out the word is supplied in brackets, with a question mark if the judgment is uncertain. For illegible words the transcriber has written "[illegible]" or "[two words illegible]," etc. Where a version of the text has been crossed out and rewritten but is still legible, the transcriber has included the crossed-out version, followed by the corrected version. Illegible crossouts, or errors crossed out and rewritten, have been omitted. Words inserted above the line are indicated in the transcription by curved brackets.

When a writer used a symbol for "and" (or a plus sign), as EVD often did, the transcriber has used an ampersand. When a writer used a dash in place of a period, as EVD often did, the transcriber has used a period. Hyphens and dashes have been standardized in the transcription: - indicates a hyphen, and — indicates a dash, regardless of the usage of the letter writer.

Fig. 4.7a Constantine, Debs, 1:xxxiii–xxxiv

The editors of the *Papers of Martin Luther King, Jr.* also specified how they would address the stylistic issues of their manuscripts:

> Our transcriptions are intended to reproduce the source document or recording as accurately as possible, adhering to the exact wording and punctuation of the original. Errors in spelling, punctuation, and grammar have been neither corrected nor indicated by *sic*. Such errors and stylistic irregularities may offer important insights into the author's state of mind and conditions under which a document was composed. Other features that could not be adequately reproduced, such as signatures and handwritten marginal comments, are noted and described in the text or footnotes.

* * * *

1. Capitalization, boldface, symbols, subscripts, abbreviations, strikeouts, and deletions are replicated regardless of inconsistency or usage.
2. The line breaks, pagination, and vertical and horizontal spacing of the original are not replicated. A blank line signals a break in the text other than a straightforward paragraph break. The transcription regularizes spacing and indentation of paragraphs, outlines, and lists, as well as the spacing of words, initials, and ellipses.
3. The underlining of book titles, court cases, or other words and phrases in typescripts is reproduced. Since underlining practices were often inconsistent (sometimes breaking between words, sometimes not), we regularized the various types to continuous underscoring.
4. Silent editorial corrections have been made only in cases of malformed letters, single-letter corrections of typescript words, and the superimposition of two characters.
5. The author's use of hyphens is replicated, but end-of-line hyphens have been silently deleted unless the usage is ambiguous. Dashes between numbers are rendered as en-dashes. Em-dashes, which appeared in several styles in the original manuscripts, have been regularized.
6. Insertions in the text by the author (usually handwritten) are indicated by curly braces ({ }) and placed as precisely as possible.

Fig. 4.7b Carson, King, 2:50–51,53

Technical or Professional Documents

4.8   In the course of performing their work, many professionals—including but not limited to architects, doctors, lawyers, business people, and scientists—produce documents that can be difficult to transcribe because of their technical terminology and unusual format. To transcribe professional documents, editors acquaint themselves with the language of the profession. They then develop methods for transcribing documents that present problems of size, layout, complexity, quantity, or organization. Different types of professional or technical documents pose their own unique challenges and require editors to consider how best to convert them into print.

4.9   Business documents, especially ledgers or account books, present editors with tables of numbers or monetary amounts and abbreviations that are difficult and often expensive to transfer into type. The editors of the *Papers of John Marshall* created a tabular format for Marshall's account book that presented information without replicating the exact layout of the original page:

	£			
Stockins for P.[5] 6 Dollars, mustard pot 9		5	14	
		5	17	9
7 yds. Oznabrugs[6] at 1/3			8	9
Inkstand 8/, pomatum[7] 1/6			9	6
Land warrants for my Father[8]		1	15	
Fee to the Attorney[9] for Do.		1	2	6
Fee to the Register[10] for a Patent for Do.		0	15	10
For Oats 36 Bushels		3	10	6
To one pair of Stockings		1		
To trimmings for Mr. Keith		1	4	9
To advice fee given the Attorney for opinion on surveyors fees[11]		1	2	6

Fig. 4.9 Johnson, *Marshall,* 1:294

4.10   Documents produced by scientists often use technical language and symbols that make them difficult to present in type. Editors need to exercise care not to distort the notation of scientific documents. The editors of the *Papers of Joseph Henry* used a combination of type and facsimile to represent Henry's notes:

"RECORD OF EXPERIMENTS"
Henry Papers, Smithsonian Archives

Monday Oct 23rd 1843

$\left\{ \begin{array}{l} \text{Exper. on the holes pierced} \\ \text{in cards by the secondary current}^1 \end{array} \right.$

Commenced this morning the Repetition of Matteucci's experiments to determ the direction of the induced current by means of the pierced card.

The points were placed ¼ of an inch apart, with one *jar* charge 60 <*three*> two small hol[e]s near the — *minus* point current adverse.

Charge 80 *three* holes nearer the minus pole. The larger hole was ragged—one jar distance same

Charge 90. Distance same *three* holes neare the minus side. When these holes are exami[n]ed with a magnifying class the larger appears ragged and triangular

Fig. 4.10a Reingold, *Henry*, 5:424

The editors of the *Collected Papers of Albert Einstein* also used both type and facsimile to reproduce Einstein's notes:

$$\int_T \int |\mathfrak{E}||\mathfrak{H}|r^2 \, d\Omega = \frac{1}{c^4} \int \bar{f}^2 \, dt \underbrace{\int \frac{\sin^2 \vartheta \, dw}{2\pi \sin \vartheta \, d\vartheta}}_{\displaystyle 2\pi \int_0^\pi (1 - \cos^2 \vartheta)\sin \vartheta \, d\vartheta}$$

$$= \left| -\cos \vartheta + \frac{\cos^3 \vartheta}{3} \right|_0^\pi = 2 - \frac{2}{3} = \frac{4}{3}$$

Fig. 4.10b Stachel, *Einstein*, 3:396

4.11 Editors publishing documents produced by engineers and architects will need to develop techniques for presenting sketches and blueprints. The editors of the *Papers of Benjamin Henry Latrobe* presented Latrobe's architectural and engineering drawings as annotated photographic facsimiles in an oversized book edition, and they published facsimiles in the series' microfiche edition (*not shown*).

4.12   Editors transcribing governmental and legal documents should be absolutely literal when these documents may be consulted by lawmakers, lawyers, and judges in order to understand precedents and to comply with existing laws. They also may need to note stray, incorrect, or missing punctuation in variant copies; these phenomena can alter meaning or affect public policy. The effect of such errors is real, as explained in a footnote to a passage in the *Territorial Papers of the United States*:

> **The governor, and judges or a majority of them** [14] **shall adopt and publish in the district such laws of the original states criminal and civil as may be necessary and best suited to the circumstances of the**

[14] In the official printed copies of the ordinance, signed by Charles Thomson as Secretary of Congress, there appear certain variations in punctuation from the original Journals which were sufficient to leave the meaning of the former in doubt. The most significant of these differences occur in connection with the above sentence. In the printed copies no comma appears after the word "governor", as in the Journal; on the other hand, a comma is inserted after the word "judges", and after the word "them". In a contemporary manuscript copy (CC Papers, no. 175, fol. 123) the comma is likewise omitted after "governor". The punctuation in the printed copies, which were in the hands of territorial officials, provoked serious differences of opinion between Governor and Judges as to their respective legislative powers .

Fig. 4.12 Carter, *Territorial Papers*, 2:42

Machine-Created Documents

4.13   Although they offer the benefit of increased legibility, machine-created documents pose their own problems for transcribers. The conventions used by typesetters, telegraph operators, and typists need to be transferred into a readable format, and editors must decide which incidental marks bear information of use to readers. Editors create policies for transcribing machine-created documents, such as this one from the *Samuel Gompers Papers*:

> Mechanically reproduced documents, such as articles printed in newspapers or typed letters, require a different treatment. Typographical and spelling errors seem to have been endemic to the labor bureaucracy and press of the late nineteenth and early twentieth centuries. For the most part it is impossible to determine which of these errors were the work of the documents' authors and which were anonymously introduced by the typographers and secretaries of the day. Since their sheer numbers

make them distracting, however, the editors have silently corrected many of them, with the following exceptions. There are no changes in the original syntax of mechanically produced documents and no changes that would substantively alter their meaning. Errors remain if they seem essential to the particular mood or style of a document. Certain features of the documents generally appear as found, including capitalization, the spelling of contemporary personal names, errors of usage, such as the use of a noun form for a verb, and common spelling conventions of the time, for instance, the use of "segar" for "cigar," the spelling of Pittsburgh, Pennsylvania, without the final "h," or lowercasing the word "street" as part of a street name. The original punctuation usually appears as found, except where it is an apparent typographical error and tends to garble the document's meaning.

Fig. 4.13a Kaufman, *Gompers,* 1:xxiii–xxiv

The editors of the *Black Abolitionist Papers* also modernized many of the elements of nineteenth-century printed documents:

> The project adopted the following principles for documents found in published sources (newspapers, pamphlets, annual reports, and other nineteenth-century printed material): redundant punctuation is eliminated; quotation marks are converted to modern usage; obvious misspellings and printer's errors are corrected; printer's brackets are converted to parentheses; audience reaction within a speech is treated as a separate sentence with parentheses, for example, (Hear, hear.). We have let stand certain nineteenth-century printing conventions such as setting names or addresses in capital or italic letters in order to maintain the visual character of the document. A line of asterisks signals that material is deleted from a printed document. In no instance is black abolitionist material edited or deleted; but if, for example, a speech was interrupted with material extraneous to the document, the irrelevant material is not published.

Fig. 4.13b Ripley, *Black Abolitionist,* 4:xxv

4.14 Newspapers have employed a wide variety of printing styles, including typefaces of different styles and sizes, idiosyncratic use of italic and bold type, columns divided by subheadings, and extensive use of quotation marks. In transcribing newspaper documents, editors need to decide how many of these stylistic devices they wish to replicate and how best to transcribe them. The editors of the *Marcus Garvey and Universal Negro Improvement Association Papers* transcribed a newspaper story in the following manner:

Negroes Plan to Found Ship Line

Project Will Be Discussed at Palace Casino Rally To-morrow Night.

The Universal Negro Improvement Association and African Communities League, recognizing, according to its president-general, Marcus Garvey, that this is a "selfish age," will hold a mass meeting at the Palace Casino, 135th street and Madison avenue, to-morrow night to prove the Negro has caught the spirit.

According to Garvey, the Negroes are anxious to go back to Africa and the West Indies and create empires of their own as strong as that of the yellow and the white man. To go back, they need ships.

Therefore, at this mass meeting the founding of the "Black Star Line" will be attempted. The proposed steamship line will operate between American ports and those of Africa, the West Indies, Central and South America.

Fig. 4.14a *New York Call,* 27 April 1919

Newspaper Report

[*New York Call,* 27 April 1919]

NEGROES PLAN TO FOUND SHIP LINE
PROJECT WILL BE DISCUSSED AT PALACE CASINO
RALLY TOMORROW NIGHT

The Universal Negro Improvement Association and African Communities League, recognizing, according to its president-general, Marcus Garvey, that this is a "selfish age," will hold a mass meeting at the Palace Casino, 135th Street and Madison Avenue, tomorrow night to prove the Negro has caught the spirit.

According to Garvey, the Negroes are anxious to go back to Africa and the West Indies and create empires of their own as strong as that of the yellow and the white man. To go back, they need ships.

Therefore, at this mass meeting the founding of the "Black Star Line" will be attempted.[1] The proposed steamship line will operate between American ports and those of Africa, the West Indies, Central and South America.

Printed in the *New York Call*, Sunday, 27 April 1919.

  1. The *Negro World* of 3 May 1919 reported that the UNIA "has opened a special account with the Corn Exchange Bank, 125th Street and Lenox Avenue, to receive lodgment of the Black Star Line" (*Garvey* v. *United States*, no. 8317 [Ct. App., 2d Cir. Feb. 2, 1925], p. 1308). The same announcement reported that the secretary of the line was "W. T. Mitchell" and that the treasurer was George W. Tobias. The former was actually Uriah T. Mitchell, a Jamaican who at the time also held the position of UNIA secretary. However, a few weeks later Mitchell resigned from the UNIA, after temporarily serving as a member of a three-man committee auditing the UNIA's accounts. The committee also charged Garvey before New York Assistant District Attorney Edwin P. Kilroe, alleging financial mismanagement and collection of money from UNIA members under false pretenses.

Fig. 4.14b Hill, *Garvey,* 1:411

The editors of the *Documentary History of the Ratification of the Constitution* modernized the stylized type and use of quotation marks when they transcribed the following newspaper passage:

> 13th. Ex poſt facto laws have ever been conſidered as abhorrent from liberty: neceſſity and public ſafety never can require them—" If laws do
> " not puniſh an offender, let him go
> " unpuniſhed; let the legiſlature, ad
> " moniſhed of the defect of the laws,
> " provide againſt the commiſſion of fu–
> " ture crimes of the ſame ſort—The
> " eſcape of one delinquent can never
> " produce ſo much harm to the com–
> " munity, as may ariſe from the in–
> " fraction of a rule, upon which the
> " purity of public juſtice, a..d the ex–
> " iſtence of civil liberty eſſentially
> " depend"—Pæley's Principles of Moral Philoſophy, vol. 2, p. 234. Oc. Ed.

Fig 4.14c *Virginia Independent Chronicle,* 28 November 1787

13th. Ex post facto laws have ever been considered as abhorrent from liberty: necessity and public safety never can require them—"If laws do not punish an offender, let him go unpunished; let the legislature, admonished of the defect of the laws, provide against the commission of future crimes of the same sort—The escape of one delinquent can never produce so much harm to the community, as may arise from the infraction of a rule, upon which the purity of public justice, and the existence of civil liberty essentially depend"—Pæley's Principles of Moral Philosophy, vol. 2. p. 234.[17] Oc[tavo] Ed.

Fig. 4.14d Jensen, *Ratification,* 8:338

4.15   Most telegrams or cables contain transmittal symbols in addition to a message. Editors must therefore decide which portions of a telegram warrant reproduction. The editors of the *Family Letters of Victor and Meta Berger* standardized the placement of the place, date, and message of telegrams, corrected keyboarding errors, converted the word *period* used by the telegraph operators to indicate the end of a sentence into the terminal punctuation itself, and presented the text in small capital letters to distinguish it from typed or handwritten letters:

Victor to Meta (telegram)

WASHINGTON, D.C.
JANUARY 10, 1920

CRUCIFIED ONCE MORE.[1] THEY DID NOT EVEN HAVE THE DECENCY TO GRANT ME TEN MINUTES FOR MY DEFENSE. MANN SHERWOOD[2] AND VOIGHT WANTED ME SEATED AND SISSON[3] PROTESTED AGAINST THE INJUSTICE OF PROCEDURE. I WILL HAVE TO FIGHT AGAIN AND BE REELECTED ARRIVE HOME MONDAY NIGHT LOVINGLY

VICTOR BERGER

Fig. 4.15a Stevens, *Berger,* 287

The *Papers of Woodrow Wilson* used the same typeface and headings for telegrams and letters but preceded the telegrams with the date and place from which they were sent and indicated that they were telegrams in the note following the document:

To Mary Allen Hulbert Peck

Trenton, N. J. Aug. 15, 1911

Ellen joins me in begging that you and Allen come to us Friday morning   best train leaves New York at nine four morning.   Woodrow Wilson.

T telegram (WC, NjP).

Fig. 4.15b Link, *Wilson,* 23:267

The editor of the article "The Great Fire of 1871: A Nation Responds," which appeared in the magazine *Voyageur* published by the Brown County [Wisconsin] Historical Society, used the following standardized format to present telegrams:

To: Gov. Fairchild
By Telegram from: J.B. Stickney, Mazomanie
Date: October 11, 1871
    I have 11 bxs of bread & provisions brought here for the Ch[icago] sufferers   I have just rec'd notice from S.S. M— that it is not needed there   Can it be sent to those in need in our own sate & how   Answer

Fig. 4.15c Olson, *Voyageur,* 13:16

4.16   The advent of the typewriter made possible the quick production of legible texts but also created a new set of concerns for transcribers. Slips by typists and the malfunctions of typewriters could create irregular spacing, typographical errors, partial letters, typed-over letters, erasures, and uneven or raised letters. The editor of the *Letters of Eugene V. Debs* (*top*) standardized irregular spacing and the hand-inserted corrections made by Debs or his typist when he transcribed the following typewritten letter (*bottom*):

August 15, 1895
Woodstock, Illinois

My dear Sir and Friend: —
   I have received a very pitiable story from Ellen M. Lappin, now an inmate of the Vigo County Jail. She informs me she is but 16 years of age, a mere child I should judge and that she is in jail on a charge of larceny because of her failure to give bond. I, of course, know nothing of the merits of the case but have written her saying I knew you well and would write to you in her behalf. If her story is true, or but half true, it seems harsh to have imprisoned her under the circumstances. I know you will not suffer her to be subjected to a wrong and yet in your multifarious duties I thought the case might have escaped your personal attention and hence this letter. I am quite sure it is only necessary you should understand the case to insure justice being done. With cordial regards and best wishes, I am,

Yours Very Truly,
Eugene V. Debs

Dict. E. V. D.

Fig. 4.16a Constantine, Debs, 1:98

PRESIDENT.

Published by the Nobard   #2

DIRECTORS.
SYLVESTER KELIHER.
L. W. ROGERS.
JAMES HOGAN.
WM. E. BURNS.
R. M. GOODWIN.
M. J. ELLIOTT.

HEADQUARTERS OF THE

AMERICAN RAILWAY UNION.

TERRE HAUTE, INDIANA.

This letter is writt McHenry County Jail stock, Ill. Address all official correspondence to Terre Haute, Ind.

Woodstock,Ill. Aug. 15th , 1895 .

Hon. Samuel Houston,

    Prosecuting Att'y,Vigo Co.,

        Terre Haute,   Ind

My Dear Sir and Friend:-

          I have received a very pitiable story from

Ellen M. Lappin,now an inmate of the Vigo County Jail. She informs me

she is but 16 years of age , a mere child I should judge and that she

```
she is but 16 years of age , a mere child I should judge and that she
is in jail on a charge of larceny because of her failure to give bond.
I ,of course,know nothing of the merits of the case but have written her
saying I knew you well and would write you in her behalf. If her story
is true,or but half true,it seems harsh to have imprisoned her  under
the circumstances .  I know you will not suffer her to be subjected to
a wrong and yet in your multifarious duties I thought the case might have
escaped your personal attention and hence this letter. I am quite sure
it is only necessary you should understand the case to insure justice
being done. With cordial regards and best wishes,I am,

                         Yours Very Truly ,


Dict.E.V.D.
```

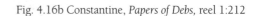

Fig. 4.16b Constantine, *Papers of Debs,* reel 1:212

Forms

4.17   Editors transcribing printed forms or tables evaluate the preprinted information on these documents and decide how much of it should be reproduced either in the text or in footnotes. Printed forms include a wide array of documents such as tax forms; census forms; applications; business forms; birth, marriage, and death certificates; military and government documents; printed date books; and diaries. Editors must also decide if it is necessary to distinguish preprinted passages from those inserted at a later time.

4.18   A common form of preprinted matter is letterhead. When documents are written on letterhead, editors decide whether to reproduce the information from the letterhead. In most cases, the content of letterhead is not printed, but in rare instances it might be transcribed or reproduced as a facsimile to provide otherwise unavailable information about organizations, places, or people. The editors of the *Marcus Garvey and Universal Negro Improvement Association Papers* transcribed an example of the letterhead of the association, probably because it provided evidence about the organization's leaders and conveyed information about its public presentation:

THE MARCUS GARVEY AND UNIA PAPERS

Marcus Garvey to Nicholas Murray Butler

One God!   **One Aim!**   **One Destiny!**

NEW YORK DIVISION
Universal Negro Improvement Association
AND
African Communities' League

Cable Address: "UNIANY", New York
Telephone 7976 Morningside

IRENA MOORMAN-BLACKSTON
President Ladies' Division

MARCUS GARVEY, President
and International Organizer

IRENE W. WINGFIELD,
1st Vice President

WALTER J. CONWAY,
1st Vice President

GEORGE A. CRAWLEY,[1]
Executive Secretary

JANIE JENKINS,[2]
2nd Vice President

EDWARD STERLING WRIGHT,
2nd Vice President

J. A. DAVIS
Chairman Advisory Board

R. H. ROGERS,
3rd Vice President

E. D. SMITH-GREEN,
General Secretary

JULIA E. RUMFORD
Secretary

ETHEL OUGHTON-CLARKE,
General Secretary

BEN. E. BURRELL
Associate Secretary

CARRIE MERO,
Associate Secretary

CLARENCE A. CARPENTER,[3]
Treasurer

LAFAYETTE BUILDING, 165 W. 131ST ST.
NEW YORK, April 29th 1918

"He created of one blood all nations of men to dwell on the face of the earth."

My dear Dr. Butler:

It is unfortunate that we have to appeal to you at this time, when the public and other financial demands are so many on one of your position, but as you will realize sometimes, one has to appeal to the old friend for help, when there is no one else to ask.

Thus, in keeping with an unanimous vote of our members, at our last general meeting in the Lafayette Hall, I was instructed to write to you asking your help by a small donation to assist our building fund.

We feel sure that whatsoever you can do for us, will be done. Trusting to receive your kind help, with return of list, with best wishes, I am   Yours respectfully,

UNIVERSAL NEGRO IMPROVEMENT
ASSOCIATION
MARCUS GARVEY PRESIDENT

Fig. 4.18a Hill, *Garvey*, 1:242

The editors of *Mark Twain's Letters* also transcribed the letterhead used for some documents:

J. LANGDON, MINER & DEALER IN ANTHRACITE &
BITUMINOUS COAL   OFFICE NO. 6 BALDWIN STREET

ELMIRA, N.Y. March 31—[1] 186 9.

Dear Mother—
    Bless you *I* don't want to go to California at all—& really I have not by any means determined to go, as yet. I know very well that I *ought* to go, but I haven't the slightest inclination to do it. Indeed, indeed,

Fig. 4.18b Branch, *Twain*, 3:184

4.19   The significant information in birth, marriage, and death certificates as well as census rolls usually consists of a few words of text written on a standard form. The editors of the *Collected Papers of Albert Einstein* presented his birth certificate, with the printed portion of the form in roman type and the inserted handwritten information in italics:

1. Birth Certificate

Ulm am *15. März 1879.*

Nr. *224.*

Vor dem unterzeichneten Standesbeamten erschien heute, der Persönlichkeit nach _____ *be*kannt,
der Kaufmann Herman Einstein
wohnhaft zu *Ulm Bahnhofstraße B Nr. 135.*[1]
israelitischer Religion, und zeigte an, daß von der
Pauline Einstein geb. Koch seiner Ehefrau
        israelitischer Religion,
wohnhaft *bei ihm*
zu *Ulm in seiner Wohnung*
am *vierzehnten März* des Jahres
tausend acht hundert *siebenzig* und *neun* *Vormittags*
um *elf ein halb* Uhr ein Kind *männlichen*
Geschlechts geboren worden sei, welches
        den Vornamen *Albert*[2]
erhalten habe
    Vorgelesen, genehmigt und *unterschrieben*
        Hermann Einstein

Der Standesbeamte.
Hartmann

Fig. 4.19a Stachel, *Einstein*, 1:1

By contrast, the editors of the *Samuel Gompers Papers* printed the 1851 London census return for the Gompers family, omitting a column from the printed form and making no clear distinction between the printed and handwritten portions of the document:

Entries for the Gompers Household
in the 1851 Census Return for London

[1851]

Liberty Old Artillery Ground		Ecclesiastical District of St Mary	Borough of Tower Hamlets						
No. of Householder's Schedule	Name of Street, Place, or Road, and Name or No. of House	Name and Surname of each Person who abode in the house, on the Night of the 30th March, 1851	Relation to Head of Family	Condition	Age of		Rank, Profession, or Occupation	Where Born	
					males	females			
113	[2 Fort St.]	Catherine Gompers[1]	Wife	M		44	General Dealer	Holland	
		Solomon	Son	M	22		Cigar Maker	do	
		Sarah	Sons Wife	M		24		do	
		Fanny[2]	Dau	UM		14	Cap Maker	do	
		Mary[3]	Dau	UM		12	do	do	
		Catherine[4]	Dau			10	do	do	
		Sarah[5]	Dau			8		do	
		Simeon[6]	Son		2			Middlesex Spitalfields	
		Samuel[7]	Gd Son		14m			do	do
		May Duggan	Servant	UM		20	General Servant	Ireland	
		Aaron [Boseen?]	Lodger	M	65			Holland	
		Isaac Goldsmith	Lodger	UM	17		General Dealer	"	
		Joel [Driazeloor?]	Lodger	UM	22		Hawker	"	
		Abraham Martin	Lodger	UM	55		Hawker	Holland	

Printed form, with handwritten entries, Census of 1851, H.O. 107/1543, folio 46, pp. 24-25, PRO. The following column was left blank by the census taker: "Whether Blind, or Deaf-and-Dumb."

1. Actually Henrietta (Jette) Salomon Haring GOMPERS (1807?-79), SG's paternal grandmother.
2. Fanny (Femmetje) Gompers COHEN, SG's aunt.
3. Clara (Mietje) Gompers LE BOSSE, SG's aunt.
4. Catherine (Grietje) GOMPERS, SG's aunt.
5. Sarah Gompers LEVY, SG's aunt.
6. Simon GOMPERS, SG's uncle and childhood companion, became a shoemaker.
7. SG.

Fig. 4.19b Kaufman, *Gompers*, 1:8

Oral Documents

4.20 Editors may be faced with the challenge of transcribing forms of communication that lack written sources. Spoken words—whether discussions, speeches, classroom lectures, or sermons—may have been delivered from brief notes or extemporaneously. To reproduce these works, editors employ the sources that preserved the information, whether outlines, shorthand transcriptions, notes, or newspaper reports. Although these sources are incomplete and introduce inaccuracies, they are often the only means for recapturing such "lost" documents.

4.21   For sermons and speeches that either were delivered before the advent of modern recording technology or were not recorded, editors must rely on text or notes used by the speaker or accounts by audience members. The editors of the *Papers of Martin Luther King, Jr.* included King's outline notes to provide information about a sermon of his for which no other source existed:

"The Challenge of the Book of Jonah"

[*1951–1955?*]
[*Boston, Mass.?*]

The following sermon outlines were found among the hundreds of notecards King prepared for his courses at Boston. In the sermons King argues that God's love is universal and inclusive of all faiths and races.

No more delightful moments can be spent than those spent reading the book of Jonah. It is one of the greatest books of the Old Testament. Its themes is both arresting and electrifying. Its unknown author appears to have possessed the vision of a Saint Paul, the satiric power of a George Bernard Shaw, and the delicious humor of a G. K. Chesterton. This book does not represent an actual occurrance any more than the parable of the prodigal son. But who can doubt the accuracy of either as portraits of ef multitude of human hearts. To often have we spent our time arguing over the historicity of Biblical stories, while failing to grasp the underlying truths.

Let us look at this story for a moment and see what it has to offer us. Recall the story

   I Tell the Story
  II This story has within it two {three} fundamental truth that I would like to set forth

     1. God's love is boundless and Universal
        (1) God loves the Ninevite
        (2) Deal with Jonah's failure to see this and the whole Jewish attitude.
        (3) Deal with Christian view. Love men because God loves them.
        (4) Story of the lost sheep.
        (5) There is no class system. Aunt June is just as significant as the Ph.D. The person who lives in the ally is just as worthful to God as the richest person in the community.
     2. All men are their brothers keepers and dependent on each other.
        (1) Deal with Jonah's failure to see this
        (2) We are all involved in a single process and whatever effects one directly effects the other indirectly. So long as there is slavery in the world I can never be totally free.
        (3) Science has made this obviously true. We must have one World or none.
        (4) Quote John Donne[1]

Fig. 4.21a Carson, *King,* 2:325–326

Editors may use notes taken by listeners to reconstruct oral documents, although such notes are often fragmentary, difficult to understand, or inaccurate because authors tend to write them for their personal reference. The notes taken by James Madison during the Constitutional Convention provide important information about that event, but as the alternative accounts in footnote 3 of the following excerpt indicate, his notes offer only one perspective on the events taking place:

Wilson and Hamilton moved to give the executive an absolute veto on laws.

Mr. Madison supposed that if a proper proportion of each branch should be required to overrule the objections of the Executive, it would answer the same purpose as an absolute negative. It would rarely if ever happen that the Executive constituted as ours is proposed to be would have firmness eno' to resist the legislature, unless backed by a certain part of the body itself.[1] The King of G.B. with all his splendid attributes would not be able to withstand the unanimous and eager wishes of both houses of Parliament. To give such a prerogative would certainly be obnoxious to the temper of this Country;[2] its present temper at least.[3]

[3]Some time after Eppes copied the Debates, JM heavily deleted a sentence and interlined the concluding clause.
   Yates's version:
   "Mr. Madison against it—because of the difficulty of an executive venturing on the exercise of this negative, and is therefore of opinion that the revisional authority is better" (Farrand, *Records*, I, 106).
   King's version:
   "Mad: I am opposed to the complete negative, because no man will dare exercise it whn. the law was passed almost unanimously. I doubt whether the Kng of Eng. wd. have firmness sufficient to do it" (ibid., I, 107).
   Pierce's version:
   "Mr. Maddison was of opinion that no Man would be so daring as to place a veto on a Law that had passed with the assent of the Legislature" (ibid., I, 109).

Fig. 4.21b Hutchinson, *Madison*, 10:24–25

For oral presentations made by noteworthy speakers, editors may be able to use newspaper reports. The editors of the *Frederick Douglass Papers* explained their methods for finding accounts of speeches in newspapers and some of the challenges they posed:

Since newspapers furnished most of Douglass's speeches, the editorial procedures adopted represent attempts to solve some of the problems caused by the special characteristics of nineteenth-century journalism. Struggling to capture the flavor of an event as well as to record the words spoken, nineteenth-century reporters often used an unpredictable combination of italics, capital letters, and quotation marks to indicate the words and phrases a speaker emphasized. Similarly, journalists' attempts to convey the rhythm of a speech frequently resulted in irregularly punctuated sentences. Usually reports included in parentheses notations of the speaker's gestures and audience reactions (cheers, hisses, interruptions). Long paragraphs often containing 2000 words were the rule. Journalists were inconsistent in capitalizing proper nouns and rarely included titles or date and place lines in their reports of speeches.

Nineteenth-century recording techniques were crude, especially in the United States, where editors had a limited number of trained stenographers upon whom they could rely.[2] Many editors—recognizing this, and trying to protect themselves from potential libel suits—began each published speech with a phrase such as "the substance of" or converted stenographically recorded speeches into third person narratives. Hampered by limited space in even the largest papers, editors often published only brief mentions of, or short extracts from, speeches.

*　*　*　*

Completeness, accuracy, and historical significance were the major criteria used in selecting the speeches included in this edition. In an effort to obtain the most accurate copies of Douglass's orations, we attempted to locate all of the extant versions of each speech. We have not, however, published each version we discovered. Extracts and brief mentions, lacking detail and context, are generally excluded. Summaries of speeches are included only when, in the editors' judgment, their topics are of special historical significance. The few extant handwritten copies of Douglass's speeches have been treated as pretexts and compared to all pamphlet copies and newspaper reports of them to determine whether he said what he intended to say.

Variants of stenographically recorded speeches posed special problems. When considering variants the editors tried to determine the "best copy." Fortunately, Douglass and his friends were quick to praise journals reporting his speeches accurately and to castigate those printing garbled versions of them.[15] It was possible, in many instances, to determine the most accurate of two or more variant stenographic copies by comparing each to long narrative accounts of the same speech. The final test for the best of several versions of a speech was close textual analysis. Intuition and familiarity with Douglass's life and work inevitably played a role in our selections.

Fig. 4.21c Blassingame, *Douglass*, ser.1,1:lxxv,lxxxi

The editors of the *Papers of Woodrow Wilson* explained in the introduction to volume 24 how they corrected obvious transcription errors introduced by Wilson's personal stenographer. The editors converted questionable passages back into shorthand and looked for misinterpretations the stenographer might have made of his own shorthand symbols. See Arthur S. Link, et al., eds., *Papers of Woodrow Wilson* (Princeton: Princeton University Press, 1977), 24:viii–xiii.

4.22   In some cases, editors may have access to sound or video recordings. The editors of *Women Remember the War, 1941–1945,* described some of the methods they used for transferring oral interviews to the written page:

> The transcripts of oral interviews conducted during 1992 and 1993 form the basis of the text printed here. We have tried to create a clean, readable text without sacrificing the original language of the interviews. Because written English differs from spoken English, we employed a number of conventions to deal with variations. We did not add or change any words, and we did not tamper with grammar or sentence structure. Words added to clarify the text always appear in brackets. The transcripts omit false starts as well as filler words, such as "you know" or "um." We made no attempt to preserve dialect or pronunciation. The original tapes are available for those interested in such nuances.
>
> The interviews ranged in length from one hour to more than three hours, and the texts presented here are excerpts. Questions and answers are presented in the order in which they occurred. When part of the answer to a question has been deleted, we note it with ellipsis points, although we have not used them to indicate omissions of entire questions and answers. The questions asked by the interviewers appear in italic type and have been edited for clarity.
>
> In every case, we contacted the interviewees and asked them to review the text selected for inclusion in this book. In several cases they requested (and we made) minor changes that correct inaccuracies or clarify statements.

Fig. 4.22a Stevens, *Women,* ix

The editors of the *Papers of Martin Luther King, Jr.* transcribed tape-recorded sermons, including descriptions of audience responses in italics within square brackets, such as: [*laughter*]. Audience comments and interjections were inserted in italic type within parentheses (*Go ahead*), and passages emphasized by King were set in *italics*:

> Now that isn't the only thing that convinces me that we've strayed away from this attitude, (*Go ahead*) this principle. The other thing is that we have adopted a sort of a pragmatic test for right and wrong—whatever works is right. (*Yes*) If it works, it's all right. Nothing is wrong but that which does not work. If you don't get caught, it's right. [*Laughter*] That's the attitude, isn't it? It's all right to disobey the Ten Commandments, but just don't disobey the Eleventh, Thou shall not get caught. [*Laughter*] That's the attitude. That's the prevailing

attitude in, in our culture. (*Come on*) No matter what you do, just do it with a, with a bit of finesse. (*All right*) You know, a sort of attitude of the survival of the slickest. Not the Darwinian survival of the fittest, but the survival of the slickest—who, whoever can be the slickest is, is the one who right. It's all right to lie, but lie with dignity. [*Laughter*] It's all right to steal and to rob and extort, but do it with a bit of finesse. (*Yes*) It's even all right to hate, but just dress your hate up in the garments of love and make it appear that you are loving when you are actually hating. *Just get by!* That's the thing that's right according to this new ethic. (*Lord help him*)

Fig. 4.22b Carson, King, 2:252

The editors of *George C. Marshall: Interviews and Reminiscences for Forrest C. Pogue* transcribed a series of oral histories, including both questions and responses, and added headings to indicate the date and number of the original recording:

TAPE 8

Recorded December 7, 1956

1. What were the basic weaknesses of the National Guard and how did you attempt to eliminate these?

As to the basic weaknesses: There were some of these that could not be eliminated, as they were inherent in the basic laws governing the National Guard. The principal trouble was the very short training period for the men, and as a few hours once a week would not suffice to replace the basic training which required us in the regular service on a twelve-hour day, very strenuous work, many months—six or more—in getting men ready for the war. Now it is only possible in a National Guard organization to get the men but once a week except for the two weeks in the summer. I did find it

Fig. 4.22c Bland, Marshall: Interviews, 255

Revised, Altered, and Collaborative Documents

4.23 Some editing projects may need to transcribe documents that have been altered or revised. Documents that have undergone heavy editing, either as part of the original composition process or after a period of time, require editors to decide how much of the revision should be made apparent to readers.

4.24 In an attempt to show the changes that occurred to bills during the process of legislative deliberation, the editors of the *Documentary History of the First Federal Congress* printed documents with extensive notes to describe proposed amendments and alterations:

ARTICLE THE ELEVENTH.

No appeal to the Supreme Court of the United States, shall be allowed, where the value in controversy shall not amount to one thousand dollars, nor shall any fact, triable by a Jury according to the course of the common law, be otherwise re-examinable, than according to the rules of common law. [16]

[16] On September 4, the Senate disagreed to a motion to strike out Article 11 and insert the following:

> The Supreme Judicial Federal Court, shall have no jurisdiction of causes between citizens of different States, unless the matter in dispute, whether it concerns the realty or personalty, be of the value of three thousand dollars, at the least: Nor shall the Federal Judicial Powers extend to any actions between citizens of different States, where the matter in dispute, whether it concerns the realty or personalty is not of the value of fifteen hundred dollars, at the least—And no part, triable by a Jury according to the course of the common law, shall be otherwise re-examinable, than according to the rules of common law.

Also on September 4, the Senate agreed to amend Article 11 to read as follows:

> No fact, triable by a Jury according to the course of common law, shall be otherwise re-examinable in any court of the United States, than according to the rules of common law.

On September 9, the Senate struck out Article 11, after incorporating it into Article 8. Otis noted, "10th. and 11th. incorporated."

Fig. 4.24 De Pauw, *Congress,* 4:38

4.25   Some authors revised documents years after their original composition. In his old age, James Madison significantly edited his papers but made many of the changes in writing that could be readily distinguished from that of the original. To note these changes, the editor of the *Records of the Federal Convention of 1787* placed the revised portions in angled brackets and included the original text in footnotes:

> of business in which he was to act, lamented his want of ⟨better qualifications⟩,[7] and claimed the indulgence of the House towards the involuntary errors which his inexperience might occasion.
>
> ⟨The nomination came with particular grace from Penna, as Docr. Franklin alone could have been thought of ⟨as a competitor⟩.[8] The Docr. was himself to have made the nomination ⟨of General Washington, but the state of the weather and of his health confined him to his house.⟩[9]⟩

[7] Crossed out "the requisites for it ".

[8] Crossed out "for the President ".

[9] Crossed out "of the Genl. but the season of the rain did not permit him to venture to the Convention chamber."

Fig. 4.25a Farrand, *Convention,* 1:4

Some documents are revised by both the author and third parties. The editors of the *Papers of James Madison* noted in a footnote both Madison's revisions and those made by his brother-in-law, John C. Payne:

> closed there. But the palpable urgency of the Ex. & its partizans to press war in proportion to the apparent chance of avoiding it, ought to open every eye to the hypocrisy [2] which has hitherto deceived so many good

> 2. JM originally wrote "hypocrisy & perfidy." Probably at a later time "& perfidy" was crossed out, and someone, probably John C. Payne, interlined "course" in place of "hypocrisy."

Fig. 4.25b Hutchinson, *Madison,* 17:142

4.26　Editors transcribe documents written by more than one author in such a way as to give both authors credit for their work. In a letter drafted by Dwight Eisenhower and edited by George Marshall, the final draft is used as the source for the version printed in the *Papers of Dwight David Eisenhower,* while the contribution of each author is identified in the footnotes:

[2] Marshall wrote the three preceding sentences (beginning "This weakness is now . . . . ") on Eisenhower's draft, replacing a sentence that read, "Since that time the enemy has not had to fear an attack involving a large scale sea campaign." The copy showing Marshall's handwritten corrections, given here and in the following notes, is in WPD 4639–31.

[3] Marshall made several stylistic changes on Eisenhower's draft, as well as writing the two preceding sentences, replacing a sentence that read, "A fleet undertaking offensive operations through island areas must be preceded by land based aircraft firmly established on suitable fields from which a protective umbrella may be maintained." As the authors of the text of the *West Point Atlas* make clear, the Japanese fully recognized this point. Their pattern of advance was to select the objective, concentrate their land-based aircraft and wipe out the Allied air units there, and then land sufficient troops to overwhelm the local Allied ground force. They next made operational the airfield they had captured before moving on. "Japanese naval task forces seldom moved beyond the combat range of their supporting land-based planes" (Esposito, ed., *West Point Atlas,* II, map 128). Later in the war in the Pacific the Americans did, of course, make longer "leap-frogs," but by then they had a large enough superiority in aircraft carriers to cover the operation with fighter planes.

[4] Marshall wrote this entire paragraph by hand.

[5] In his #201 MacArthur had concluded: "If agreeable to you I would appreciate greatly the presentation of this view to the highest authority." In his draft Eisenhower had concluded: "I welcome and appreciate your views on these subjects and invariably submit them to the very highest authority." Marshall penciled in the changes.

Fig. 4.26 Chandler, *Eisenhower,* 1:103

Original Missing or Destroyed

4.27   When a document has been copied and the original subsequently destroyed, editors are forced to rely on the copied version as their source text. The editors of the *Papers of Benjamin Franklin*, for example, used earlier printed editions as their source text for letters when the originals could not be located, indicating the circumstances and source text in the headnote:

To Jane Franklin[4]   MS not found; reprinted from Duane, *Works*, VI, 3.

Dear Sister,   Philadelphia, January 6, 1726–7
    I am highly pleased with the account captain Freeman[5] gives me of you. I always judged by your behaviour when a child that

Fig. 4.27 Labaree, *Franklin*, 1:100

4.28   In rare cases, missing or no longer extant documents may be reconstructed using drafts, outlines, or other sources of information. For example, the editors of *Jefferson's Extracts from the Gospels: "The Philosophy of Jesus"* and *"The Life and Morals of Jesus"* reconstructed Jefferson's vanished compendium of Biblical passages by using his notes and the original copies of the Bible from which he cut out passages. For more on the methods used to reconstruct the book and to verify its accuracy, consult the chapter "The Reconstruction of the Philosophy of Jesus," in *Jefferson's Extracts from the Gospels* (Princeton: Princeton University Press, 1983).

Other Types of Sources

4.29   Information can be acquired from sources other than verbal texts. Photographs, drawings, music, inscriptions, material objects, and maps all provide historical evidence but often defy easy transfer to the printed page.

4.30   When documents include both textual and nontextual elements, editors devise solutions for presenting them on the printed page. The editors of the *Papers of Thomas A. Edison* followed a policy of producing facsimiles of drawings along with the accompanying text:

In practice it may be found necessary to feed the paper drum by a seperate magnet, which will take an Intermittent work off from the Engine and perhaps add to the acuracy of the Unison of the two machine   It may be done in This manner   Fig 23

Fig 23

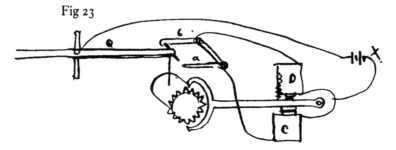

Fig. 4.30a Jenkins, *Edison,* 1:325

The editor of the *Complete Works of Washington Irving: Journals and Notebooks* separated drawings from text, indicating through footnotes in the text where drawings had appeared. Facsimiles of drawings appeared as illustrations in the middle of the volume:

385. All the writing on the page and also a small drawing of a profile (Figure 4) are in brown or black ink.

Figure 4. Small profile,
mentioned on page 171, n. 385.

Fig. 4.30b Wright, *Irving,* 1:171, figure 4

4.31   Editors present editorial cartoons through photoreproduction combined with enlargement or reduction if necessary. The editors of the *Documentary History of the Ratification of the Constitution* reproduced political cartoons as documents with appropriate annotation:

Massachusetts Centinel, 16 January[4]

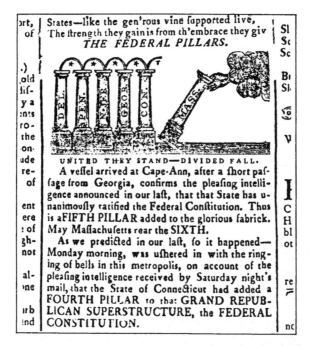

4. The two-lines of verse, the cartoon, and the two paragraphs appeared at the top of the second column on the third page of the *Massachusetts Centinel*. The original cartoon is approximately 3¹/₂″ × 2¹/₄″. Benjamin Russell reprinted the two paragraphs, with minor variations, from the *Massachusetts Gazette*, 15 January. Russell reversed the order of the paragraphs placing news of Georgia's ratification ahead of news of Connecticut's ratification, but he did not correct the references to Connecticut and Georgia as the fourth and fifth pillars, respectively. The cartoon, however, correctly labels Georgia as the fourth pillar and Connecticut as the fifth.

Fig. 4.31 Jensen, *Ratification*, 15:566–567

4.32   Maps require special handling for inclusion in a documentary edition. The editors of the *Expeditions of John Charles Frémont* (Champaign: University of Illinois Press, 1970) produced a "Map Portfolio" as part of their edition. It contained five folded maps and a descriptive pamphlet, all held in a box placed in a binding identical to the preceding volumes. This format allowed readers to remove the facsimile maps and open them to their full size. The editors of the *Atlas of the Lewis and Clark Expedition* (Lincoln: University of Nebraska Press, 1983) created a separate oversized volume (14″ × 20″) in which the large maps were printed as full-sized or reduced-size facsimiles.

4.33   The editors of the *Documentary History of the Ratification of the Constitution* included sheet music as a document:

> *799–G. Alexander Reinagle: The Federal March*
> *Philadelphia, 4 July*[1]

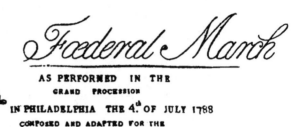

1. Alexander Reinagle composed "a grand march" called the "Fœderal March" for the "Grand Federal Procession" that paraded in celebration of the Fourth of July in Philadelphia (Evans 21421). Reinagle's "Fœderal March" was played by a band which made up division XII of the procession. On 10, 12, 15, and 17 July the sheet music

for the march, adapted for pianoforte, violin, or German flute, was advertised in the *Pennsylvania Packet* as "Just PUBLISHED" and for sale by John Aitken, an engraver, for the price of one shilling. The sheet was decorated with a liberty pole and cap.

Alexander Reinagle (1756–1809), an English-born composer, conductor, pianist, teacher, and theatrical manager of Austrian descent, arrived in the United States in 1786 and settled the same year in Philadelphia, where he revived the series of "city concerts." In 1791 he was cofounder of the New Theatre in Philadelphia which gave its first series of concerts in 1793. This company also performed in New York City and Baltimore on a regular basis.

Fig. 4.33 Jensen, *Ratification*, 18:248–249

4.34   Three-dimensional artifacts may warrant reproduction in historical editions. Some of Thomas Edison's inventions were presented in the *Papers of Thomas A. Edison* with a series of photographs from various angles:

–107–   [Newark or New York, Summer 1870]

And Franklin Pope
Production Model:
Printing Telegraphy[1]

M (historic photograph) (est. 17 cm dia. × 17 cm), NjWOE, Cat. 551:6, 18, 39. See Doc. 54 textnote. The machine frame is stamped "G. C.

Fig. 4.34 Jenkins, *Edison*, 1:188

Conflated Documents

4.35   On occasion, editors may create new texts by combining together, or conflating, information contained in several documents. The editors of the *Documentary History of the Ratification of the Constitution* combined information from three different documents—the text of the draft constitution of August 6, the notes from the Journal of the Convention, and James Madison's notes of the debate—to reconstruct how the Constitutional Convention's debates altered the text of the draft constitution. The editors created an original synthetic document that contained information from the three sources, with the retained portions of the text of the original draft in roman type, portions deleted from the draft in strikethrough type, and additions set in italics. The result was a document for which no original source text existed but that represented information about the transformation of the text of the U.S. Constitution:

> We the People of the States of New-Hampshire, Massachusetts, Rhode-Island and Providence Plantations, Connecticut, New-York, New-Jersey, Pennsylvania, Delaware, Maryland, Virginia, North-Carolina, South Carolina, and Georgia, do ordain, declare and establish the following Constitution for the Government of Ourselves and our Posterity.
>
> ARTICLE I. The stile of this Government shall be, "The United States of America."
>
> II. The Government shall consist of supreme legislative, executive and judicial powers.
>
> III. The legislative power shall be vested in a Congress, to consist of two separate and distinct bodies of men, a House of Representatives, and a Senate. ~~each of which shall, in all cases, have a negative on the other.~~ The Legislature shall meet *at least once in every year; and such meeting shall be* on the first monday in December ~~in every~~

Fig. 4.35 Jensen, *Ratification,* 1:271

Chapter Five

Presenting the Text

Textual Issues

5.1   Editors who use expanded transcription must consider how they will present documents on the page, screen, or microform frame and decide how much they will emend documents to present them in a readable fashion. Most editors standardize the presentation of parts of their documents, creating datelines, placelines, signatures, salutations, or complimentary closings whose placement is consistent from document to document. Uniform presentation helps the reader locate important information such as the dates and recipients. It also helps editors avoid the difficulty and expense of reproducing the irregular physical layout of many documents, elements that are not important to most users and that are best studied in the original manuscripts. Within each document, editors also need to decide to what extent they will emend the text to facilitate its presentation. Some editors intervene only minimally, presenting a near-literal transcription of the text, while others standardize many parts of the document and make significant emendations to produce a text with a modern, standard appearance. The variety of possibilities within expanded transcription requires editors to explain to their readers exactly how they have standardized and emended the documents they publish.

Date and Placeline

5.2   If a document indicates date and place of composition, editors usually want to include this information in the published version. Most editors standardize the placement of this information regardless of where it appears in the document, although the exact format of this information varies among editions. The editors of *Freedom: A Documentary History of Emancipation* standardized placement on a single line at the beginning of the document, but retained the original form:

> **207: Commander of the 2nd Division of the Army of Kentucky to the Commander of the Army of Kentucky, Enclosing an Order by the Former and a Letter to a Citizen of Ohio**
>
> **near Lexington Ky. Dec 11th 1862**
> **Sir   I have never, until now, felt disposed to take notice of attacks**

Fig. 5.2a Berlin, *Freedom*, ser.1,1:550

The editor of the *Letters of Eugene V. Debs* standardized both the placement and format of the date and place of composition. Each document's date was presented as a month spelled out, date, and year with the place appearing directly below it as a city and state. This information was placed one line above the salutation, regardless of its format or placement in the original document:

Katherine Metzel Debs to Grace D. Brewer

October 11, 1910
Terre Haute, Indiana

Dear Mrs. Brewer:
  Your letter with enclosure is received. Yes, they are a long way

Fig. 5.2b Constantine, *Debs*, 1:381

The editors of the *Documentary History of the First Federal Elections* placed the date and place of composition in a heading for each document. The year of composition did not appear in the heading but could be found in the running head at the top of each page:

To the German Inhabitants of the State of Pennsylvania, Philadelphia, 13 November[1]

  The character of the German (at least in Pennsylvania) has never been to demand privileges he is not intitled to. From natural diffidence, he rather steps

Fig. 5.2c Jensen, *Elections*, 1:339

The editor of *A Confederate Nurse: The Diary of Ada W. Bacot* placed the date above and to the right of each diary entry:

hope to awake in the morning to find the New Year coming in with a
bright smile as the old has left us weeping.

Tuesday Jan 1st 1861

1861 yes little did I think four year ago, I would live to write the
year 1861. But alive I am thank God, & far better than I was four years

Fig. 5.2d Berlin, *Nurse*, 23

The editor of the *Diary of Elizabeth Koren* placed the date in italic type on the
first line of each new diary entry:

**Monday, January 30. Just as I was about to drink my coffee
this morning, Embret came very opportunely and gave**

Fig. 5.2e Nelson, *Koren*, 151

5.3   When possible, editors supply datelines and placelines when the information is missing in the original document. When editors can provide this
information with certainty, the supplied portion is placed in square brackets,
as was done by the editors of *Lydia Maria Child, Selected Letters*:

Chauncey St. Wednesday
[25 March 1857]

My Dearly Beloved David,

I am getting homesick already, and meditating how I can get through all

Fig. 5.3a Meltzer, *Child*, 308

When part of the supplied date was conjecture, the editors of the *Letters of
Jessie Benton Frémont* followed that portion with a question mark:

Monday [Sept. 23?, 1878]

Dear Nell,

I have been in bed three days—fatigue &c.—we go tomorrow and

Fig. 5.3b Herr, *Frémont*, 447

The editor of the *Selected Letters of Charles Sumner* placed editorially supplied
information in italic type inside brackets. When supplied dates were conjectural, the editor marked them with a *c.* or *ca.* for circa. In this example, the

editor supplied both the date and place of composition, although only the date was conjecture:

> [*Washington*]
>
> [*c. 24 January 1874*]
>
> Dear Mr Bolles,
>   I wonder if I deserve this.[1] The remarks I made were unprepared &

Fig. 5.3c Palmer, Sumner, 2:628

Salutations and Closings

5.4   Most editors standardize the placement of salutations in letters. The editors of the *Papers of John Adams* employed a common method, placing all salutations at the top left of the body of the document, with no space between the salutation and the letter:

From Jonathan Trumbull

Gentlemen   Lebanon 25th March 1776
    Two accounts of loss by hostilities committed by the Ministerial

Fig. 5.4a Taylor, Adams, 4:64

The salutation was placed on the first line of the text by the editor of *Dear General: Eisenhower's Wartime Letters to Marshall:*

8   LONDON   *September 23, 1942*

Dear General: Admiral Ramsay[1] brought to me a verbal message from you to the effect that you hoped I would not be compelled to make a visit

Fig. 5.4b Hobbs, Dear General, 43

The editors of the *Documentary History of the Ratification of the Constitution* did not print the common salutations of their documents (e.g. Dear Sir). They did print salutations that provide unusual information (e.g. Dear Friend):

Gov. Edmund Randolph to Meriwether Smith, Charles M. Thruston, John H. Briggs, and Mann Page, Jr., Richmond, 10 December[1]

Your favor of the second instant,[2] requesting permission to publish my letter on the new Constitution, gives me an opportunity of making

Fig. 5.4c Jensen, Ratification, 8:229

5.5   Editors generally standardize the placement of complimentary closings, regardless of their location in a document. The editors of the *Papers of Alexander Hamilton* ran together four closing lines in a single paragraph, separating the elements with space:

I am   with great respect   Sir   your most humble and obedient
Servant   John Foncin

Fig. 5.5a Syrett, Hamilton, 26:169

Other editions place the closing one line below the last line of the body of the letter, set off to the right, as done by the editors of the *Papers of Henry Laurens*:

by that Eternal God to whom all hearts are open & before whom
the most Secret thoughts cannot be hid
   I am Sir
                         Your most Obd^t & most Hble Servt
                         Alex^r Innes

Fig. 5.5b Hamer, Laurens, 10:332

The editors of the *Documentary History of the Ratification of the Constitution* did not print the standard complimentary closings of their documents:

particular, the Convention reciting the powers by which they were convened. I was exactly in time as the 1st of February was set down for taking up and entering the several ratifications, and I delivered ours before they began that business.

1. FC, Stevens Family Papers, NjHi. This letter, with minor differences in wording, is printed in Livingston Rutherfurd, *Family Records and Events: Com-*

Fig. 5.5c Jensen, Ratification, 3:191

5.6   Editors transcribe authors' signatures in different ways. The editors of Abraham Lincoln's *Speeches and Writing* (New York: Library of America, 1989) omitted Lincoln's signature from his signed documents. The editors of the *Papers of Henry Laurens* transcribed signatures using upper- and lowercase letters:

Sir / Y^r mo. obed^t & very hble Servt
                                 P. Henry

Fig. 5.6a Hamer, Laurens, 14:529

The editors of the *Papers of James Madison* transcribed the same signature using large and small capital letters:

Sir Yr. Mo. obedt. & very hble Servt.

P. HENRY

Fig. 5.6b Hutchinson, *Madison,* 1:267

If more than twelve signatures appeared at the end of a document, the editors of *Free at Last: A Documentary History of Slavery, Freedom, and the Civil War* did not print them but indicated the number of signers in brackets:

your faithful friends in all the perils and dangers which threaten our

beloved country.

[*59 signatures*]

And many other colored citizens of Nashville[45]

Fig. 5.6c Berlin, *Free,* 505

For documents with many signers, the editors of the *State Records of South Carolina: Journals of the House of Representatives* included the first signer and the number of additional signatures in the footnotes:

[The Petition of Sundry Inhabitants of the Village of Granby in the County of Lexington humbly sheweth That the present Road in the said County leading from Granby to Charleston was some time ago order'd to be laid off by the County Court of the said County and that shortly after the said Court was suspended and no Commissioners being appointed put it out of the power of your petitioners of Applying for the said road to be alter'd which is at present so bad as to render it almost impassable and is about four Miles further round your petitioners therefore pray that the old road may be open'd which is much nearer and easier kept in repair and that your Honble. House would take the Matter into Your Consideration and appoint Commissioners for the purposes aforesaid and your petitioners as in Duty bound will ever pray.][21]

[21] Petitions, 1791, No. 107. The petition was signed by Alex. Blair and twenty-three other persons.

Fig. 5.6d Stevens, *House: 1791,* 388

The editors of *Free at Last: A Documentary History of Slavery, Freedom, and the Civil War* transcribed the mark (X) of illiterate men and women:

his

Archy X Vaughn[16]

mark

Fig. 5.6e Berlin, *Free,* 113

Paragraphs

5.7   Editors decide how their editions will note irregular paragraphing, and many explain their procedure in their statement of editorial method. The editors of the *Political Correspondence and Public Papers of Aaron Burr* standardized the length of paragraph indentations but did not add indentations that did not appear in the original text:

> Paragraph indentations are standardized to the customary five-character indentation. When an author has chosen not to indent the first line of a new paragraph, that format is respected.

Fig. 5.7a Kline, Burr, 1:xxxvii

The editors of *Friends and Sisters: Letters between Lucy Stone and Antoinette Brown Blackwell* interpreted the long dashes and elongated spaces of their subjects' letters as standard paragraphs:

> Particularly in the early letters, the writers seemed reluctant to waste space, so they apparently used a long dash or an elongated space to separate the end of one paragraph and the beginning of the next on the same line. We have rendered these into standard paragraphs.

Fig. 5.7b Lasser, Friends, xxvi

The editors of the *Papers of Jefferson Davis* modernized all paragraphing in their edition:

> Standard PARAGRAPH INDENTION is used. It is commonplace in nineteenth-century manuscripts for the writer to end a paragraph in midline and return to the left margin without indention. Whenever this occurs, extraneous punctuation, if any, is eliminated and the modern form of paragraphing is employed.

Fig. 5.7c Monroe, Davis, 1:xxvi

Capitalization

5.8   Editors usually retain the capitalization employed by the authors of documents, but a few editions standardize some elements of capitalization. When transcribing manuscript documents, it may be difficult to determine whether authors intended to use uppercase or lowercase letters, a situation made more difficult when transcribing seventeenth- and eighteenth-century manuscripts that include irregularly capitalized words. The editor of the

Complete Works of Washington Irving: Journals and Notebooks attempted to transcribe literally Irving's writings but explained the challenge posed by his penmanship and erratic use of capital letters:

> The most frustrating part of transcribing Irving's handwriting stems from his whimsical and indiscriminate use of capital and lower-case letters, as much for common as for proper nouns, and occasionally for other parts of speech as well, so that the old-fashioned custom of capitalizing nouns does not explain Irving's peculiar use of capitals. His capital and lower-case formations of letters, particularly "a," "c," "g," "m," "n," "o," "s," "v," and "w" (and occasionally "d," "l," and "t") are often indistinguishable. Their size in relation to following or preceding comparable letters is seldom a clear index to whether a capital or lower-case form is intended, although the initial capitals "B," "F," "H," "I," "J," "K," and "Q," are seldom left in doubt. The conformation of the letter is often more helpful, but in letters like "a," "c," "m," "n," "o," "s," and "r," it is of little use because the formation of lower-case and capital letters is often nearly identical. Place names appear in varying forms, occasionally in successive lines and often on the same page. "Peter," "Paris," "French," and "Italian" are as likely to be lower-case as not. The initial "o" in "o'clock" (almost always without the apostrophe) appears in from pigmy to giant size and usually in the same conformation; whereas "Evg" occurs regularly and becomes routine form regardless of its location in the sentence. The initial flourish with which a capital is likely to begin is an unreliable index, for when it is used (especially in such a letter as "s"), it is used in varying forms – some long, some short, most of them in-between. It is the in-between cases, where the eye cannot decide, that the doubtful cases are resolved in Irving's favor, and the form that usage dictates is rendered. That is, doubtful words that are customarily capitalized are so transcribed, the only exception being those cases in which the letter is clearly a lower-case form – judged so by its distinctive conformation and by comparison with adjacent and comparable characters. In converse cases, where Irving seems to use capitals for normally lower-case words, he is given the benefit of the doubt by transcribing as capital only those letters which are clearly so – all intermediate forms being rendered lower-case.[2]

Fig. 5.8a Wright, *Irving,* 1:xxi

The editors of the *Papers of Benjamin Franklin* generally maintained Franklin's capitalization, but they chose to begin every sentence with a capital letter, regardless of the form of the original:

b. *Capitalization.* Franklin himself was a life-long advocate of the use of initial capitals for all substantives, as he explained in a long letter to Noah Webster, December 29, 1789, and the editors, obedient to his views, will follow his practice in printing his manuscripts. We shall likewise retain all other capitalization as written, except that we shall begin every sentence with a capital letter. Some eighteenth-century writers, however, were so erratic and the size of their initial letters often varied so much in the same manuscript, that it is sometimes uncertain whether the writer meant to use a capital or a small letter, especially with such letters as "C" and "P." In these circumstances we shall render doubtful initial letters as like letters are in the same manuscript or, such a guide failing, employ modern usage.

Fig. 5.8b Labaree, *Franklin,* 1:xli

The editor of the *Correspondence of Roger Williams* retained original capitalization with the exception of proper nouns:

Capitalization

Capitalization is retained as found in the original manuscripts, except in the following instances. Personal names and geographical names have been capitalized. When it is not certain whether Williams or other writers intended to use a capital or lowercase letter, modern usage is followed.

Fig. 5.8c LaFantasie, *Williams,* 1:lxxi

Interlineations, Marginalia, and Canceled Passages

5.9   Editors treat interlineations in several ways. Many editors incorporate interlineated passages silently into the text at the point indicated by the document's author, as was done for most interlineations by the editors of the *Papers of Joseph Henry:*

In a number of documents there are interlineations, canceled matter, variant texts, marginalia, and even footnotes by the original author. The first are silently brought into line unless there is some point in their position. In that event we generally use a footnote to elucidate the significance, retaining the original position only in exceptional cases.

Fig. 5.9a Reingold, *Henry,* 1:xxxvi

The editors of the *Journals of the Lewis and Clark Expedition* indicated interlineations by inserting an editorial explanation set in italic type within brackets:

> Thursday 29th   Rained last night   a violent wind from the N this morng with rain, Some hail   we have a trial of John Shields. John Colter & R Frasure which take up the greater part of the day, in the evening we [*we written over 1*] walk to Higgens   a blustering day all day, the blacksmiths return with part of their work finished, river Continue to rise, Cloudy Day

Fig. 5.9b Moulton, Lewis and Clark, 2:182

The editors of the *Papers of Zebulon Baird Vance* placed interlineations between diagonal lines (//) at the point of insertion:

> upon ourselves these ties of /unity &/ common fellowship? With men who have slaughtered our sons & brothers in battle, murdered our citizens in cold blood, burnt our homes into cinders, stolen our property and inflicted upon our mothers /sisters/ and daughters the crowning outrage of humanity, and now send against

Fig. 5.9c Johnston, Vance, 2:244

The editors of *Mark Twain's Letters* inserted interlineations into the text, marking single-word insertions with a single caret (∧) (*not shown*) and putting multiple-word interlineation between two carets:

> hold him in grateful remembrance if he did that which made it possible for you & me to‑⊢ ₐbecome all in all to each other.ₐ[4] Oh, Livy! The clock has just struck 3! Another night without sleep! I am terrified. With kisses & blessings, good-bye my own darling.

Fig. 5.9d Branch, Twain, 3:154

Interlineations may be placed at the point of insertion between up and down arrows (↑↓), as did the editors of the *Autobiography of Benjamin Franklin: A Genetic Text:*

> the Assembly; your ↑equivocal↓ Project would be ↑just↓ a Match for their Wheat *or other Grain*.

Fig. 5.9e Lemay, Franklin: Genetic Text, 115

5.10   Marginalia (writing placed in the margins of a document) is transcribed by editors in different ways. The editors of the *Papers of General Nathanael Greene* incorporated marginalia and other nonlinear passages into the body of the text. The editors of the *Autobiography of Benjamin Franklin: A Genetic Text* indicated marginalia by placing those passages between double up and down arrows (↑↑marginalia↓↓):

> scatter'd Counsels thus into a Focus, enabled them to make greater Impression. The Piece ↑↑being universally approv^{ed}↓↓ was copied in all the Newspapers of the Continent, reprinted in

> Fig. 5.10a Lemay, *Franklin: Genetic Text*, 94

The editor of the *Diary of Samuel Sewall* indicated marginalia by preceding those passages with the bracketed and italicized phrase *In the margin*:

> Mr. Noyes pray'd at the beginning, and Mr. Higginson concluded. [*In the margin*], Væ, Væ, Væ, Witchcraft.

> Fig. 5.10b Thomas, *Sewall*, 1:289

The editors of the *Papers of Thomas A. Edison* placed marginalia in angled brackets and used lettered footnotes to describe unusual placement or authorship, such as the note below the following passage, which described the marginal text as having been written by Edison's assistant, Charles Batchelor:

> With this relay we were enabled to repeat & record on chemically prepared paper at the rate of 250 words per minute perfectly;[2] ⟨The sentence we took was "Now is the winter of our discontent made glorious summer by this son of York & all the clouds that lowered upon" with this we got 250 words per minute but counting 5 letters to a word we got 228.⟩[c]
>
> [c]Marginalia written by Batchelor.

> Fig. 5.10c Jenkins, *Edison*, 2:146

5.11   Editors establish policies for determining if and how they will transcribe passages that have been canceled out or erased from original documents. The editor of the *Papers of George Mason* did not transcribe most canceled passages but included significant crossed-through passages in the notes:

> I beg to be kindly remembered to Mrs. Mercer & my Young Relations; [and] am Dr Sir Yr affecte. Kinsman & obdt. Servt.
>
>   G MASON
>
> GM first wrote "my little Cousins," but crossed it through and settled for MY YOUNG RELATIONS (Mercer and GM were first cousins).

> Fig. 5.11a Rutland, *Mason*, 1:427

The editors of the *Papers of William Penn* indicated canceled passages with strikethrough type:

> lead not out of the Sence & Unity of that living Word of God, ~~For that is the defiled Bed & Dishonerable Marriage, where the Love & Affection that goe forth from either Male or Female, to each other, are not honoured with the unity, Blessings, & Holy Leadings of the Spirit, & Word of God in the Heart, & not preserved in the undefiled Life~~; So that this, the Lord God eternal requires at the hand of every Male & Female, that are convinced of his pure Light, & Way, &

Fig. 5.11b Dunn, Penn, 1:233

The editors of the *Letters of Jessie Benton Frémont* transcribed canceled passages as italic type within angled brackets:

> Mr. Pryor re-married a Miss Gray within ⟨*a very short time*⟩—as soon as a ⟨*month afterwards*⟩. Legislature in session granted divorce at once. woman housekeeper.

Fig. 5.11c Herr, Frémont, 116

The editors of the *Marcus Garvey and Universal Negro Improvement Association Papers* marked erased passages with the bracketed word *erasure:*

> WORLD, I do not see anything therein upon which this Department can base any action whatever. There is, [*erasure*], in a democratic form of government like ours the right to agitate to influence governmental policy, and so far as

Fig. 5.11d Hill, Garvey, 1:389

The editors of the *Papers of Alexander Hamilton* used several different procedures for canceled passages:

IV. CROSSED-OUT MATERIAL IN MANUSCRIPTS

Words or sentences crossed out by a writer in a manuscript have been handled in one of the three following ways:
1. They have been ignored, and the document or letter has been printed in its final version.
2. Crossed-out words and insertions for the crossed-out words have been described in the notes.
3. When the significance of a manuscript seems to warrant it, the crossed-out words have been retained, and the document has been printed as it was written.

Fig. 5.11e Syrett, Hamilton, 26:xvi

Superscripts and Abbreviations

5.12   When documents contain superscript letters, editors may either transcribe them literally or bring them down to the line. The editors of the *Papers of Henry Laurens* literally reproduced the superscript letters found in the complimentary closing of this letter from Patrick Henry to Henry Laurens, while the editors of the *Papers of James Madison* brought them down to the line:

> I beg to be presented to Congress in the most acceptable manner & in Terms expressive of that high Regard with which I have the Honour to be__
>   Sir / Y^r mo. obed^t & very hble Servt
>
> P. Henry

Fig. 5.12a Hamer, *Laurens,* 14:529

> I beg to be presented to Congress in the most acceptable manner & in Terms expressive of that high Regard with which I have the Honour to be
> Sir Yr. Mo. obedt. & very hble Servt.
>
> P. Henry

Fig. 5.12b Hutchinson, *Madison,* 1:267

5.13   When documents contain abbreviations and contractions, editors may transcribe them literally or expand them into full words to make them more easily understood. The editors of the *Diary of Martha Ballard* literally transcribed all abbreviations and contractions, while the editor of the version of the diary found in the *History of Augusta* expanded most abbreviations into the full words they represented:

> Deacon Coney made ye 1st prayer, Esqr Petingil ye Last foren^n.   Col^o Sewal ye 1st aft & red Doc^t Dodridges Discoarses,   mr Liverm^a Last prayer, but few attended.

Fig. 5.13a McCausland, *Ballard,* 176

> Deacon Coney made the 1st prayer; Esqr. Petengil the last, forenoon; Colonel Sewall the 1st, afternoon, and red Doctor Dodridge's Discoarses; Mr. Livermore, last prayer; but few attended.

Fig. 5.13b Nash, *Augusta,* 296

The editors of the *Papers of Ulysses S. Grant* lowered superscript letters used in abbreviations but otherwise transcribed abbreviations as they were written:

> The undersigned having been duly appointed Colonel of the 7th Congl Dist Regt. of Ills Volts. Militia by order of Govr Richard Yates, duly promulgated hereby assumes command.

Fig. 5.13c Simon, Grant, 2:45

Abbreviations were transcribed literally by the editor of *A Plantation Mistress on the Eve of the Civil War: The Diary of Keziah Goodwyn Hopkins Brevard,* although missing letters in brackets were supplied if an abbreviation was unclear:

> $13.35 cts. in my purse after paying D[ick], N[ed] & John. Paid this (87½ cts.) for lard (Ned) leaf lard.[5] This is right, 7 lb. of l[eaf] lard at 12½ cts. per lb.

Fig. 5.13d Moore, Plantation Mistress, 59

The editors of the *Correspondence and Miscellaneous Papers of Benjamin Henry Latrobe* noted in their statement of editorial method that they expanded abbreviations that they regarded as difficult to understand:

> Ampersands have been changed to "and" except in the names of business firms and in the abbreviation "&c." Superscript letters have been lowered to the line of type, and the resulting abbreviation silently expanded if it is not easily recognizable (e.g., while "Pha." has been rendered "Philadelphia," "Phila." has been let stand).

Fig. 5.13e Van Horne, Latrobe, 1:xxii

The editors of the *Papers of Thomas Jefferson* altered the abbreviated portions of their texts significantly, expanding all abbreviations into full words:

> As for contractions and abbreviations, these will normally be expanded in ordinary documents, and raised letters at the close of such contractions or abbreviations will in all cases be lowered. In many instances, however, particularly in such a document as Jefferson's notes and outlines of his argument in behalf of religious freedom in 1776, the text will be presented quite literally even though many of the contractions present a difficult problem of decipherment. A single example of the kind of expansion that the editors have in mind in adopting this conventionalized practice will suffice. If presented literally, what Jefferson wrote as he took down hasty notes in a congressional investigating committee in

the busy summer of 1776 would read as follows: "Carleton havg hrd yt we were returning with considble reinfmt, so terrifd, yt wd hve retird immedly hd h. nt bn infmd by spies of deplorble condn to wch sm pox hd redd us." Such a passage, by the conventionalization to be followed in these volumes, will read: "Carleton having heard that we were returning with considerable reinforcement, [was] so terrified, that [he] would have retired immediately had he not been informed by spies of [the] deplorable conditions to which small pox had reduced us." This expanded text represents the kind of clear and readable form that Jefferson himself would have used for a document intended for formal presentation in print. It makes for clarity and readability and yet sacrifices nothing of Jefferson's words or meaning. Among the typical forms to be expanded, except in those outstanding documents in which a literal presentation is adopted, are the ampersand and the thorn, though the ampersand will be retained in the names of firms, the form "&c." will be employed since it was widely used in eighteenth-century printing, and the thorn, much as the editors object to the attempt to represent it by the letter "y," will be employed in the case of a few highly important documents which are given with literal exactness. Among other typical forms to be expanded are the following: *agst* (against), *cos* (companies), *commee* (committee), *dft* (defendant), *exors* (executors), *plt* (plaintiff), and *pr* (per; though the symbol ℔ will be retained when employed for per, pre, and pro).

Fig. 5.13f Boyd, Jefferson, 1:xxxi

Typefaces

5.14 Editors decide how literally they wish to represent the different sizes and styles of typefaces used in original documents. In the first volume of the *Documentary History of the Ratification of the Constitution*, the editors explained why they did not reproduce the typefaces of original documents:

Reproduction of Newspaper, Pamphlet, and Broadside Material

Eighteenth century printers sometimes used several varieties of type in a single item—large capitals, small capitals, and italics, as well as ordinary type. No attempt is made to reproduce varieties of type except when capital letters and italics were evidently used for emphasis by the author or the printer. In a few cases we have reproduced, so far as possible, the format of newspaper items.

Fig. 5.14a Jensen, Ratification, 3:19

The editors of the *Papers of Benjamin Franklin* described their method for transcribing the various typefaces of printed documents:

> b. Proper nouns, such as the names of persons and places, which were conventionally printed in italics in the eighteenth century, will be printed in roman type.
>
> c. Prefaces to pamphlets or other publications and passages of substantial length in other pieces were often printed in italics for typographical reasons that were cogent in the eighteenth century but no longer seem persuasive. These also will appear in roman type. Italics will be preserved, however, for words or phrases of emphasis and in other special cases as, for example, in some instances of dialogue or conversation.
>
> d. Single words originally printed in full capitals for emphasis or other similar reasons will usually be printed in small capitals in harmony with modern typographical taste.

Fig. 5.14b Labaree, *Franklin*, 1:xl–xli

Underlined Passages

5.15   Editors transcribe underlined passages by representing them literally with underlined type or, more often, by representing them with italics. The editors of the *Papers of Thomas A. Edison* transcribed underlined passages literally with underscored type and indicated double-underlined passages, such as the words *sixty-thousand* in the example below, by printing them in underscored type and then indicating the second underlining in the textual note marked with a superscript letter:

> A girl of ordinary intelligence and a few hours or days of practice, works either machine with perfect accuracy.
>
> We found that where a single wire was tumbling messages into the office at the rate of sixty thousand[b] words per hour, that we must have something more rapid than the hand-pen
>
> [b]Underlined twice.

Fig. 5.15a Jenkins, *Edison*, 1:251–252

The editors of *Lafayette in the Age of the American Revolution* presented underlined passages in italic type:

> Before settling any thing the french generals want to hear from theyr Second division. *Don't fear By any means* theyr acting *Rashly* and Be assur'd that you may very far depend on theyr *Caution*.[5] But our

Fig. 5.15b Idzerda, *Lafayette*, 3:114

The editor of the *Selected Letters of Charles Sumner* placed underlined passages in italics but indicated double-underlined passages by presenting them in italicized, underscored type:

> This proposition, if pres[sed] to a vote, will split our party—as no other party ever has been split. *Seward will not vote for it.* He will use it as a lure; *but not vote for it.* I deplore its introduction, & think of it constantly with tears. My constant hope is that events in their rapid

Fig. 5.15c Palmer, Sumner, 2:55

Single-underlined passages were placed in italics (*not shown*), while double-underlined passages were placed in small capital letters by the editors of the *Salmon P. Chase Papers:*

> those positions of the Slave Power which are most exposed. Our first and chief effort should be directed to the DENATIONALIZATION OF SLAVERY—to the absolute and complete divorce of the General

Fig. 5.15d Niven, Chase, 2:119

Slips of the Pen and Other Errors

5.16   Editors need to establish policies on how to treat writing, typing, or printing errors. The editors of the *Samuel Gompers Papers* silently corrected many of the errors created by typesetters and typists (see Section 4.13), as did the editors of the *Frederick Douglass Papers:*

> Obvious printer's errors have been corrected. The most common of these were the transposing of letters within a word, the repetition of words and punctuation marks, and transposition of numbers within dates. Misspelled names have been treated as printer's errors when it was apparently impossible for anyone to pronounce them as transcribed or when the correct spelling appeared elsewhere in the same document.

Fig. 5.16a Blassingame, Douglass, 1:lxxxiii

The editors of the *Papers of Woodrow Wilson* printed all documents exactly as they appeared, without correcting errors, because of the insights such errors could provide:

> We think that it is very important for several reasons to follow the rule of *verbatim et literatim*. Most important, a document has its own integrity and power, particularly when it is not written in perfect literary form. There is something very moving in seeing a

Texas dirt farmer struggling to express his feelings in words, or a semiliterate former slave doing the same thing. Second, in Wilson's case it is crucially important to reproduce his errors in letters which he typed himself, since he usually typed badly when he was in an agitated state. Third, since style is the essence of the person, we would never correct grammar or make tenses consistent, as one correspondent has urged us to do. Fourth, we think that it is very important that we print exact transcripts of Charles L. Swem's copies of Wilson's letters. Swem made many mistakes (we correct them in footnotes from a reading of his shorthand books), and Wilson let them pass. We thus have to assume that Wilson did not read his letters before signing them, and this, we think, is a significant fact. Finally, printing typed letters and documents *verbatim et literatim* tells us a great deal about the educational level of the stenographic profession in the United States during Wilson's time.

Fig. 5.16b Link, *Wilson,* 51:ix

The editor of the *Correspondence of Mother Jones* marked slips of the pen using the word *sic* in brackets:

would have to suffer the result. I *want to say right here,* I may never see him again, but one thing one thing [*sic*] certain, I will fight to death

Fig. 5.16c Steel, *Jones,* 52

5.17   If an edition has erratic or missing punctuation, an editor may literally transcribe those passages to maintain the character of the original document or emend the passages to produce a document that may be easier to read. Following the revision of the editorial policy in volume 10, the editors of the *Papers of Henry Laurens* retained all original punctuation. The editors of *Witness to the Young Republic: A Yankee's Journal* emended some forms of punctuation to make the documents easier to read:

Our intent throughout has been to present the text as French wrote it; the words are all his except for the few that have been bracketed. In the interests of consistency and clarity, however, we have made a few changes in punctuation and spelling. Some of the commas and dashes, which French used much too liberally, have been removed or replaced silently by other marks of punctuation. To avoid incomplete or run-on sentences we have occasionally created new ones, and sentences without periods have had them added, in each case without mention. Otherwise, when marks of punctuation have been added, brackets have been used. The punctuation of dates and addresses has been regularized silently, and the datelines at the start of each entry have been made uniform in style. The place at which an entry was written is cited only when it differs from the previous entry.

Fig. 5.17a Cole, *Witness,* xi–xii

The editor of the *Diary of Isaac Backus* altered the erratic punctuation of the original text quite significantly:

> Misleading punctuation is corrected where the meaning is not in doubt. Punctuation is regularized between the members of a series, in dates, and after abbreviations. A period used as a comma is replaced by a comma, and superfluous interior periods are omitted. Also omitted are dashes used to fill out manuscript lines and dashes or other superfluous marks at the ends of sentences. A quotation mark or parenthesis omitted at the end of a quoted or parenthetical passage is silently supplied if there is no question as to its placement. Brackets used to enclose parenthetical phrases are replaced by parentheses to avoid confusion with the brackets that enclose editorial insertions.

Fig. 5.17b McLoughlin, *Backus,* 1:xxxvi

5.18   Editors must decide how to present words misspelled by the authors of documents. The editor of the *Correspondence of Mother Jones* retained all misspellings:

> Reynoldsville Pa
> Dec the 9 1901
>
> Der Mother Jones
>   I write to inform you that I had hoped by this tim you would have been able to have made your way to Reynoldsville according to both telegrams and letters   I made arrangements for you to speak and you would have had a rousing meeting but unfortenly you was Debared from coming   now Mother Jones you will not be able to do much until after the Holladays and I hope you will see your way clear to com here about Christmas time if so let me know   I don think I will return to W Va til after new years   Com if you can as these People is anishius for you aspishely the textile workers

Fig. 5.18a Steel, *Jones,* 18

The editors of the *Journals of the Lewis and Clark Expedition* retained the authors' original spelling, clarifying confusing orthography in brackets:

> I took Collins &
> went to the place he found a Hog Skined & Hung up, the Crows[1] had devoured the meet, Killed Prary fowl[2] and went across a Prary to a 2nd Bank where I discovered an Indian Fortification,[3] near the Second bank I attempted to cross a Bond [pond] of about 400 yds wide on the Ice &

Fig. 5.18b Moulton, *Lewis and Clark,* 2:153

All spelling (and many other features) was normalized by the editor of *Children of Pride,* as explained in the volume's introduction:

> The Joneses and their friends wrote extraordinarily careful English, but for ease of reading it has seemed wise to reduce a varying text to a consistent standard. To this end I have normalized all spelling, capitalization, punctuation, and paragraphing.

Fig. 5.18c Myers, Children, xiv

Nontextual Elements

5.19   Editors decide how to handle symbols, drawings, and other unusual elements that appear in documents. The editors of the *Joseph Henry Papers* reproduced drawings, doodles, and sketches found in Henry's documents as facsimiles (see Section 4.10). The editors of the *Documentary History of the First Federal Congress* reproduced some elements, such as the hand symbol used by William Maclay in his diary:

> favour of Titles from these Motives, but that in conformity to the Practice of the other House, for the present they resolv'd to address the President without Title ☛
>
> {☛ Mr. Muh   Yesterday G⟨eneral⟩. M.(Muhlenberg) accosted me with the with, *Your highness of the Senate.*   on my pausing he said Wynkoop had

Fig. 5.19a De Pauw, Congress, 9:37

The editors of the *Journals of the Lewis and Clark Expedition* represented the sun, moon, and star symbols with typographical equivalents:

> *Note*—The *Longitude* of the mouth of the River Dubois was calculated from four sets of observations of the ⊙ & ☽, in which the ⊙ was twice West, and twice East; two sets with Aldebaran, ☆ East in one, and W. in the other; and one set with Spica, ☆, ☆ East. the Longtd. above stated is

Fig. 5.19b Moulton, Lewis and Clark, 2:228

Flourishes and decorative marks were not transcribed by the editors of the *Documentary History of the Supreme Court of the United States:*

> We delete from our transcription all textual marks that are of strictly decorative or design function. Thus, end-of-line dashes used to justify texts to the right margin are deleted as unnecessary since our typeset lines do not break at the same point as the document lines. Dashes employed in the same fashion within braces are not reproduced either. Any dash, however, that might serve

some purpose as punctuation is retained. Elaborately self-conscious changes in the style of handwriting—textual enlargement, ornate capital letters—are not reproduced as such; nor are idiosyncratic decorative or aesthetic marks whether meant to balance or serve some other purpose inherent in the layout of the original document page. To reproduce such idiosyncratic embellishment would be technologically difficult and prohibitively expensive. We make this decision fully aware that the meaning of a document inheres as much in its appearance as in the words it contains. But the meaning that derives from the physical appearance of a document can be discerned only by examining it in person. The experience of personal contact with a document cannot be duplicated in a typeset edition.

Fig. 5.19c Marcus, *Supreme Court*, vol.1,1:lvii–lviii

Terminal Punctuation

5.20 Because authors end sentences in a variety of ways, editors need to decide how to indicate terminal punctuation. The editors of *Jonathan Carpenter's Journal* literally transcribed the long dashes and extra spaces Carpenter used to punctuate and terminate his sentences:

Dec'r ye 10   Last night 5 of our men made their escape   joy go with 'em   They tell us we shall soon be exchanged but I sopose they lie as they used to do—our Money is Reduced to 1s pr week[8]   we have had 2 heretofore ever since I have bin in this troublesome scene in high Life below stairs[9] —

Fig. 5.20a Herwig, *Carpenter*, 51

The editors of the *Book of Abigail and John: Selected Letters of the Adams Family* literally transcribed long dashes, even when they followed a period as terminal punctuation:

But I must bid you adieu or the post will go of without my Letter.—

Fig. 5.20b Butterfield, *Abigail and John*, 191

If a sentence did not have terminal punctuation, the editors of the *Papers of Andrew Johnson* inserted the appropriate punctuation in brackets:

Give my best respects to Messrs Browns[11] & Dosser,[12] tell dosser he must write to me and send me all the news[.]
      Please accept for your Self my best wishes[.]   A. Johnson

Fig. 5.20c Graf, *Johnson*, 1:34

The editors of the *Naval War of 1812: A Documentary History* changed long dashes into modern forms of punctuation:

> The punctuation used is that of the original document, with one exception. In the early 19th century, dashes were often used in place of periods, commas, semi-colons, and question marks; most of these dashes will be replaced by appropriate modern punctuation.

Fig. 5.20d Dudley, *1812*, 1:xii

Interpolation and Missing Text

5.21   In cases where words or passages are missing from a document, editors sometimes use their knowledge of the topic and the surrounding words to interpolate the meaning of the missing portions. The editors of the *Papers of James Madison* printed a letter with several pieces missing, supplying the lost portions in brackets; information about which the editors were uncertain is followed by question marks:

> [adverse to?] the American Cause. Independ[ent] of the Recommendation[8] [to detain the?] person and papers of Govr. Eden and to form a New Gove[rn]mt. [representative?] of the people, they have re-

Fig. 5.21a Hutchinson, *Madison*, 1:182

When the editors of the *Papers of Alexander Hamilton* supplied missing or indecipherable words or letters, they placed them in angled brackets (< >):

> **The answer to this is, that however true it may be, that th⟨e⟩ right of the Legislature to declare wa⟨r⟩ includes the right of judging whether the N⟨ation⟩ be under obligations to make War or not**

Fig. 5.21b Syrett, *Hamilton*, 15:40

The editors of *Mark Twain's Letters* provided their interpolation as part of the document's text, without brackets, but noted the reconstruction and interpolations of missing information at the back of the volume:

> ■ 12? September 1861 · To Mary E. (Mollie) Clemens · Carson City, Nev. Terr. · *UCCL* 02715
>
> ■*Copy-text:* MS, Jean Webster McKinney Family Papers, Vassar College Library (NPV). Only the last leaf of the MS survives. As the illustration shows, a piece has been torn out of the leaf at the upper right corner, affecting seven lines; the missing text has been conjecturally supplied by emendation. Accompanying the MS facsimile is a type facsimile of the same lines with the emended readings

in place. ■*Previous publication:* none known. ■*Provenance:* see McKinney Family Papers, pp. 459–61. ■*Emendations and textual notes:*

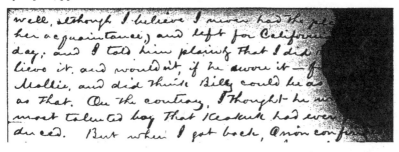

> well, although I believe I never had the pleasure of
> her acquaintance,) and left for California the same
> day, and I told him plainly that I did not be-
> lieve it, and wouldn't, if he swore it—for I didn't,
> Mollie, and did think Billy could be as stupid
> as that. On the contrary, I thought he was the
> most talented boy that Keokuk had ever pro-
> duced. But when I got back, Orion confirmed

Fig. 5.21c Branch, *Twain,* 1:499

5.22   If a source text is defaced or damaged, an editor may want to indicate this information to the reader. The editors of the *Collected Works of Abraham Lincoln* marked missing words or letters with dots in brackets ([...]) and indicated the extent of the missing portion in the footnotes. The editors of the *Papers of Ulysses S. Grant* marked lost letters and words with dots and dashes in brackets ([...] or [- - -]), with the number of such marks approximating the number of lost letters or words. Two sets of approximately four lost letters are indicated by the bracketed dots in the following passage:

I would have been able to call you *Wife.* Dearest Julia if you have been just as constant in your love it *shall not* [. . . .] long until I will be entitled to call you by the [. . . .] affectionate title. You

Fig. 5.22a Simon, *Grant,* 1:113

The editor of the *Papers of Josiah Bartlett* marked missing portions of documents with a set of empty brackets ([ ]):

Cold that I took on my Jorney. The Small Pox is in the City. Some of the members of the Congress are now under Innoculation & some have taken [   ] as hitherto to Escape it. Which I Shall Do I am not fully

Fig. 5.22b Mevers, *Bartlett,* 18

The editors of the *Salmon P. Chase Papers* indicated missing portions of documents with the word *torn* italicized and in brackets:

instant destruction. All [*torn*] things I wished you to see and enjoy with me. And besides I wanted [*torn*] society and to feel your heart

Fig. 5.22c Niven, *Chase*, 2:231

5.23   When editors transcribe documents, they often find words or passages that are illegible. The editor of the *Correspondence of Mother Jones* indicated illegible passages in brackets (i.e. [three words illegible]):

I am scraching this off in a hurry. It goes out underground   I am watched on all sides of my room   My old [three words illegible] this off   I am writing it blindly for I have to watch the windo I'll take no

Fig. 5.23a Steel, *Jones*, 109

The editors of the *Letters of Delegates to Congress* described the system used in the edition to signify missing or illegible words and numbers. Three bracketed ellipses points [...] were used for missing words within sentences and four bracketed ellipses points for words missing from the end of sentences:

The following devices will be used in this work to clarify the text.

[. . .], [. . . .]	**One or two words missing and not conjecturable.**
[. . .][1], [. . . .][1]	**More than two words missing; subjoined footnote estimates amount of material missing.**
[ ]	**Number or part of a number missing or illegible.**
[ ][1]	**Blank space in manuscript; explanation in subjoined footnote.**
[roman]	**Conjectural reading for missing or illegible matter; question mark inserted if reading is doubtful.**

Fig. 5.23b Smith, *Delegates*, 1:xii

Text with Original Annotation

5.24   When a document contains footnotes, editors must devise a system to prevent the reader from confusing those notes written by the document's author with those written by the editor. The editors of *John Franklin Jameson and the Development of Humanistic Scholarship in America* distinguished Jameson's footnotes (*top*) from the editor's (*bottom*) by placing the number of the editor's notes in braces:

1. Lecture before the Trustees of the Carnegie Institution of Washington, December 12, 1912.

{3.} Edward Waterman Townsend (1855–1942) created the character of Chimmie Fadden in a series of stories that first appeared in the *New York Sun* and were collected and published in 1895 as *Chimmie Fadden, Major Max and Other Stories* and *Chimmie Fadden Explains, Major Max Expounds.*

Fig. 5.24a Rothberg, *Jameson,* 1:229,304

The editors of the *Papers of Martin Luther King, Jr.* replaced King's numbered footnotes with a series of symbols and numbered the editor's notes sequentially:

nal life. And this is why Christianity rejects the doctrine of natural immortality in favor of the belief that eternal life is given by God alone.*[46]

Tillich concludes that the dialectical problem of nonbeing is inescapable. It is a problem of finitude. Finitude involves a mixture of being and nonbeing.[47] "Man's finitude, or creatureliness, is unintelligible without the concept of dialectical nonbeing." †

---

* Tillich, ST, I, 188.
† Tillich, ST, I, 189.
‡ Tillich, ST, I, 189.
§ Tillich, ST, I, 190.

---

46. Roberts, "Tillich's Doctrine of Man," pp. 119–120: "The Christian doctrine of *creatio ex nihilo* attempts to solve the problem by denying that there is a second principle co-eternal with God; but it affirms that there is an element of nonbeing in all finite existence. Tillich denies that when Augustine attributes sin to nonbeing he is following a purely privative theory; rather, Augustine is asserting that although sin has no positive ontological status it nevertheless *actively* resists and perverts being. Indeed, since anything created originates out of nothing, it must return to nothing. This is why any view which regards the Son as a creature (Arianism) had to be rejected by the Church on the ground that a creature cannot bring eternal life. And this is why Christianity rejects the doctrine of natural immortality in favor of the belief that eternal life is given by God alone."

47. Tillich, *Systematic Theology,* p. 189: "The dialectical problem of nonbeing is inescapable. It is the problem of finitude. Finitude unites being with dialectical nonbeing."

Fig. 5.24b Carson, *King,* 2:397

The editor of the *Papers of Chief John Ross* incorporated the footnotes of the original documents sequentially into the editor's notes, distinguishing them within the notes themselves:

> [3] A footnote here reads: "The meaning here probably is that the names of beloved towns, which are exchanged between nations of indians when they made peace, were in this instance speedily exchanged back again; and this sudden return to each others' names is considered as indicating a sudden breaking of friendship—like the return of love tokens when courtships are broken off."
> [4] A footnote here reads: "Mohawks & Seneces both bore this name."

Fig. 5.24c Moulton, Ross, 1:121

Enclosures, Attachments, and Envelopes

5.25   Editors should evaluate information found in enclosures, attachments, and envelopes and should determine if and how this material should be noted in the edition.

5.26   Frequently the author of a letter encloses in it other documents. These may include not only textual documents such as orders, newspaper clippings, wills, receipts, contracts, and the like but also such nontextual items as drawings, pictures, and maps. The editors of the *Papers of Woodrow Wilson* marked such items with the word *enclosure* in small capital letters and printed the full text of the enclosed document:

E   N   C   L   O   S   U   R   E

> ### Vira Boarman Whitehouse to Joseph Patrick Tumulty
>
> Dear Mr. Tumulty: New York Oct. 13th, 1917.
>   Your letter of October 12th has brought rejoicing to the suffrage camp. You say the President asks what would be the best

Fig. 5.26a Link, Wilson, 44:384

The editors of the *Booker T. Washington Papers* chose not to reproduce an article enclosed in a letter, but instead provided a brief summary of the work and a full citation:

> I enclose a very bad proof of an article which will appear in the July issue of the A.M.E. Church Review.[1] It is an abstract of a fragment of my talks to the Hampton and Tuskegee students a year ago. My recol-

----

[1] Durham's article, "Three Growths," *A.M.E. Church Review,* 14 (July 1897), 121-30, concluded that the establishment of trade schools and the movement to open factories, workshops, and businesses were in harmony with natural economic

development. Durham discussed the different economic roles of slaves and how they evolved after the Civil War. He had high praise for the ex-slave craftsmen and suggested that schools such as Tuskegee continued that tradition.

Fig. 5.26b Harlan, *Washington*, 4:310

It is not unusual for a letter to mention an enclosure that cannot be located. The editors of the *Papers of Robert Morris* speculated on the content of a missing enclosure in a footnote:

Office of Finance 23. Sept. 1782

Sir,

I enclose you Copy of a Letter of the thirteenth Instant from Mr Webb Receiver of Taxes for Virginia.[1] In Consequence of which I also

1. George Webb's letter has not been found, but apparently suggested purchase of public tobacco from Virginia with Morris's notes in order to enable the state to make payment on the congressional specie requisition for 1782. Although the arrangements

Fig. 5.26c Ferguson, *Morris*, 6:419

In some cases, enclosures can be found but not their cover letters. The *Political Correspondence and Public Papers of Aaron Burr* printed an enclosure for which a cover letter could not be located, alerting the reader in the document's endnote:

ALS (NHi:Burr), enclosed in an unlocated letter to AB of the same date.

Fig. 5.26d Kline, *Burr*, 1:52–53

5.27 When documents contain address information on their reverse side, on envelopes, or on wrappers, editors may wish to transcribe that information. The *Papers of George Mason* quoted that information in a note following the document's text, after the word *Addressed:*

RC (Morristown National Historical Park, N.J.). Addressed: "To Mr. John Craig Mercht. in Port Tobacco."

Fig. 5.27a Rutland, *Mason*, 1:146

The editors of *Mark Twain's Letters* used a small envelope icon to separate the body of the letter from information taken from its envelope:

W^m. H. Clagett, Esq. | Unionville | Humboldt Co. | N. T. [*partly boxed, lower left:*] *Via* Carson [*postmaster's hand:*] Esmeralda Cal, | April 21st 1862 [*brace*] [*three-cent U.S. postage stamp, canceled with a pen*]

Fig. 5.27b Branch, *Twain*, 1:193

5.28   Editors often preserve endorsements—that is, notations written on the back of a document or a wrapper. The editors of the *Political Correspondence and Public Papers of Aaron Burr* placed endorsements in an unnumbered note at the end of the document following the provenance note:

> AL (DLC:Monroe). Endorsed: "5. July 1795 / A Burr."

Fig. 5.28a Kline, *Burr*, 1:224

The editors of the *Papers of Robert Morris* marked endorsements with the word *endorsed* in small capital letters and placed it before the provenance note:

> ENDORSED: 26th Augt 1782/Office of Finance/de Jno Bradford Esqr./received 16th Septr. seq. enclosed

Fig. 5.28b Ferguson, *Morris*, 6:259

Endorsements are particularly common on military and government documents, with each subsequent recipient writing a response or order directly onto the original document or its wrapper. Such endorsements occasionally take up several pages of text. The editors of *Freedom: A Documentary History of Emancipation* transcribed sequential endorsements in the following manner:

99: Commander of U.S. Forces at Fort Donelson, Tennessee, to the Headquarters of the 3rd Division, Reserve Corps, Army of the Cumberland

Fort Donelson Tenn.   October 14th 1863.
      There are at this Post about one hundred and twenty negroes who have been at work for the Government of the U.S. without pay since the first of June last. In order to get paid they must be mustered into the service as Infantry soldiers and detailed in the Engineer Department. Their services will be needed here for some time. Can there not be an officer sent here to muster them at once?
HLcSr   (sgd) E. C. Brott.

[*Endorsement*] Hd. Qur^s Com^r Org. U.S.CT. Nashville Nov 5″ 1863. Respectfully referred to Major Genl Thomas Comdg Dep^t of Cumberland, Chattanooga Tenn. There is a large amount of money due negroes for work on the fortifications in the Department and I am informed by Lieut Burroughs (Eng. Corps) that there is money in his hands to pay them. Many families are suffering for want of money earned from six to twelve months since. The 1st Reg^t U.S. Col^d Vol^s of Tenn. earned by labor on the fortifications previous to Aug 15 Eighteen to twenty thousand dollars which is still due them. (sgd) Geo. L. Stearns Maj. & A.A.G. USV. Com^r Org^n U.S.C. Troops

[Endorsement] Hd. Qurs. Dep[r] Cumb[d] Chattanooga *[Tenn.]* Nov 11 /63 Respy referred to Brig Gen[l] W F Smith. Chief Engineer. It was understood that Lt Burroughs had instructions to settle these arrears of pay By order of Maj Gen[l] Thomas. (sgd). C. Goddard. A.A.G.

Fig. 5.28c Berlin, *Freedom,* ser.1,2:408–409

5.29 Editors often transcribe docketing—that is, information placed on a document to identify it. The editors of the *Papers of James Madison* placed docketing information in an unnumbered note following the document, after the letter code indicating the location of the document:

RC (DNA: RG 59, DD, Netherlands, vol. 4). Marked duplicate; docketed by Wagner as received 21 Nov.

Fig. 5.29a Brugger, *Madison: State,* 1:417

The editors of the *Papers of John Adams* also placed docketing in the note following the document, following the word *docketed:*

RC (NHi:Misc. MSS, Adams); docketed: "Mr J A Lettr June 1775."

Fig. 5.29b Taylor, *Adams,* 3:43

Previously Published Documents

5.30 In the case of new editions of previously published works or manuscripts, it may be important for editors to preserve references to the original pagination and page breaks. Readers may want to use a modern edition but still be able to find references or citations to the original work made in previous scholarship. The editor of the *Complete Works of Captain John Smith* placed the page number from the source text in the margin, in bold type and brackets, and indicated the exact location of page breaks in the original with two vertical lines (‖):

your knowledge: now though some bee hurt by your misprision, yet he is your friend, and so wil continue: and since the ice is open hee **[65]** would have you send a- ‖ waie your corne; and if you would have his companie send also your armes, which so affrighteth his people, that they dare not come to you, as he hath promised they should.

Fig. 5.30 Barbour, *Smith,* 1:250

Foreign Languages and Encoded Documents

5.31 Editors of documents written in languages other than the primary language of the edition's audience establish translation policies that balance fidelity to the original work with the desire to provide readers access to the content of the documents.

5.32   Editors of English-language documents containing frequently used foreign-language phrases may create a list of these phrases and their meanings. The editors of the *Diary of Elizabeth Drinker* provided at the beginning of the edition a list of French words and phrases in Drinker's phonetic spelling:

Glossary of French Words and Phrases

Accouchement: delivery; childbirth

allez cet matin chez un person a mon desire: went this morning to the home of a
person at my request

allez de: left; went out

a mon Chere: to my dear

a point du purpose: to no purpose

Fig. 5.32 Crane, Drinker, 1:lxiii

5.33   Editors may choose to translate documents originally written in a foreign language entirely into English. For example, the editor of A *Documentary History of the Indiana Decade of the Harmony Society* translated all documents into English but indicated that a document had been translated with *Tr.* in an unnumbered note at the end of the document:

and wish you continuous well-being while with friendship and respect I
remain your sincere friend

CASIMIR KURTZ

[Endorsed:] Casimir Kurtz   July 25th 1817

ALS. Tr. Since there is no postmark the letter was probably delivered by
an immigrant. Kurtz was a reliable contact in Amsterdam for the Harmony
Society. However, in 1805 he had been involved in an emigration scheme so
questionable that the Duke of Württemberg on May 20, 1805, issued an order
for the arrest of anyone connected with it and a similar order was issued by
the Free City of Frankfurt am Main.

Fig. 5.33a Arndt, Harmony, 1:369

The editors of the *Papers of Daniel Webster: Diplomatic Papers* preceded translated documents with the italicized word *Translation:*

COUNT NESSELRODE TO ALEXANDER DE BODISCO

Translation.   [March 18/30, 1841]

Copy of a despatch from the Vice Chancellor Count [Karl Robert] de Nesselrode to M. [Alexander] de Bodisco dated Saint Petersburg 18/30th March 1841.[1]

Fig. 5.33b Shewmaker, *Webster: Diplomatic*, 1:51

5.34   Editors may choose to print foreign-language documents in their original language. Some editors believe that such a decision preserves the exact text of the original, while others maintain that it denies access to those readers who are unfamiliar with the language of the document. Although the editors of the *Papers of Benjamin Franklin* did preface some non-English documents with abstracts in English, they printed the text of all foreign-language documents without translation:

From Paul-Pierre le Mercier de la Rivière

LS: American Philosophical Society

This odd letter seems to be Franklin's only contact with a noted French *philosophe*. Le Mercier de la Rivière (1720–93) had been a councilor at the Parlement of Paris, intendant at Martinique, guest of Catherine the Great to advise her on a new legal code for Russia, and popularizer of Quesnay's economic doctrines.[1] The accession of Louis XVI in May, 1774, and his appointment of Turgot were beginning a new if short-lived era of economic reform. An edict of Sept. 13, which permitted the importation of foreign grain and its free circulation in France,[2] was doubtless the background for Mercier's proposal to buy five thousand tons of Philadelphia flour, in return if possible for wine. But how did he expect Franklin to arrange such a massive purchase in Pennsylvania? or to take French wine in trade, despite the restrictions of the Navigation Acts and the colonists' well developed partiality for port and madeira?[3] We cannot answer these questions, and presume that Franklin could not either. If he ever troubled to respond to the letter, his reply has been lost.

De Paris ce 21 7bre 1774.

Je me flatte, Monsieur, que mon nom ne vous est point inconnu, puisque vous avez à Paris pour amis ceux qui sont les miens. C'est aussi parceque je vous connois très bien de réputation, que je n'hésite point à m'adresser à vous, par préférence à tous autres, pour l'affaire dont je vais vous entretenir.

Je voudrois, Monsieur, tirer de vos Colonies angloises pour Paris 100 mille quintaux, et même plus, de vos plus belles fleurs

Fig. 5.34a Labaree, *Franklin*, 21:309

The editors of the *Letters of Henry Adams* translated difficult phrases but assumed a basic foreign-language literacy among the readers of the edition:

> We have translated difficult and deceptive foreign words and phrases, but tried to avoid the obvious. We have assumed the modest acquaintance with French, German, Italian, and Spanish that tourists, schoolboys, or stamp-collectors might have. Three letters from Paris, which Adams wrote in the summer of 1860 and which we have left untranslated, provide a rough measure of what we call understandable French (even with his errors of spelling and usage intact). Our rule was not to gloss words, English or foreign, which can be found in a standard desk dictionary.

Fig. 5.34b Levenson, *Adams,* 1:xlii

The editors of the microfilm edition of the *Papers of General Friedrich Wilhelm von Steuben* did not translate foreign-language documents but preceded them with brief abstracts:

```
-Abstract
```

```
                              Paris  Sept. 10, 1777

        Beaumarchais recommends St. to Robert Morris.  He describes St.'s
   former duties as aide-de-camp to Frederick II in the Prussian Army and
   as court Chamberlain to the Prince of Hohenzollern; that he served 22
   years under the Prussian king and will be honored to serve under Gen.
   Washington in the cause of liberty.
```

Fig. 5.34c von Zemenszky, *von Steuben,* reel 1:10

5.35   Some editions contain both the text in its original language and a translation. The editors of the *Collected Papers of Albert Einstein* presented French and German documents in their original languages and produced a companion volume with translations of these documents into English. The editors of *Lafayette in the Age of the American Revolution* printed documents in their original languages with translations in an appendix. The editors of the *Papers of George Washington* translated foreign-language documents into English but provided the full text in the original language in the footnotes:

From Ségur

Sir,   St Petersburg [Russia] 24th August 1789.
I take the advantage of the departure of Mr Paul Jones to
bring myself to the recollection of your Excellency,[1] and to con-
gratulate you upon the ratification of the new Constitution by
the United States and electing you their President—They will
not be deceived in their experience—Your wisdom will mantain
the splendor of that liberty which your courage established.

2. The original letter reads: "Je veux profiter du depart de Monsieur Paul-
jones pour me rappeller au Souvenir de Votre Excellence Et pour la feliciter
Sur le choix que les Etats unis ont fait d'Elle lorsqu'ils ont adopté la nouvelle
Constitution Et nommé un president du Congrês. ils ne Seront point trompés
dans leurs Esperances Et Votre Sagesse Saura maintenir dans toute Sa Splen-
deur la liberté qu'a Etablie votre courage. Je desire infiniment que les circon-
stances me mettent à portée d'aller un jour contempler la prosperité d'un
Pays pour le quel je m'estime heureux d'avoir Combattu, Et la gloire d'un
general celebre Sous le quel je regrette de n'avoir pas plus longtemps Servi.

Fig. 5.35a Twohig, *Washington: Presidential*, 3:535

The editors of the *Family Letters of Victor and Meta Berger* retained German
phrases in English-language letters, providing translations in the footnotes:

That's all I can tell you to night. I must take a walk—because I feel
that I don't get enough exercise.
Im übrigen hab' ich Dich sehr lieb.[4] Kiss the babies for me, and
remember I am ever

Your
V.L.B.

4. By the way, I love you very much.

Fig. 5.35b Stevens, *Berger*, 154

5.36   Editors decode documents written in code to make them accessible to
readers. The editors of *John Jay* presented decoded passages in small capital
letters:

know every thing that passes in Holland. Our Minister there is zealous
and laborious BUT I WILL NOT ANSWER FOR HIS PRUDENCE. TRULY HIS DIS-
PLAY OF HIS PUBLIC CHARACTER, WHEN EVERY THING WAS AGAINST IT CAN NOT
be accounted for on principles that will do him honor. But I am sliding

Fig. 5.36a Morris, *Jay*, 2:114

The editors of the *Papers of James Madison* presented decoded passages in italics with an indication in the unnumbered source note following the document that the passage was written in code:

to 32 & 30/ on James River & 28/ on Rappahannock. The scarcity of cash is one cause. *Harrison the late governor* was *elected* in *Surry* whither *he previously removed with his family. A contest* for *the chair* will *no* doubt *ensue.* Should *he fail it he* will be *for Congress.*

RC (DLC). Cover missing. Docketed by JM and in an unknown hand. Also headed "No. 8." Italicized words, unless otherwise noted, were encoded by JM in the code first used by Jefferson on 14 Apr. 1783

Fig. 5.36b Hutchinson, *Madison*, 8:346–347

5.37   Many editors convert documents written in shorthand into standard written English. The editor of *An Education in Psychology: James McKeen Cattell's Journal and Letters from Germany and England* preceded documents originally written in shorthand with a note explaining the condition of the original text:

1.10 Journal, Paris, 7 June 1881

(Transliterated from Pitman shorthand except for proper names, titles, and place names, which were originally written in longhand.)

The evening before leaving London I heard Patti sing in Rosinni's Semiramidis.[1]
Wednesday the 25th we came over via Dover & Cal.[2] *We went to the Hotel de la*

Fig. 5.37a Sokal, *Cattell*, 33

The editors of the *Papers of Woodrow Wilson* presented his shorthand diary in standard English but alerted readers in the heading that the text was written in shorthand:

From Wilson's Shorthand Diary

[July] 19th Thursday. Spent most of the day playing croquet[,] riding etc. Made satisfactory progress on my speech and read the introduction of Fox's speech on parliamentary reform—his great effort in support of Mr. Gray's bill. Went with Jessie in buggy to

Fig. 5.37b Link, *Wilson*, 1:285

Exceptions to Transcription Policies

5.38   Editors may make exceptions to their transcription policies as long as exceptions are clearly defined. Exceptions should be made to reflect differences among documents or to highlight specific, unusual cases for the reader. Before abandoning their policy of modernizing transcription, the editors of the first three volumes of the *Documentary History of the Ratification of the Constitution* also pursued a more literal policy for documents of exceptional significance:

Literal Reproduction of Official Documents

Official documents such as the Constitution, resolutions of the Confederation Congress, state acts calling conventions, forms of ratification, and proclamations are reproduced as literally as possible. A few other documents, because of their character or importance, are also reproduced as literally as possible. The literal reproduction of such documents is indicated by the symbol "LT" (i.e., literal transcript) in the footnote citation to the source.

Fig. 5.38 Jensen, *Ratification*, 2:14

Chapter Six

Principles of Annotation

Reasons for Annotation

6.1   Annotation, the information added by editors to improve readers' understanding of historical documents, can serve several different functions. Editors may explain the history of documents; supply missing parts of the text such as a date, place, or word; or offer editorial commentary that helps the reader understand the text. Annotation may appear as bracketed insertions in the text, footnotes, endnotes, headnotes, microform targets, or supplemental materials such as tables, illustrations, charts, glossaries, directories, and introductory essays. Annotation makes the text of documents more readable, clarifies unusual terms, offers background on events and people, supplies missing information, and provides readers with historical context.

6.2   The quantity and specificity of annotation will be determined by the needs of the audience, the characteristics of the documents being edited, the resources available for researching and printing annotation, and the judgment of the editors. Editors of complex documents may need to provide extensive annotation to assist their readers, while easily understood documents may require little annotation. Editions produced for academic audiences may assume a high level of background knowledge and thus provide readers with more technical information, while editions for general audiences may assume their readers have little historical background and thus use their annotation to contextualize and clarify documents. Editors balance the value of providing useful information that will enhance the accessibility of documents with the cost of producing and printing notes. Furthermore, excessive annotation may preclude printing additional documents and can diminish an edition's readability by cluttering the page.

6.3   The editors of *Freedom: A Documentary History of Emancipation*, which is intended primarily for an academic audience, provided narrative introductions to their volumes and chapters but offered no introduction to individual documents:

153: Missouri Unionist to the Commander of the Department of the West, and the Latter's Reply

Saint Louis Mo. May 14, 1861.
Sir: In common with thousands who have perused your admirable proclamation of this morning,[1] I return you the thanks of a citizen of Missouri for its pratriotic tone and tranquilizing assurances.

Fig. 6.3a Berlin, *Freedom*, ser.1,1:413

When the editors published the same document in *Free at Last: A Documentary History of Slavery, Freedom, and the Civil War*, an edition for a general audience, they introduced the document with a narrative headnote that linked it to the preceding document and provided the background and context that a general reader might need:

> While some Confederate partisans foresaw a threat to slavery, President Abraham Lincoln and the U.S. Congress reiterated that the North sought only to preserve the Union. Desiring to reassure unionists in the slave states—particularly the border states of Maryland, Kentucky, and Missouri, which had not seceded—Lincoln promised that the army would respect the property rights of slaveholders. In the early months of the war, federal field commanders hewed closely to the president's policy. Writing to General William S. Harney, the commander at St. Louis, a Missouri unionist sought assurances that the government would protect slavery.

Saint Louis Mo. May 14, 1861.
Sir: In common with thousands who have perused your admirable proclamation of this morning,* I return you the thanks of a citizen of Missouri for its pratriotic tone and tranquilizing assurances.

Fig. 6.3b Berlin, *Free*, 6

Types of Annotation

6.4   Editors create three general categories of notes: provenance notes, textual notes, and contextual/informational notes. Provenance notes report the current location of source documents and, in some instances, their publication history. Textual notes provide commentary on the appearance and physical condition of the document or on words used within it. Contextual notes provide information that situates the events described in documents in their proper historical setting or provide additional information needed to understand the substance of documents.

Provenance Notes

6.5 Editors frequently include provenance notes to indicate documents' location, genre, and publication history. Editions drawn from documents at a single repository or from within a single collection may be able to provide this information concisely in their introductions unless the documents cannot be located in the repository or collection without more detailed guidance. For editions containing documents drawn from multiple archives and manuscript repositories, editors provide this information for each document.

6.6 The quantity of information provided in a provenance note varies, but in all cases it should be sufficient to lead readers to the original document. The editors of the *Documentary History of the Ratification of the Constitution* provided readers with the document type (RC for recipient's copy), collection (Washington Papers), and repository (DLC for Library of Congress), as well as the document's publication history (Rutland, *Madison*, X, 253–255):

> 1. RC, Washington Papers, DLC. Printed: Rutland, *Madison*, X, 253–55.

Fig. 6.6a Jensen, *Ratification*, 8:167

For documents taken from newspapers, the editors of the *Documentary History of the Ratification of the Constitution* provided the name of the newspaper and the date when the article or letter appeared, as well as contextual information about the item's circulation:

> 1. Charleston *Columbian Herald,* 22 October. Reprinted twelve times from Richmond to Boston by 26 November.

Fig. 6.6b Jensen, *Ratification*, 3:223

Some editions are more specific about the location of manuscripts, providing box numbers for archival collections. While this information can be helpful for readers, box numbers may change if collections are moved, processed, or reorganized. In large repositories, record group and file numbers are essential provenance information. The *Marcus Garvey and Universal Negro Improvement Association Papers* provided information on the repository, record group, and specific file where documents were located:

> DNA, RG 165, File 10218–77/5 2-1.

Fig. 6.6c Hill, *Garvey*, 1:337

Editors of documents that have been microfilmed may cite the microfilm reel as part of their provenance information. The *Samuel Gompers Papers* led readers to both reel 9 of the microform *Letterbooks of the Presidents of the American Federation of Labor* and the original manuscripts (SG Letterbooks) housed at the Library of Congress (DLC):

> TLpS, reel 9, vol. 14, pp. 365-66, SG Letterbooks, DLC.

Fig. 6.6d Kaufman, *Gompers,* 4:140

The *Collected Papers of Albert Einstein* provided a note citing the source for Einstein's published writings:

2. "The Principle of Relativity and Its Consequences in Modern Physics"

[*Einstein 1910a*]

PUBLISHED 15 January and 15 February 1910

IN: *Archives des sciences physiques et naturelles* 29 (1910): 5–28; 125–144

Translated by Edouard Guillaume

Fig. 6.6e Stachel, *Einstein,* 3:130

The editors of *Mark Twain's Letters* provided a section at the end of the volume describing the provenance and publication history of all documents included in the volume:

> ■ 30 January 1862 · To Jane Lampton Clemens · Carson City, Nev. Terr. · *UCCL* 00034
> ■ *Copy-text:* PH, "Model Letter from Nevada," Keokuk *Gate City,* 6 Mar 62, 4. Newsprint of the *Gate City* is in the Iowa State Historical Department, Division of the State Historical Society, Iowa City (IaHi), and the Historical Library, The State Historical Society of Iowa, Des Moines. We have not been able to use the original newspaper as copy-text. ■ *Previous publication:* Paine, 419–20, and *MTB*, 1:183–84, paraphrase and excerpts; Lorch 1938, 345–49; Rogers 1961, 29–34. ■ *Provenance:* Paine cites the Keokuk *Gate City* as his source for the excerpts published in *MTB*; he evidently did not see the MS, which is not known to survive.

Fig. 6.6f Branch, *Twain,* 1:505

The provenance of documents may be noted in an editorial statement or introduction, as was done by the editors of the *Family Letters of Victor and Meta Berger*:

> All the letters printed here are recipients' copies found in the Victor L. Berger Papers at the State Historical Society of Wisconsin, with the exception of Victor's letter of July 28, 1926, to Jan Edelman, which is a retained carbon copy from the same collection.

Fig. 6.6g Stevens, *Berger*, 29–30

The *Papers of Joseph Henry* provided provenance information in document headings (see Section 7.2).

Textual Notes

6.7   Textual notes provide information about the physical appearance of a document that is not conveyed through transcription. Common textual notes describe details such as deletions, insertions, interlineations, tears, amendments, evidence of multiple authorship, enclosures, and marginalia. They are also used to compare variant copies of the same text. Some textual notes appear as editorial insertions within the text. Others are placed in footnotes or headnotes.

6.8   The editors of *John Jay* used a footnote to describe William Laight's unusual method of deleting and inserting passages:

> 1 Laight did not actually cross out the word "address" when he added "shor[t] Epistle" above the line as a substitute. This peculiarity is repeated several times throughout the draft, and such incomplete deletions and substitutions have been transcribed as though the material to be omitted has been struck out.

Fig. 6.8a Morris, *Jay*, 1:170

The editors of the *Papers of George Washington: Colonial Series* used a footnote to explain the mutilated condition of the original manuscript and the method used by the editors to transcribe it:

> LS, DLC:GW; MH: Sparks Papers. The letter was written on both sides of a sheet of paper, and the sheet was torn approximately in half. The top part of both pages of the letter are in DLC; the bottom parts are in MH. The letter appears to be in the hand of John Kirkpatrick. The second postscript, dated "27th," is in Dinwiddie's shaky hand, a rare sample of his handwriting from his years in Virginia.
>
> 1. The portion of the first page, at DLC, ends here; and the portion at MH begins with the lower half of the words taken to be "a detachment." The left-hand margin of the lower part of the first page has been torn off. The letters in angle brackets in this and the next paragraph are the letters that are missing as a consequence of the tear. In his *Writings of Washington*, Stanislaus

Hamilton prints only the top, or DLC, portion of the letter, but he does supply the letters missing from words on the lower half of the page at MH, indicating that the scrap torn from the lower left margin remained with the upper half of the letter in DLC. Hamilton also supplies words or parts of words that he mistakenly supposed came at the end of the lines that were missing to him.

Fig. 6.8b Abbot, *Washington: Colonial,* 4:158

6.9   Notes may be used to describe documents or enclosures that were not selected for publication but may contain information of value. Such notes may take the form of abstracts that quote or excerpt the most significant passages of documents (see Section 2.23), or they may be footnotes or headnotes that describe the document.

Contextual/Informational Notes

6.10   Contextual notes include any type of editorially supplied information that helps readers more fully understand and appreciate the content of a document. Contextual notes generally amplify or clarify the information in a document by providing historical background, biographical data, fuller descriptions of mentioned events, clarification of ambiguous passages or words, unstated outcomes, corrections of erroneous information in the text, or other information about people and events that could not be found by reading the documents alone. Contextual notes allow editors to share their expertise with the reader, who can then more fully appreciate the meaning, background, and content of a document.

6.11   Biographical notes present information about authors, recipients, or individuals named or mentioned in a document, providing readers with sufficient background to understand the role of an individual within, and occasionally beyond, the context of a document. Not all individuals need to be identified, and those who are identified do not need to be described with equal detail. Moreover, information cannot always be found about every person mentioned in a document. Editors choose whom they will identify and how much information they will provide. Basic biographical information should be provided only once, usually the first time an individual is mentioned or within a biographical directory placed at the beginning of the edition or in an appendix. The editors of the *Papers of Andrew Johnson* provided full biographical notes for most individuals mentioned:

1. **Alexander Outlaw Anderson (1794–1869)** at the time of this letter was unsuccessfully seeking the position of American minister to Mexico. An East Tennessean who was with Jackson at New Orleans, he served briefly as U. S. senator (1840–41), filling out the unexpired term of Hugh Lawson White. Later he participated in the gold rush and briefly held office in California. During the Civil War he lived in Alabama, but returned to Knoxville before his death. *BDAC*, 477.

Fig. 6.11a Graf, *Johnson,* 1:153

The editor of the *Correspondence of Mother Jones* provided brief biographical descriptions that place individuals in the context of the document in which they are mentioned:

> **ALS (William B. Wilson Papers)**
> 1. William Warner, a UMWA organizer, had led the strike of the Maryland miners in 1900, when Mother Jones was an associate in the field. Later in life he became a mine superintendent.
> 2. Albert Manka, like Warner an international organizer, had worked in West Virginia the preceding year, when Warner was still involved in the Maryland strike.

Fig. 6.11b Steel, *Jones,* 13

The editors of the *Black Abolitionist Papers* wanted to improve understanding of the contributions of members of the black community whose lives had received little attention from historians. Consequently, they provided longer biographical entries for people and events that could not be found in standard reference sources:

> People and events that are covered in standard biographical directories, reference books, or textbooks are treated in brief notes. We have given more space to subjects on which there is little or no readily available information, particularly black individuals and significant events and institutions in the black community. A full note on each item is presented at the first appropriate point in the volume.

Fig. 6.11c Ripley, *Black Abolitionist,* 1:xxviii

6.12   Editors seldom record information that is common knowledge to their audience in the annotation. For example, most editions aimed at American audiences would not need to note that George Washington served as the first president of the United States, but they might include lesser-known information about him if necessary to understand the documents.

6.13   Editors will find individuals who merit identification but about whom they cannot locate authoritative sources. Most editors pass over these people without comment; some acknowledge the lack of information with a note such as that employed by the *Papers of Daniel Webster: Correspondence:*

> 1. Not identified.

Fig. 6.13a Wiltse, *Webster: Correspondence,* 1:125

When a small quantity of information is available, an editor may provide it but acknowledge other areas of uncertainty, as did the editor of the *Letters of Eugene V. Debs:*

> 2. Samuel Howell is listed as a carpenter in the Terre Haute city directories of 1871-73. The basis of his notoriety in Terre Haute has not been discovered.

Fig. 6.13b Constantine, *Debs*, 1:4

6.14 Literary references, Biblical references, and foreign phrases can be identified and explained in an edition's notes. Passages that would have been readily understood by a document's intended recipient or audience may otherwise be difficult for a contemporary reader to grasp. For example, the editors of the *Documentary History of the Ratification of the Constitution* provided notes locating literary quotations or misquotations and explaining their relevance:

> the very idea of which, is enough to make every honest citizen exclaim in the language of Cato, O liberty, O my country![3]—
>
> 3. The phrase, taken from Joseph Addison's play, *Cato. A Tragedy* (1713), actually reads: "O liberty! O virtue! O my country!" (act 4, scene 4). First performed in London, this play was about Marcus Porcius Cato Uticensis (Cato the Younger), a republican opponent of Julius Caesar, who committed suicide in 46 B.C. rather than accept the triumph of Caesar over Pompey and his followers, of whom he was one. (See "Cato Uticensis," *Virginia Independent Chronicle*, 17 October [above] which defended Mason.)

Fig. 6.14a Jensen, *Ratification*, 8:211

The editors of the *Papers of Martin Luther King, Jr.* provided sources and more complete quotations for fragmentary literary references:

> This universe hinges on moral foundations. (*Yeah*) There is something in this universe that justifies Carlyle in saying,
>
> No lie can live forever.[3]

> 3. King may have been paraphrasing Carlyle's *French Revolution* (1837), part 1, book 3, chapter 1: "No lie you can speak or act but it will come, after longer or shorter circulation, like a bill drawn on Nature's Reality, and be presented there for payments—with the answer, No effects."

Fig. 6.14b Carson, *King*, 2:253

6.15 Geographical descriptions that were evident to the author or recipient of a document may be meaningless to the readers of a documentary edition without editorial assistance. Editors help their readers place geographical references in context by providing maps or descriptions. For example, the editors of the *Diary of Elizabeth Drinker* used a note to identify the location of a bridge:

> —WD. and self, walk'd as far as the draw Bridge this evening—The name of Drawbridge is continued, tho there has not been one there since my memory[47]

> 47. By 1740 a stone bridge had replaced a drawbridge erected in the early 1690s to extend Front Street over Dock Creek. During the course of the eighteenth century the creek was filled in and paved to form Dock Street (Joseph Jackson, *Encyclopedia of Philadelphia* (Harrisburg, Pa.: The National Historical Association, 1931], 2:601, 591).

Fig. 6.15a Crane, *Drinker*, 3:1678

The editors of the *Papers of General Nathanael Greene* also used annotation to help readers understand cursory references to geography:

> Our purpose in crossing Santee was to fight [Col. John] Watson but unluckily We was one day to Late. He crossed at Buckenhams Yesterday & is gone toward Camden with about two hundred men & two field p[iece]s.[3]

> 3. On Watson's earlier movements, see note at Wade to NG, 19 April, above. From Georgetown, where he had retreated after breaking off pursuit of Marion, Watson marched toward the Santee River; his detachment was "much reduced in Number, thro' Casualties, Sickness and a Reinforcement which he had left to strengthen the Garrison at Georgetown." (Rawdon to Cornwallis, 24 May, PRO 30/11/6) He crossed the Santee at Lenud's Ferry, near the river's mouth, and waited for a day or two by order of Nisbet Balfour to cover the possible return of Lord Cornwallis or Banastre Tarleton to South Carolina. Watson's detachment of about 500 men then moved toward Nelson's Ferry, on the Santee. (Balfour to Germain, 1 May, PRO 30/11/109; Balfour to Clinton, 6 May, ibid.; Rankin, *Swamp Fox*, p. 200) Henry Lee later stated that NG's position prevented Watson from reaching Camden "on the usual route from Motte's post." Watson, who was moving up the south side of the Santee, was thus left with two other options, according to Lee: he could cross the Congaree at Motte's and the Wateree below the High Hills of Santee or else cross the Santee below Motte's and move up the north side of the Santee by way of the High Hills. (Lee, *Memoirs*, 2: 70) Guessing that Watson would take the former route, Marion and Lee crossed to the south side of the Santee at Scotts Lake and moved "with celerity" toward Mottes. (Lee, *Memoirs*, 2: 70–71; Rankin, *Swamp Fox*, p. 201) Watson, however, who was now ahead of them, crossed the Santee at Buckenham's—or Buchanan's—a small ferry near the confluence of the Congaree and Wateree, which, he later wrote, had been "left unguarded" because it was supposedly "impracticable" to cross. His detachment then proceeded to Camden "without molestation," though not without difficulty, by a route that required the troops to wade across six creeks, build a sixty-foot bridge over a seventh, and cut "for about a Mile and half through the canes that grow in those swamps."

Fig. 6.15b Showman, *Greene*, 8:215

The editor of "'As to the People': Thomas and Laura Randall's Observations on Life and Labor in Early Middle Florida," published in the *Florida Historical Quarterly*, used a footnote to provide historical information about Tallahassee in the 1820s:

> 5. Tallahassee had been established as the territorial capital in 1823. The village that Randall visited on business was the home of about a thousand people, and claimed a church, school, several hotels, and various businesses. Mary Louise Ellis and William Warren Rogers, *Favored, Land Tallahassee: A History of Tallahassee and Leon County* (Norfolk/Virginia Beach, 1988), 33-36.

Fig. 6.15c Rogers, *Florida*, 75:443

6.16 Collected documents often provide a fragmentary narrative because some documents are lost or not printed and because authors frequently fail to follow up on events discussed in their documents. Editors can bridge the narrative of documents by providing readers with the missing parts of the story in the notes. Such notes are particularly useful in explaining responses when editors choose to publish only a single side of a correspondence, such as Felix Frankfurter's responses to Louis Brandeis's letters provided by the editors of *"Half Brother, Half Son": The Letters of Louis D. Brandeis to Felix Frankfurter:*

> It occurred to me that you might know of some New York (or other) lawyers, who would be glad to join in making this gift.[3]
>
> [3] On 27 January FF replied: "I have gladly written to several New York lawyers of the opportunity to ease their swollen fortunes."

Fig. 6.16 Urofsky, *Brandeis*, 21

6.17 Notes can clarify passages that are confusing, ambiguous, or unclear. For example, the editors of the *Papers of Ulysses S. Grant* used a footnote to explain the meaning behind Grant's cryptic phrase "urgent family reasons":

> I am induced to make this application at this time for the reason that my services can probably be better dispensed with at present than at any future time, there being at this Post, with one comp.y, a Commanding officer, Adjutant and three Company officers besides myself. Urgent family reasons also induce me to respectfully submit this application.
>
> The "urgent family reasons" mentioned by USG probably involve the birth of USG's son Frederick Dent Grant on May 30, 1850, in St. Louis. Julia Dent Grant had been advised by Maj. Charles Stuart Tripler, surgeon at Detroit, to return to her parents for the birth of her first child. Unpublished memoirs of Julia Dent Grant.

Fig. 6.17a Simon, *Grant*, 1:194

The editors of the *Letters of Delegates to Congress* used contextual notes to clarify oblique references, such as this one made by John Adams:

> The People of England, have thought that the Opposition in America, was wholly owing to Dr. Franklin: and I suppose their scribblers will attribute the Temper, and Proceedings of this Congress to him: but there cannot be a greater Mistake. He has had but little share farther than to co operate and assist. He is however a great and good Man. I wish his Colleagues from this City were All like him, particularly one,[2] whose Abilities and Virtues, formerly trumpeted so much in America, have been found wanting.

---

[2] That is, John Dickinson. Adams' disparaging remarks about Dickinson were extended in a letter the next day to James Warren, which was subsequently captured and published by the British. John Adams to James Warren, July 24, 1775.

Fig. 6.17b Smith, *Delegates*, 1:649

The editors of the *Papers of William Livingston* used notes to define unfamiliar terms such as *draught:*

> The Draught[1] from my Battallion serving on the Woodbridge Department is not yet returned, as they have been out six Times since

ALS, MHi.

1. draught: a group of soldiers posted from a larger body to some special duty.

Fig. 6.17c Prince, *Livingston*, 1:182

Editors can use notes to clarify misstatements of fact in original documents, such as in this passage from *Letters of Delegates to Congress:*

> The Secretary for Foreign Affairs yesterday read to us a passage in a letter from a correspondent at Boston which positively asserts that General Sullivan had marched with 1000 men to reduce to obedience to their government the revolters on the East side of Connecticut River.[3]

[3] Although the New Hampshire legislature had authorized the raising of two regiments commanded by John Sullivan "to be sent to the western part of the State" to subdue those border towns attempting to join Vermont, the governor did not call the force into service because the legislature subsequently voted to pardon those residents who had previously revolted. See *N. H. State Papers*, 10:476–78; and Charles P. Whittemore, *A General of the Revolution. John Sullivan of New Hampshire* (New York: Columbia University Press, 1961), p. 184.

Fig. 6.17d Smith, *Delegates*, 18:377–378

Editors may use contextual notes to provide follow-up information about events, such as when the editors of the *Papers of George Washington: Revolutionary War Series* used a note to tell their readers the outcome of a request by the Six Nations to have an audience with the Continental Congress in Philadelphia:

> These Indians reached Philadelphia by 25 May when they requested an audience with Congress. That audience was held at 11:00 A.M. on 27 May, and preceding it at 9:00 A.M. Congress staged a military review "in order," as one delegate candidly remarked, "to give those savages some idea of our strength and importance" (Joseph Hewes to Samuel Johnston, 26 May 1776, in Smith, *Letters of Delegates*, 4:77–78; *JCC*, 4:392–93, 396–97). "Coll. Dickinson's, Coll. Robertdoe's, Coll. Cadwallader's, Coll. Mckean's and Coll. MatLock's Battalions [of associators], three companies of Artillery & the Light-horse of the Militia; and Coll. Shee's and Coll. Magaw's Battalion's of the Continental Troops Were all Reviewed," Caesar Rodney wrote Thomas Rodney on 29 May, "the day before Yesterday, on the Common, by the Congress, Generals Washington, Gates and Mifflin accompanied by a great number of other officers, most of the Assembly, the Presbiterian Clergey who were here at the Sinod—and 21 Indians of the Six Nations, who gave the Congress a War-dance Yesterday" (Smith, *Letters of Delegates*, 4:99–100). The Indians appeared in Congress again on 11 June when a speech pledging American friendship and various gifts were delivered to them (*JCC*, 4:410, 5:421, 430–31, 471).

Fig. 6.17e Chase, *Washington: Revolutionary*, 4:320

Editors may use contextual notes to alert readers when documents they may expect to find in the edition are not included, such as when the editors of the *Papers of James Madison* chose not to publish two documents previously attributed to Madison that they believed he did not write:

EDITORIAL NOTE

Few editors and scholars would question that the drafting of the Virginia Resolutions was JM's most important contribution to the proceedings of the 1798–99 session of the Virginia General Assembly. Earlier generations of editors have maintained, however, that JM was responsible not only for the resolutions of 21 December 1798 but also for three resolutions criticizing the foreign policy of the Adams administration that were approved by the General Assembly on 10 January 1799; and more importantly they have claimed that he wrote another attack on the Alien and Sedition Acts in the form of the "Address of the General Assembly to the People of the Commonwealth of Virginia" of 23 January 1799 as well. Both the compilers of the congressional edition and Gaillard Hunt included these last two documents in their canons of JM's papers, and several of JM's biographers, from John Quincy

Adams to Irving Brant, have concurred with this attribution, at least to the extent of asserting that the "Address" of 23 January 1799 was the product of JM's pen (Madison, *Letters* [Cong. ed.], 4:508–14; Madison, *Writings* [Hunt ed.], 6:331–40; John Quincy Adams, *An Eulogy on the Life and Character of James Madison, Fourth President of the United States; Delivered at the Request of the Mayor, Alderman, and Common Council of the City of Boston, September 27, 1836* [Boston, 1836], p. 57, later republished as *The Lives of James Madison and James Monroe* [Buffalo, 1850], see p. 70; Brant, *Madison,* 3:464).

The present editors do not believe that JM composed these last two documents, and for that reason they have decided to exclude them from this edition of his papers. This decision was not taken lightly, nor without an awareness of its significance for the body of important scholarship that exists in relation to the contents of these two documents, particularly the "Address" of 23 January 1799. If JM did not write this last document, historians will have to reconsider some aspects of the lengthy and complicated debate about the development of thinking on the freedom of the press in the United States, especially with respect to the claim that JM changed his views markedly on this subject between January and December 1799. The author of the "Address" of 23 January 1799 denied that the federal government could institute prosecutions for seditious libel, but at the same time he explicitly left open the possibility of punishing "libellous writing or expression" in state courts by "juries summoned by an officer, who does not receive his appointment from the President." The power of state courts over matters of seditious libel, however, was denied by JM barely twelve months later when he wrote his Report of 1800 on the Virginia Resolutions, a document that has become justly celebrated as one of the most important expositions of the meaning of the freedom of the press clause in the First Amendment (Madison, *Letters* [Cong. ed.], 4:150; see Walter Berns, "Freedom of the Press and the Alien and Sedition Laws: A Reappraisal," in *1970: The Supreme Court Review* [Chicago, 1970], ed. Philip B. Kurland, pp. 129–30; Levy, *Emergence of a Free Press,* pp. 319–26; Jeffrey A. Smith, *Printers and Press Freedom: The Ideology of Early American Journalism* [New York, 1988], pp. 71–73).

It is, unfortunately, not possible to address and resolve all these significant issues in an edition of JM's papers. As it is, little enough is known about JM's activities at this time, and historians do not understand a great deal more about the proceedings in the Virginia General Assembly as it ratified these two documents of protest in January 1799. The shreds of information that are available, however, cannot be adduced to support the contention that JM was responsible for either of them. In this context, it should be stressed above all else that there exists no good contemporary evidence of any sort, direct or circumstantial, to substantiate the claim that JM had either composed the two documents in question or contributed in any way to their adoption by the General Assembly.

Fig. 6.17f Hutchinson, *Madison,* 17:199–200

6.18   Editors may bridge gaps between documents by writing transitional passages, such as the one below, written by the editors of the *Papers of Daniel Webster: Correspondence*, that took the reader from international relations to domestic politics and provided the necessary context for understanding the documents that followed:

> *Although Webster's energies during the winter of 1851–1852 were largely absorbed in his conduct of foreign affairs, including delicate negotiations regarding a canal across Central America, his attention was never far from politics. Despite his age, and the practical obstacles to a nomination in 1852, Webster's presidential ambitions burned as strongly as ever—perhaps more so, since he well knew this would be his last chance for the elusive prize.*
>
> *Unfortunately, a long list of prominent backers in the major cities of the Eastern Seaboard did not translate into popular enthusiasm for his cause, or add up to delegate strength for the upcoming Whig National Convention. Moreover, although Webster was loathe to admit the fact, southern support for his candidacy was almost entirely lacking. With the decline of fears for the Union, his efforts in 1850 made less of a difference to southern moderates, many of whom looked to Millard Fillmore as their best hope in 1852. For his part, the President, avowedly not a candidate, nonetheless declined to withdraw ;from the race, a "nondecision" that was announced on January 24 by the Republic, Fillmore's organ in Washington.*
>
> *Under the circumstances, Webster's best chance for the nomination lay in a brokered convention, in which Winfield Scott and Fillmore supporters, failing to gain the necessary majority, would each turn to Webster as their second choice. For such an event to occur, however, Webster had to demonstrate substantial delegate support of his own. As the correspondence below suggests, this proved a frustrating quest.*

Fig. 6.18 Wiltse, *Webster: Correspondence*, 7:301

Chapter Seven
Forms of Annotation

Choosing Annotation Forms

7.1   Editors have tremendous latitude in deciding how to annotate documents. In selecting a system of annotation, they employ methods that provide the greatest clarity in the most economical fashion. They consider the characteristics of their documents and the needs of their audience in order to create annotation that is appropriate for the content and format of the edition.

Headings

7.2   Many editors precede each document with a heading. The information included in headings varies from edition to edition. The editors of the *Papers of Ulysses S. Grant* listed only the name of the author or recipient of correspondence, because most letters in the edition were written by or to Grant:

To Julia Dent

———

Corpus Christi Texas
Jan. 12th 1846

My Dear Julia
I have just been deligted by ~~the~~ recieving a long and inter-

Fig. 7.2a Simon, *Grant,* 1:69

Many editors use headings to note both the author and the recipient of letters, as in those created by the editor of *Religious Philanthropy and Colonial Slavery: The American Correspondence of the Associates of Dr. Bray:*

Robert Carter Nicholas to Rev. John Waring

Fig. 7.2b Van Horne, *Dr. Bray,* 164

The editor of *A Documentary History of the Indiana Decade of the Harmony Society* included the author, the recipient, and an abstract of the document:

JEREMIAH WARDER, JR., TO GEORGE FLOWER: Requests information on the Harmonists; questions George Rapp's motives; expresses concern for redemptioners purchased by the Society.

Fig. 7.2c Arndt, *Harmony,* 1:382

The editors of the *Naval War of 1812: A Documentary History* used larger type to introduce new topics and smaller type, in small capitals, to identify the author and recipient of each document:

Diplomatic Arrangements
for Prisoner Exchanges

ANTHONY ST. JOHN BAKER TO
SECRETARY OF STATE JAMES MONROE

Fig. 7.2d Dudley, *1812,* 1:236

The editors of the *Papers of Joseph Henry* included in the heading both the title of the document and its provenance:

"RECORD OF EXPERIMENTS"
Henry Papers, Smithsonian Archives

Fig. 7.2e Reingold, *Henry,* 5:193

The editor of *German-American Pioneers in Wisconsin and Michigan: The Frank Kerler Letters* placed the year of composition in the heading of all letters:

1852
Louise Foerster to August Frank.

Fig. 7.2f Anderson, *Kerler,* 178

Introductory Essays

7.3   To provide readers with more context for understanding the documents, editors may include historical essays in their editions. While such essays can be valuable in guiding readers through unfamiliar historical terrain, editors must remember that pages occupied by interpretive essays deny space to a greater number of documents. The editors of the *Samuel Gompers Papers* included short essays on Gompers's life and the labor movement in their edition:

Samuel Gompers' Participation in Workingmen's Organizations in the 1870s

Gompers began attending meetings of the International Working-men's Association (IWA) in 1873 and soon became a participant in an inner circle of the Association that called itself "Die Zehn Philosophen" or the ten philosophers.[1] By the mid-1870s "Die Zehn Philosophen" had evolved into the loosely organized Economic and Sociological Club, whose members included Gompers and many of his early associates, including David Kronburg, Ferdinand Laurrell, Fred Bloete, Louis Berliner, Henry Baer, Hugh McGregor, and J. P. McDonnell. George E. McNeill and Ira Steward, leaders of the Boston eight-hour movement, were also associated with the club.

    The Economic and Sociological Club rejected what Gompers, in his memoirs, called "Socialist partyism," and favored "trade unions, amalgamated trades unions, and national or international amalgam-

Fig. 7.3 Kaufman, *Gompers,* 1:83

7.4   The *Papers of George Catlett Marshall* introduced each chapter with a brief introductory essay:

OPERATIONS OFFICER with the first division sent to France was the job Marshall "particularly desired." General Sibert's telegram meant duty in France, but Marshall did not know that the general was to command the First Division, and he did not know in what general staff capacity he was to serve. On June 8, when Sibert formally took command of the division, Marshall learned that he was to be the assistant chief of staff for Operations. (*Memoirs,* p. 5.)

    The troops began boarding their hastily and inadequately prepared ships on the night of June 10. The next day, the division's staff assembled for the first time aboard the United States Army Transport *Tenadores,* formerly a United Fruit Company banana boat. Marshall shared a stateroom with the division's

Fig. 7.4 Bland, *Marshall,* 1:109

Headnotes

7.5   Editors may use headnotes to explain or provide context for documents, as did the editors of the *Papers of Martin Luther King, Jr.*:

"A Study of Mithraism"

[*13 September–23 November 1949*]
[*Chester, Pa.*]

During the first semester of his second year at Crozer, King wrote this paper for Enslin's course on Greek religion. Mithraism, a sect of Zoroastrianism characterized by the worship of Mithra as the defender of the truth, was a monotheistic mystery religion prevalent in the Roman empire before the acceptance of Christianity in the fourth century. Followers of Mithra became less common after the Roman emperors banned their cults, and Christianity gained the popularity that once belonged to Mithraism. Enslin gave the essay an A and wrote: "This is an exceedingly good paper. You have given a very complete picture of the essential details and you have presented this in a balanced and restrained way. And furthermore you know how to write. You should go a long way if you continue to pay the price."

Fig. 7.5a Carson, *King*, 1:211

Editors of popular editions often use headnotes to provide readers with basic historical and contextual information that will enable them to understand and appreciate the documents. The editors of *Voices from Vietnam* preceded a letter describing the United States withdrawal from Vietnam with a headnote noting the date of the Paris peace accords and the rapid removal of troops that followed, giving readers a context for the events described in the letter:

On January 25, 1973, the Paris peace accords were signed, officially ending direct U.S. participation in Vietnam as well as military assistance to South Vietnam. Over the next sixty days, all American combat troops were withdrawn from the country. In the following letter, Weidner describes the final months of the war.

January 29, 1973

Dear Mom & Dad,
    The war has never been so bad as since the peace was declared. You've heard already—TSN was rocketed Sunday AM. Also Bien Hoa, Pleiku,

Fig. 7.5b Stevens, *Voices*, 130

Footnotes and Endnotes

7.6   Editors may place annotation in footnotes—that is, notes placed at the bottom of the page—such as those employed by the editors of the *Colonial Records of North Carolina: Second Series:*

> [79]GO 116.1 here includes the following: "At a Council held at Brunswick the [*blank*] day of June 1766. Present His Excellency the Governor, James Hasell, John Rutherfurd, Lewis Henry DeRosset, William Dry, Robert Palmer, Benjamin Heron. [*Blank*].
> [80]Pp. 532, 539-540, below.

Fig. 7.6 Parker, *North Carolina,* 9:161

7.7   More commonly, notes directly follow the text of a document and are numbered sequentially, with new numbering for each document's notes. The editors of the *Letters of Delegates to Congress* used an unnumbered note for provenance and textual information and numbered notes for contextual information:

> LB (DNA: PCC, item 16). There is no indication in Hanson's presidential letterbook why this appeal to the states was addressed only to the governor of New York.
> [1] The enclosed resolution recommending that the state legislatures "make suitable provision for staying all suits" instituted against Continental officers "for debts contracted by them for supplies furnished or services rendered to the United States," was adopted in response to a letter of February 25 from Quartermaster General Timothy Pickering. See *JCC*, 22:138–39; and PCC, item 19, 5:171–73, item 192, fols. 89–98. Pickering's letter had been referred the same day to a committee consisting of Elias Boudinot, Daniel Carroll, Thomas McKean, Edmund Randolph, and John Morin Scott, whose report was in turn referred on March 7 to a second committee consisting of Abraham Clark, Samuel Livermore, and James Madison. For the work of these committees and Madison's authorship of the committee recommendation eventually adopted by Congress, see Madison, *Papers* (Hutchinson), 4:91–92.

Fig. 7.7 Smith, *Delegates,* 18:416

7.8   When an edition consists of a single document, such as the *Diaries of David Lawrence Gregg: An American Diplomat in Hawaii,* editors sometimes place endnotes at the back of a volume:

Notes

NOTES

INTRODUCTION

1. Biographical material on Gregg's family was collected from the letters of David L. Gregg, Jr., of Glendale, Calif., to Ralph S. Kuykendall, 1923-1939, in Gregg Folder, Hawaiian Collection Letter File, University of Hawaii, hereafter cited as Gregg Folder; St. Patrick's Church records, La Salle, Ill., in Florence Clarke to Pauline King Joerger, November 3, 1973;

D. L. Gregg to William Gregg, August 26, 1856, in Gregg Letter Books, Gregg Collection, hereafter cited as Gregg LB and Gregg Coll.
  2. The Gregg Collection is made up of diaries, letter books, and letter files and is on deposit at the Archives of Hawaii, hereafter cited as AH.

Fig. 7.8a King, Gregg, 503

Editors who want to keep their annotation unobtrusive may also choose to use endnotes, as did the editors of *Abraham Lincoln: Speeches and Writings,* who referred readers to page and line numbers rather than using numbered notes:

Notes

In the notes that follow, the reference numbers denote page and line of this volume (the line count includes item headings). No note is made for material included in a standard desk-reference book. Correspondents and names mentioned by Lincoln are identified only when they are essential to an understanding of the text. Prefatory and end notes within the text are Lincoln's own. For more detailed notes and references to other studies, see *The Collected Works of Abraham Lincoln,* 8 volumes plus index (New Brunswick: Rutgers University Press, 1953–55), edited by Roy P. Basler, Marion Dolores Pratt, and Lloyd A. Dunlap; *The Collected Works of Abraham Lincoln: Supplement 1832–1865* (Westport, Connecticut: Greenwood Press, 1974), edited by Roy P. Basler; *Lincoln Day by Day: A Chronology,* 3 volumes (Washington, D.C.: Lincoln Sesquicentennial Commission, 1960), edited by Earl Schenck Miers, William E. Baringer, and C. Percy Powell; and Mark E. Neely, Jr., *The Abraham Lincoln Encyclopedia* (New York: McGraw-Hill, 1982).

7.1   *Mary S. Owens*] Owens (1808–77), the only woman besides Mary Todd whom Lincoln is known to have courted, came to New Salem from Kentucky in 1836 for an extended visit with her sister, Elizabeth Owens Abell.

9.5   *Mr. Linder*] Usher F. Linder (1809–76), an attorney and Democratic legislator. In 1838 Linder became a Whig, but his hatred of abolitionism caused him to return to the Democrats in the 1850s. He appeared with and against Lincoln in many law cases.

Fig. 7.8b Lincoln, Speeches and Writings, 858

Endnotes may also be placed at the end of a short magazine article, such as was done by the editor of "A Thousand Mile Motor Trip" published in *Nebraska History:*

O.K. here. So end[s] the Thirteenth Day
and the Thousand Mile Motor Trip. We
traveled about 800—eight hundred
miles. We had seen a lot of country; had
enough new experiences to suit anyone.
But like little Pollyanna we are Glad:
the Buick is battle-scared; we are motor
veterans!!!

Notes

¹ John A. Jakle, *The Tourist: Travel in Twentieth
Century North America* (Lincoln: University of Nebraska Press, 1985), xi.

² Ibid.

³ Sara Mullin Baldwin, ed., *Who's Who in Lincoln:
Biographical Sketches of Men and Women of
Achievement* (Lincoln: Robert M. Baldwin, 1928), 96.

⁴ *Polk's Lincoln City Directory, 1925* (Kansas City:
R. L. Polk and Co., 1925), 53.

⁵ The 1910 *Cornhusker* Yearbook lists Maggie
May Gehrke as a member of the Y.W.C.A., English

Fig. 7.8c Koelling, *Nebraska*, 78:27

Intratextual Annotation

7.9   Editors may also choose to place annotation within the text of documents. Editorial interpolations and brief textual comments may be indicated
through words or symbols and placed within sentences (see Chapter 5), but
extended annotation may also appear within the text of documents, as it did in
the *Papers of John C. Calhoun*, whose editors placed intratextual editorial notes
in italic type in brackets:

received there, the abolitionists had gained all they wanted; and so
long as they were permitted to come there he would take the liberty
to speak of them in the terms they deserved.

*[Bedford Brown of N.C. praised the resolutions as showing the
weakness of abolition sentiment in Me. and remarked that it was
impracticable "to expect a State to eradicate every folly or infatua-
tion from the minds of all its citizens." He further remarked that,
while the language of the petitions "was bad enough," he did not
believe any had used the words "pirates, robbers, and murderers" for*

*the people of the South. Calhoun thereupon asked Thomas Morris
of Ohio for the petitions that he had presented and then withdrawn
earlier in the session. Morris gave Calhoun some petitions but said
he could not consent for them to be used "at that time."*]

Mr. Calhoun said he was utterly astonished at the remarks of the
gentleman from North Carolina. These charges were made when
the Ohio petitions were presented and read, and in the gentleman's

Fig. 7.9 Meriwether, *Calhoun*, 13:145

Specialized Directories

7.10   Editors sometimes find that a glossary or directory is more convenient
for readers and requires less space than separate notes, especially when the
persons, places, or terms to be described recur throughout the edition. The
editors of *Circular Letters of Congressmen to Their Constituents* created biographical entries that provide brief identification of each congressman whose
letters appear in the volumes:

DIRECTORY OF CONGRESSMEN

The following directory contains identifications of the members of Congress
represented in these volumes and a listing, under each congressman, of the
circular letters here published. More detailed biographical information can be
found in the *Biographical Directory of the American Congress, 1774–1971* (Washington, D.C., 1971). A party identification as a Republican refers to the Jef-
fersonian Republican party. Since the old party labels of Federalist and
Republican were not very meaningful for some members who entered Congress after 1815, party identification has not been made for all members.

ALLEN, ROBERT (1778–1844). Republican representative from Tennessee in
    16th–19th Congresses, 1819–1827; not a candidate for reelection.
    Circular letter: Feb. 22, 1825.

Fig. 7.10a Cunningham, *Circular Letters*, 1:liii

Editors may explain in an introductory headnote how they produced specialized directories, and may detail the problems they encountered. The editors of
the *Diary of Elizabeth Drinker: The Life Cycle of an Eighteenth-Century Woman*
preceded their biographical directory with such an introduction:

Biographical Directory

Elizabeth Drinker recorded the names of several thousand people over the nearly fifty-year period during which she penned her entries. Some, such as her husband and children, were mentioned almost daily, others less frequently, and many only sporadically. The directory has been compiled for the purpose of identifying as many people as possible in all three categories. A surprising quantity of biographical information has surfaced in the attempt, although the amount and nature of that information vary from person to person.

Where feasible, birth, death, and marriage dates have been included, as well as occupation, public roles, religion, and relationship to the Drinkers. Some dates are prefaced by a *c.*, which means that the genealogical source was ambiguous. Thomas Coombe, for example, "d. 1799 in the 79th year of his age," and his birthdate, therefore, is listed as "c. 1720." Although some of the information obtained from the various sources is suspect, the editor has attempted to amend the reference material only when ED herself inscribes a birth or death date that conflicts with secondary evidence.

Because of the length of the diary and its eighteenth-century qualities, certain problems arise of which the reader should be aware. Most important, family members with the same last name frequently had the same given name even within a single generation, and as Drinker herself realized, "several of one name in a family occasions confusion and mistake—oftentimes." To compound matters, ED knew a number of distantly related or unrelated people with similar names. Thus, when she refers simply to Ann Emlen, for example, it is sometimes unclear whether she has Ann Emlen Mifflin or Ann Emlen Pleasants in mind. (The former married in 1788, the latter in 1796.) Where the context makes it possible to narrow the choice to a specific person, or where two or three equally strong candidates seem likely, the alternatives have been included in the directory. Where, however, there are several possibilities but no clue to a positive identification, the name has been omitted from the directory altogether. Jacob Taylor is a case in point: three men of that name were members of the Northern District Monthly Meeting during the late eighteenth century, but no supporting evidence exists to indicate which one appears in the diary.

Spelling variations have been cross-indexed. The main entry may be found under the currently accepted spelling of the name; ED's departures are included as guides to the main entry, since some bear little similarity to contemporary references.

Since the diary covers nearly five decades, many women appear in it under two names: their name at birth and their name after marriage. In the directory, the full identification may be found under the name by which a subject first appears in the diary. A cross-reference under the married name will direct the reader to the name at birth if the full entry appears at the latter location. A word of caution, however: given the relative similarity of first names (the profusion of Sarahs, Marys, and Anns is bewildering), and the frequency of intermarriage among people who answered to no more than six different surnames, it is possible that in a few cases the cross-reference may not be to the same person, as intended, but rather to a mother or cousin with the same name.

The directory entry for each person always refers to the subject's formal name. ED, however, referred to many acquaintances by their diminutives. The following list, therefore, provides the reader with the nicknames that appear most often in the diary:

Ann	Nancy
Catherine	Caty, Katy

Fig. 7.10b Crane, *Drinker: Life Cycle,* 305

The editors of the *Samuel Gompers Papers* included a biographical glossary at the back of each volume of their edition:

INDIVIDUALS

APPEL, George W. (b. 1860?), served as the general secretary of the Metal Workers' National Union of North America from 1886 to 1889. Born in Maryland, he worked as a silver plater and brass finisher in Baltimore.

ARCH, Joseph (1826-1919), was a founder (1872) and leader of the National Agricultural Labourers' Union and a Member of Parliament (1885-86, 1892-1900).

Fig. 7.10c Kaufman, *Gompers,* 1:473

The editor of *The Children of Pride* provided a list of "principal characters" at the front of his volume to simplify identification of the individuals who wrote and received letters or who were discussed in the documents:

The Principal Characters

At Maybank, Montevideo, and Arcadia

Rev. Dr. Charles Colcock Jones, *a retired Presbyterian clergyman*
Mary (Jones) Jones, *his wife*

In Savannah

Charles Colcock Jones, Jr., *a lawyer, elder son of Dr. and Mrs. C. C. Jones*
Ruth Berrien (Whitehead) Jones, *his wife*
Julia Berrien Jones, *their daughter*

Fig. 7.10d Myers, *Children*, 3

7.11   The editor of the *Papers of George Mason* included a joint biographical-geographical glossary in his edition:

FAIRFAX PARISH: Fairfax County; divided from Truro Parish in 1764; contained Alexandria and vicinity; built Fall's (1767) and Alexandria (Christ's) churches.

FALCONER, NATHANIEL: capt. of ship *Friendship* on Philadelphia-to-London run, 1760; sought and may have obtained command in U.S. navy during Revolution.

FALLS WAREHOUSE: (Falls of the Potomac), Fairfax County; about one mile north of Difficult Run; built by Thomas Lee in 1742 as a public tobacco warehouse, it had little success.

FARGUSON, JOHN: Fairfax County freeholder; Truro Parish vestry, 1733–1744.

Fig. 7.11 Rutland, *Mason*, 1:li

7.12   For editions that contain numerous technical terms, a glossary may be a useful addition. The editors of the *Papers of General Nathanael Greene* included a glossary of eighteenth-century military terms:

A GLOSSARY OF MILITARY TERMS

ABATIS	A barrier of felled trees, with limbs pointing toward the enemy, usually temporary.
ACCOUNT	A financial record.
ACCOUTREMENTS	Soldiers' outfits, usually not including clothing or weapons.
ARTILLERY PARK	An encampment for artillery.
ARTILLERY TRAIN	An army's collection of cannon and material for firing them.

Fig. 7.12a Showman, *Greene*, 8:xxxvii

The editors of the *Samuel Gompers Papers* included a glossary of labor organizations:

> The Journeymen BAKERS' National Union of the United States was organized in 1886, participated in the formation of the AFL that year, and was chartered by the AFL in 1887. In 1890 it adopted the name Journeymen Bakers' and Confectioners' International Union of America and, in 1903, Bakery and Confectionery Workers' International Union of America.
>
> The BRICKLAYERS' and Masons' International Union of America was organized in 1865. It did not affiliate with the AFL until 1916.

Fig. 7.12b Kaufman, Gompers, 1:507

The editors of the *Documentary History of the First Federal Congress* included a glossary of legislative and legal terms:

GLOSSARY

ACT: (1) A bill that has been passed by one or both Houses of Congress. (2) A bill that has been passed by both Houses of Congress and signed by the President or passed over his veto.

AMENDMENT: (1) A proposal to alter a bill, act, amendment, or resolution after it has been formally introduced. Amendments vary in importance from slight word changes to major substantive alterations. To be adopted, an amendment must be agreed to by a majority of the Members voting. (2) A change in the Constitution. Such an amendment is usually proposed in the form of a joint resolution of Congress, which may originate in either House. If passed, it does not go to the President for his approval but is submitted directly to the states for ratification.

BILL: A proposal of specific legislation presented to Congress for enactment into law. Bills may originate in either House; two exceptions, however, are those for raising revenue, which, according to the Constitution, must originate

Fig. 7.12c De Pauw, Congress, 1:xvii

Tables, Lists, and Calendars

7.13   Tables and charts may be created to distill important information, as does this table created by the editors of the *Documentary History of the*

Ratification of the Constitution to show the attendance of the delegates to the Georgia Ratification Convention:

Convention Roster and Attendance Record
25 December 1787–5 January 1788

	Dec. 25	Dec. 26	Dec. 27	Dec. 28	Dec. 29	Dec. 31	Jan. 1	Jan. 2	Jan. 5
CHATHAM									
William Stephens	X	X		X	X	X	X	X	X
Joseph Habersham				X	X	X	X	X	X
Thomas Gibbons									X
EFFINGHAM									
Jenkin Davis						X	X	X	X
Nathan Brownson				X	X	X	X	X	X
Caleb Howell									
BURKE									
Edward Telfair		X		X	X	X	X	X	X
Henry Todd	X	X		X	X	X	X		
George Walton									

Fig. 7.13 Jensen, *Ratification*, 3:270

7.14   Genealogical tables provide readers with a quick and easy method of understanding complex family relations, as does this chart included in *The Secret Eye: The Journal of Ella Gertrude Clanton Thomas:*

The Thomas Family

Joseph J. Thomas was a descendant of John Thomas, who settled in Jamestown, Virginia, in 1622. Joseph married Elizabeth Eskridge of Virginia, a descendant of Col. George Eskridge, patriot and guardian of George Washington's mother, Mary Ball. Their children of record were Pierce Butler, Nathaniel, Joseph Darius, and Nancy. Some members of this family emigrated to Edgefield County, South Carolina, and Burke County, Georgia. Joseph Darius Thomas of Burke County married Louisa (Loula) Kettles (Kittles) of Screvin County, Georgia.

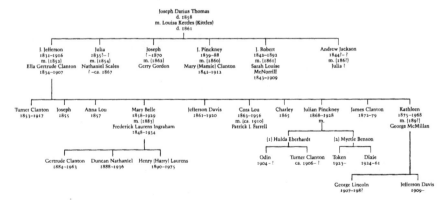

Fig. 7.14a Burr, *Secret Eye*, xviii

The editor of *"Dear Master": Letters of a Slave Family* used another format for showing genealogical relationships:

> ### Skipwith Family
> Children of Lucy Nicholas, who cohabited with Jesse Skipwith
>   Peyton Skipwith (d. 1849)
>   m. Lydia Randall (1804?–1834)
>   Diana (1822–1844?) m. Moore James (b. 1820?)
>   Matilda (b. 1824)
>   m. Samuel Lomax (1823?–1850)
>   infant (died)
>   Eliza Adala
>   Lydia Ann
>   child (died)

Fig. 7.14b Miller, *Dear Master*, 20

7.15 A calendar of the years covered by the documents in an edition assists readers in following the chronology of events, especially when many of the documents refer regularly to days of the week without specifying dates. This one was included in the *Documentary History of the First Federal Elections:*

Fig. 7.15 Jensen, *Elections*, 1:xxx

7.16 Chronologies help readers understand the relationship of documents to the broader sweep of events. The editors of the *Papers of Thomas A. Edison* provided a chronology of Edison's inventions for the period covered in each volume:

1873
25 June   Returns to Newark from England.
2 August   Drafts caveat that contains the basis of the quadruplex.
25 August   Executes patent application for his roman-letter automatic-
                        telegraph perforator.
2 September   Sells British rights for his automatic telegraph to a London
                        company.
6 September   A carbon rheostat for use in artificial-cable telegraph experi-
                        ments is finished in the shop.

Fig. 7.16a Jenkins, *Edison*, 2:xxx

The editor of the two-volume *Selected Letters of Charles Sumner* printed a chronology spanning Sumner's entire life, focusing on his education, orations, and
political career:

1811   6 January. Born to Charles Pinckney and Relief Jacob Sumner in
                  Boston.

1821–   Attends Boston Latin School.
1826

1830   25 August. B.A., Harvard.

1831   September. Enters Harvard Law School.

1834   January. Completes studies at Harvard Law School (LL.B. awarded
                  June 1834). Begins practice at office of Benjamin Rand, Boston.
                  September. Admitted to bar and enters partnership with George
                  Hillard at 4 Court Street, Boston.
                  Writes for *American Jurist* and *North American Review.*

1835–   Lectures at Harvard Law School; edits *Sumner's Reports*.
1837

1837–   European tour.
1840

1839   24 April. Charles Pinckney Sumner dies.

1840   3 May. Returns to United States, resumes Boston law practice.

1845   4 July. Oration, "The True Grandeur of Nations," in Boston.

Fig. 7.16b Palmer, *Sumner*, 1:xv

Maps and Illustrations

7.17 Editors include maps to provide readers with a better understanding of the geographical areas discussed in documents. The editors of the *Papers of Ulysses S. Grant* provided a map to explain the location of Union and Confederate units around Richmond and Petersburg:

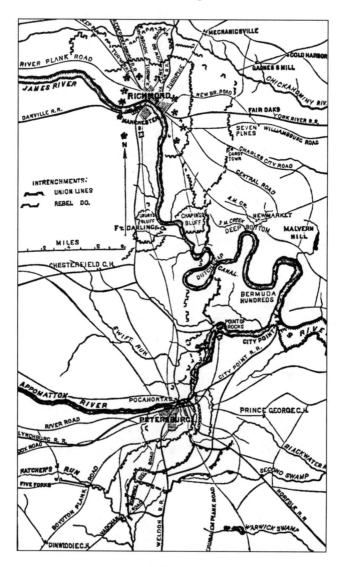

Area of Operations around Richmond and Petersburg
From Horace Greeley, The American Conflict: A History of the
Great Rebellion (Hartford, Conn., 1866), II, 594

Fig. 7.17 Simon, *Grant*, 12:115

7.18 Editors may provide readers with illustrations as a way to enhance the information provided within documents. Information about the medium, artist, and institution holding copyright on the image should be provided in a caption or in a note. Commonly used illustrations include portraits and photographs of individuals, facsimiles of significant documents, and pictures of buildings or scenes associated with the topic. When presenting illustrations to complement documents, editors should strive to include only relevant materials.

Annotation in Microform and Electronic Editions

7.19 Microform editions may be annotated with many of the same types of notes found in a book edition, although the microform format often makes it difficult to refer to tables, charts, or other reference tools located in the first or last frames of an edition. As this example from the microfiche supplement to the *Documentary History of the Ratification of the Constitution* demonstrates, a document in microform can be accompanied by headings and footnotes containing provenance notes, just like a document in a book edition:

5   Williamsburg Meeting, 6 October, 1787[1]

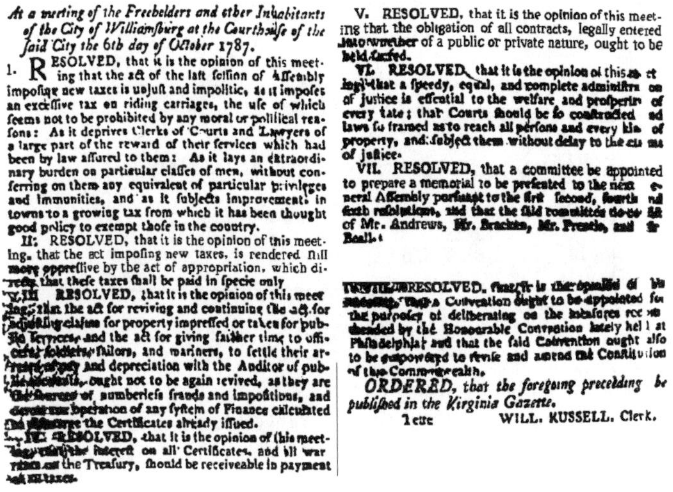

1. *Virginia Gazette and Weekly Advertiser*, 18 October. All eight resolutions were reprinted in the *Pennsylvania Mercury* and the *Pennsylvania Packet*, 26 October. Resolution VIII was reprinted in the New York *Daily Advertiser*, 26 October; *Albany Gazette*, 15 November; and Poughkeepsie *Country Journal*, 21 November.

Fig. 7.19a Jensen, *Ratification*, supplement to vols.viii–x, frame B05

Microform targets—cards containing annotation that are filmed alongside a document—are more common. The editors of the *Guide to the Thomas A. Edison Papers: A Selective Microfilm Edition* described different ways their edition employed targets:

Targets

Targets are editorial aids that appear on the microfilm to assist the reader in using the materials in the collection. Targets introduce each series, each major subseries, and the individual volumes and folders that appear in the edition. The series and subseries targets are essentially more detailed versions of the Series Notes on pages 19–30 of this guide. The target preceding each bound volume provides information about authorship, inclusive dates, and number of pages, as well as a brief description of the character and contents of the volume and, wherever appropriate, cross-references to related materials. The target preceding each folder in the Document File Series lists the types of documents in the folder, any variations from chronological order, and cross-references to related materials. The target also provides a brief description of materials in the folder that were not selected for filming. Where the contents of a particular folder were not filmed, an explanatory target appears on the microfilm.

Occasionally, explanatory targets accompany individual documents in order to: (1) explain relationships among documents (for example, the target ENCLOSURE); (2) describe multiple versions of a document (for example, the targets TRANSLATION FOLLOWS and TRANSLATION); (3) supply missing information (for example, the date or author of a letter); and (4) note the existence of missing information (for example, the target INCOMPLETE).

Fig. 7.19b Jeffrey, Edison, part 1:15

The editors of the *Papers of Eugene V. Debs* filed a rectangular card at the top of each document; it provided the date, author and recipient, type of document, length of document, and provenance:

```
1905 March 17
EVD to Marguerite Bettrich Debs
ALS 4pp
InTI, Debs Coll.
```

Fig. 7.19c Constantine, Papers of Debs, reel 1:445

The editors of the microfilm edition of the *Emma Goldman Papers: A Microfilm Edition* also used targets describing the type of document and its date, place, author, recipient, number of pages, and physical size, as well as its provenance and copyright holder:

860512003

The Emma Goldman Papers

[Postcard] 1906 March 6, New York [to] Leon Malmed, Albany, N.Y. / E[mma] G[oldman]. — 2 p. ; 9 × 14 cm.
Permission to reproduce or quote in any form must be obtained from the Schlesinger Library, Radcliffe College.

Fig. 7.19d Falk, Goldman, reel 2:14

The editors of the microfilm edition of the *John Muir Papers* filmed each document with an editor's control card. The sample card below shows the information provided:

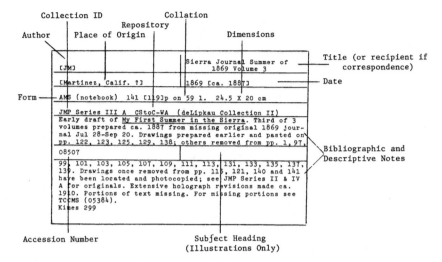

Fig. 7.19e Limbaugh, *Muir*, 7

7.20 Hypertext links make special types of annotation possible in electronic editions. By selecting certain highlighted areas on the screen, readers may bring forth text, pictures, sounds, or visual images related to the particular image or passage. For further information on the creation and annotation of electronic editions, editors should consult the home page of the Model Editions Partnership (URL: *http://mep.cla.sc.edu/*), a consortium of seven historical editing projects working in conjunction with the Text Encoding Initiative and the Center for Electronic Texts in the Humanities to establish guidelines for electronic documentary editing and to develop model electronic editions. For links to home pages of various historical editions, see the Web site of the Association for Documentary Editing (URL: *http://etext.virginia.edu/ade/*).

Abbreviations

7.21 Editors use many symbols and abbreviations to convey information about documents. Abbreviations are commonly used to refer to the archival repository of documents, the form of the source text, and frequently used reference works. Because there are no standardized abbreviations for provenance or short titles, editors must borrow these symbols from other editions or create their own. When referring to provenance, modern editions often use the symbols established by the Library of Congress and found in the most current edition of *Symbols of American Libraries* (Washington, D.C.: Cataloguing Distribution Services). Editions that began to be published before these abbreviations were standardized developed their own systems or used one of numerous other systems established regionally or locally by libraries or bibliographers.

7.22   Documentary editions commonly describe the form and genre of documents by using abbreviations devised for individual projects. For example, the editors of the *Papers of Thomas Jefferson*, the *Papers of Woodrow Wilson*, and the *Papers of Thomas A. Edison* employed different sets of abbreviations, highlighting different aspects of documents:

Dft	draft (Usually a composition or rough draft; later drafts, when identifiable as such, are designated "2d Dft," &c.)
Dupl	duplicate
MS	manuscript (arbitrarily applied to most documents other than letters)
N	note, notes (memoranda, fragments, &c.)
PoC	polygraph copy
PrC	press copy
RC	recipient's copy
SC	stylograph copy
Tripl	triplicate
FC	file copy (Applied to all forms of retained copies, such as letter-book copies, clerks' copies, &c.)
Tr	transcript (Applied to both contemporary and later copies; period of transcription, unless clear by implication, will be given when known.)

Fig. 7.22a Boyd, *Jefferson*, 1:xxxix–xl

ABBREVIATIONS

ALI	autograph letter initialed
ALS	autograph letter signed
att.	attached
enc.	enclosure, enclosed
env.	envelope
hw	handwritten, handwriting
JRW	Joseph Ruggles Wilson
JWW	Janet Woodrow Wilson
miscl.	miscellaneous
sh	shorthand
shLS	shorthand letter signed
shP(S)	shorthand postal (signed)
WW	Woodrow Wilson
WWhw(S)	Woodrow Wilson handwriting or handwritten (signed)
WWsh	Woodrow Wilson shorthand
WWshL(S)	Woodrow Wilson shorthand letter (signed)
WWshP(S)	Woodrow Wilson shorthand postal (signed)

Fig. 7.22b Link, *Wilson*, 1:xxxi

AD	Autograph Document
ADf	Autograph Draft
ADS	Autograph Document Signed
AL	Autograph Letter
ALS	Autograph Letter Signed
AX	Autograph Technical Note
AXS	Autograph Technical Note Signed
D	Document
Df	Draft
DS	Document Signed
L	Letter
LS	Letter Signed
M	Model
PD	Printed Document
PDS	Printed Document Signed
PL	Printed Letter
TD	Typed Document
TL	Typed Letter

Fig. 7.22c Jenkins, *Edison,* 1:lxi

7.23 The editors of *Freedom: A Documentary History of Emancipation* listed the different types of abbreviations used throughout the edition, including those describing the physical characteristics of documents, the provenance of collections, general and military abbreviations, and short-title references to published sources:

SYMBOLS AND ABBREVIATIONS

SYMBOLS USED TO DESCRIBE MANUSCRIPTS

Symbols used to describe the handwriting, form, and signature of each document appear at the end of each document.

The first capital letter describes the handwriting of the document:
A   autograph (written in the author's hand)
H   handwritten by other than the author (for example, by a clerk)
P   printed
T   typed

The second capital letter, with lower-case modifier when appropriate, describes the form of the document:

L	letter	c	copy
D	document	p	press copy
E	endorsement	d	draft
W	wire (telegram)	f	fragment

The third capital letter describes the signature:
S   signed by the author
Sr   signed with a representation of the author's name
I   initialed by the author
     no signature or representation

For example, among the more common symbols are: ALS (autograph letter, signed by author), HLS (handwritten letter, signed by author), HLSr (handwritten letter, signed with a representation), HLcSr (handwritten copy of a letter, signed with a representation), HD (handwritten document, no signature).

ABBREVIATIONS FOR RECORD GROUPS IN THE
NATIONAL ARCHIVES OF THE UNITED STATES

RG 11   General Records of the United States Government

RG 15   Records of the Veterans Administration

RG 21   Records of District Courts of the United States

* * * *

SHORT TITLES

Freedom

Freedom: A Documentary History of Emancipation, 1861–1867.

Series 1, volume 1, *The Destruction of Slavery,* ed. Ira Berlin, Barbara J. Fields, Thavolia Glymph, Joseph P. Reidy, and Leslie S. Rowland (Cambridge, 1985).

Series 1, volume 2, *The Wartime Genesis of Free Labor,* ed. Ira Berlin, Thavolia Glymph, Steven F. Miller, Joseph P. Reidy, Leslie S. Rowland, and Julie Saville (Cambridge, forthcoming).

Series 2, *The Black Military Experience,* ed. Ira Berlin, Joseph P. Reidy, and Leslie S. Rowland (Cambridge, 1982).

Navy Official Records

U.S. Navy Department, *Official Records of the Union and Confederate Navies in the War of the Rebellion,* 30 vols. (Washington, 1894–1922).

Official Records

U.S. War Department, *The War of the Rebellion: A Compilation of the Official Records of the Union and Confederate Armies,* 128 vols. (Washington, 1880–1901).

MILITARY AND OTHER ABBREVIATIONS THAT APPEAR
FREQUENTLY IN THE DOCUMENTS

A.A.A.G.	Acting Assistant Adjutant General
A.A.G.	Assistant Adjutant General
A.C.	Army Corps
A.C.	Assistant Commissioner (Freedmen's Bureau)
Act., Actg.	Acting
A.D.	African Descent
A.D.C.	Aide-de-Camp
Adjt.	Adjutant
Agt.	Agent
A.G.O.	Adjutant General's Office
A.Q.M.	Assistant Quartermaster
Asst.	Assistant
A.S.A.C.	Assistant Subassistant Commissioner (Freedmen's Bureau)

Fig. 7.23 Berlin, *Freedom,* ser.1,1:xxxiv–xxxvi

Cross-References

7.24 A convenient way to save space and avoid excessive duplication of information is to refer readers to documents or notes provided in an earlier edition, especially a microform edition. Cross-references to microform editions in particular allow editors to lead readers to original documents and additional sources that they may not have published. By providing cross-references to earlier volumes, editors lead readers to their previous research and annotation, avoid repetition, and focus efforts on providing new information.

7.25 The editors of the *Papers of Robert Morris* regularly referred readers to earlier documents and notes:

1. RM had taken a weekend "excursion into the Country." See Diary, July 19, 1782.
2. On the congressional committee to investigate the Office of Finance, see Diary, June 12, 1782, and notes. James Duane's letter is dated July 19.
3. See Diary, February 14, 1782, and notes.
4. Arthur Lee was on the committee mentioned in note 2 above.
5. See RM to Duer, July 23, and notes.
6. On Crawford's case, see Diary, July 19, 1782, and notes.
7. On Campbell's application, see Diary, May 8, 1782, and notes.

Fig. 7.25a Ferguson, *Morris,* 6:4

In the following example from the *Papers of Daniel Webster: Correspondence*, the footnote following the reference to the Crafts' Case directed the reader to an earlier note in the same volume that had described the circumstances of the case:

> also to state, that I knew the correct opinions of Mr Sanger, on this subject, when the "Crafts' case"[6] came up. And I cannot but trust that

> 6. See above, headnote preceding
> DW to Fillmore, November 5, 1850,
> p. 177.

Headnote, p. 177:

Threatened and actual resistance to the new Fugitive Slave Law was not restricted to Pennsylvania. In Boston a "vigilance" committee led by Theodore Parker sprang to the aid of a fugitive couple, William and Ellen Craft, whose Macon, Georgia, master, Robert Collins, sought to reclaim them. Collins's two agents were harassed in Boston and briefly clapped in jail, until they left the city empty-handed. On November 7, prior to the Crafts' leavetaking for England to circumvent the law, they were married, in a highly charged ceremony conducted by Reverend Parker. See John Weiss, ed., Life and Correspondence of Theodore Parker *(New York, 1864), 2: 94–102, and below, pp. 189–190, Theodore Parker to DW, December 12, 1850.*

Fig. 7.25b Wiltse, *Webster: Correspondence,* 7:177,223,224

The editors of the *Papers of Andrew Johnson* used cross-references to guide readers to earlier volumes in which individuals had already been identified in biographical notes:

> 2. For Thomas, see *Johnson Papers*, V, 367n.

Fig. 7.25c Graf, *Johnson,* 6:141

Researching and Citing Annotation Sources

7.26   Although editors possess a wealth of knowledge, most projects still entail considerable research. Editors will want to provide their readers with some indication of the sources used to compile their notes, but the exact method depends on the audience of the edition, the number and type of sources used, and the judgment of the editors.

7.27   Editors may provide full citations listing the sources used to write their notes. For example, the notes of the *Papers of George Catlett Marshall* provided citations for books, newspapers, and primary documents:

1. Rogers had moved to Washington in early July 1942 to become a special assistant to William J. Donovan, head of the Office of Strategic Services. He had written to Marshall, whom he had met the previous year (see *Papers of GCM*, 2: 692), to volunteer his organization's assistance in evaluating the army's officer training schools. As Marshall was concerned with this issue (see Marshall to Bull, September 8, 1942, p. 349), and as he regarded Rogers as "an unusually able man," he had Rogers sent to investigate and report on the various institutions. (Marshall Memorandum for General McNair, August 10, 1942, GCMRL/G. C. Marshall Papers [Pentagon Office, Selected].) Rogers made his trip during the second week in September. The editors have not found his reports on the Infantry School (Fort Benning) or the Armored Force School (Fort Knox), but he commented in his diary: "The Benning school is almost perfect. It graduates 250 2nd lieutenants every day after the best officers' training of 13 weeks I ever saw. It is 90% in the field. The Armored Schools are too West Pointy—severe, silly close order drill an hour a day, no field work, all snap and dash. . . . It was a week of gun-fire, night demonstrations, tanks, cannon, machine guns to no end." (*Wartime Washington: The Secret OSS Journal of James Grafton Rogers, 1942–1943*, ed. Thomas F. Troy [Frederick, Md.: University Publications of America, 1987], p. 12.)

Fig. 7.27 Bland, *Marshall*, 3:365

7.28 Editors decide on the format of citations, including the level of detail they will include. The *Papers of Joseph Henry* cited secondary works as follows:

[12] In 1828 through the donation of a nearby resident, Yale purchased a Dollond refractor of five-inch aperture, the finest telescope in America for almost a decade to come. David F. Musto, "A Survey of the American Observatory Movement, 1800–1850," *Vistas in Astronomy*, 1968, 9:87–92.

Fig. 7.28a Reingold, *Henry*, 1:277

The *Collected Papers of Albert Einstein* borrowed their citation format from scientific texts, using author-date citations, with a list of full citations at the back of the volume:

[6] See *Thomson 1851*. As in Doc. 37, κ denotes the thermal conductivity, T, the temperature. MARIĆ's *Diplomarbeit*, which she hoped to use as the basis of her doctoral dissertation, was on heat conduction (see Docs. 63, 75, note 5, and 111).

LITERATURE CITED

Thomson 1851 Thomson, William. "On a Mechanical Theory of Thermo-Electric Currents." (15 December 1851) *Proceedings of the Royal Society of Edinburgh* 3 (December 1850 to April 1857): 91–98.

Fig. 7.28b Stachel, *Einstein*, 1:258,405

7.29   When frequent reference will be made to a small number of published and unpublished works, editors often devise short titles or abbreviations for such works. At the front or back of the volume, they then provide a list of short titles and abbreviations, along with the corresponding full citations. For example, the *Collected Papers of Charles Willson Peale and His Family* used abbreviations to indicate secondary works used in the notes:

> 1. Robert Eden (1741–84) was Maryland's last colonial governor. *DAB*.
> 2. A new state house was nearing completion at this time, and the ostensible reason for CWP's presentation of his first painting of Pitt was to contribute to the building's adornment. The painting now hangs in the State House, Annapolis. *CWP*, p. 110.

Fig. 7.29a Miller, *Peale*, 1:132

Short Titles of Sources

CWP
   Charles Coleman Sellers, *Charles Willson Peale* (New York, 1969).

DAB
   Allen Johnson and Dumas Malone, eds., *Dictionary of American Biography*, 20 vols. and supplements (New York, 1928–36).

Fig. 7.29b Miller, *Peale*, 1:xl

7.30   Editions may develop methods that address the specific circumstances of their subject or the available primary and secondary sources. For example, information about many of the individuals named in the *Booker T. Washington Papers* is accessible only in the Tuskegee Institute archives. Therefore, source

> [1] Josephine Beall Wilson Bruce, the daughter of a Cleveland dentist, taught school in Cleveland before marrying Blanche Kelso Bruce in 1878. After her husband's death in 1898, Josephine Bruce became Lady Principal at Tuskegee Institute, serving from 1899 to 1902.

notes do not list the specific locations of sources but instead mention the years when individuals were associated with the Tuskegee Institute:

Fig. 7.30 Harlan, *Washington*, 4:227

7.31   Editors may choose to provide no citations for the information contained within their notes. For example, the *Documentary History of the Ratification of the Constitution* attached no secondary source citations to its notes because the large array of sources used by the editors would have made the notes unwieldy and added considerably to the space required for annotation:

1. RC, Gratz Collection, PHi. Printed: CC:537 (a longer excerpt). In an omitted portion of the letter, Griffin speculated about the prospects of ratification in several states. Griffin (1748–1810), a lawyer, represented Lancaster in the House of Delegates, 1777–78, 1786–87. He was a delegate to Congress, 1778–80, 1787–88 (president, 1788), and a member of the Continental Court of Appeals in Cases of Capture, 1780–87. FitzSimons (1741–1811), a Philadelphia merchant and a member of the Pennsylvania Assembly, signed the Constitution in the Constitutional Convention.

2. James Madison, Griffin's fellow Virginia delegate to Congress, probably supplied him with this information about Lee and Page. (See letters to Madison from George Washington, 10 January; Archibald Stuart, 14 January; and Tench Coxe, 23 January, all above.)

Fig. 7.31 Jensen, *Ratification*, 8:382

Chapter Eight

Special Issues of Access and Indexing

Critical Nature of Indexes

8.1   Editors carefully design their editions to offer easy access to the documents. For book editions, indexes are the most important tool editors can provide, although document numbers and running heads can also help readers find their way around an edition. Modified indexes and content lists lead users of microform editions to the desired documents, while electronic links and computerized search engines provide access to electronic editions. Editors of documentary editions should familiarize themselves with general principles of indexing, which can be found in standard guides. Two useful books on the subject are Nancy C. Mulvany, *Indexing Books* (Chicago: University of Chicago Press, 1994), and Hans H. Wellisch, *Indexing from A to Z* (Bronx, N.Y.: H. W. Wilson, 1991). Editors also should consider some of the special needs of documentary editions, which will be addressed below.

Indexes

8.2   An index includes headings describing the names, places, and major subjects contained within an edition, usually presented in alphabetical order and subdivided into logical subheadings. An indexer should balance the necessity to save space with the need to provide full access to the varied material contained in the edition. Editors strive to provide access to all subjects covered within an edition, even those that may not be related to the main subject of the volume. For example, the papers of a political figure, such as Thomas Jefferson, could also be used to study agriculture in early America.

8.3   Indexers of documentary editions should be familiar with the subject of the edition, its historical significance, and the major historical issues and actors addressed by the work. Indexers should understand the significance of allusions in documents and make relevant associations. Familiarity with the work being indexed enables indexers to understand the nuances of the text and to place topics under appropriate headings. Indexing is an intellectual process of interpretation and association that should not be left to a computer's word-search program or the hands of a novice assistant. The unhappy results of these methods will be a device that heavily indexes specific names and words but overlooks substantive passages where specific terms were not used.

Statement of Indexing Method

8.4   Conventional book editions normally do not contain statements regarding the nature of the index. Because of the complexity of documentary editions and the greater detail found in their indexes, editors sometimes preface their indexes with a statement of method. For example, the editors of the *Papers of John Adams* outlined their policy for indexing variant spellings of names, wives' names, geographic references, authors and recipients of letters, books, and newspapers.

NOTE ON THE INDEX

This index, which covers the first two volumes of the *Papers of John Adams*, is designed to supplement the annotation, when possible, by furnishing the correct spellings of names, supplying forenames when they are lacking in the text, and indicating dates, occupations, and places of residence when they will aid in identification. Markedly variant spellings of proper names have been cross-referenced to what are believed to be their most nearly standard forms, and the variant forms found in the MSS are parenthetically recorded following the standard spellings. Corrections from readers are most welcome.

Wives' names, with a few exceptions for special reasons, follow their husbands' names, with *see*-references under their maiden names. Under major place names (such as Boston and Braintree) there are appended separate gatherings of "Buildings, landmarks, streets, &c.," the items in which are arranged alphabetically rather than in the order of their appearance (as other subentries are throughout this Index). No attempt has been made to list every name mentioned; particularly is this true for Adams' long essays which make repeated reference to historical persons and institutions, as in the Novanglus letters.

References under a particular name, subject, or subheading are arranged in the order in which they appear in the volumes, except that "mentions" appear at the end of the references. If documents appear by caption only or are merely calendared, the index so indicates. Letters to and from John Adams are listed only under the names of his correspondents, the letters being grouped by dates at the end of each such entry; but an alphabetical listing of correspondents is found under the John Adams entry. Two Boston newspapers are distinguished in the index by calling the *Massachusetts Gazette and the Boston Weekly News-Letter* simply the *Massachusetts Gazette*, as Adams repeatedly did, and the *Massachusetts Gazette and Boston Post-Boy and Advertiser*, the *Boston Post-Boy*. Book titles mentioned or cited by Adams and his contemporaries appear in shortened form under their authors' names; full citation is found in the notes.

Fig. 8.4a Taylor, *Adams*, 2:430

The editors of the *Colonial Records of North Carolina: Second Series* included an explanation of their indexing policy for variant spellings of names, multiple individuals with the same name, petitioners, family relationships, and variant spellings of place names:

Index

Proper names and subjects are entered in this index. For persons, one spelling of each individual's name has been selected from the spellings appearing in the manuscripts, with variant spellings provided in parentheses following the main entry for each name. A cross reference to the selected spelling is given for each variant of the surname. Cross references also are provided between names known or thought to refer to the same person. Where a distinction, such as place of residence or date of death, can be determined between or among individuals of the same name, it is indicated in parentheses following each surname entry. Two innovations have been introduced in an effort to contain the size of the index. The single designation "petitioner" has been used to indicate petitioners for land warrants, resurveys, extensions of warrants, and alterations to land grants. And family relationships have been omitted as individual designations, but can be found under the subject heading "Family, family relationship."

Modern spellings are used for place names unless the indexer has been unable to identify the place, in which case the spelling is one appearing in the documents. Variant spellings are given in parentheses, and cross references to the spelling used in the entry are provided under all variants except those closely resembling the modern spelling. Subject entries are in modern spelling. Where a subject or name is mentioned intermittently throughout four or more consecutive pages, the term "passim" follows the final page number in the sequence.

Fig. 8.4b Parker, *North Carolina,* 9:705

8.5　　Editors of multivolume series need to decide how to index their editions. Some multivolume editions, such as the *Papers of George Mason,* used continuous pagination through the entire three-volume series and provided a single index at the back of the final volume. The *Adams Family Papers* provided an index in every even-numbered volume. The editors of the *Papers of Alexander Hamilton* provided an index in each individual volume and created a cumulative index as the last volume of the series. The editors of the *Papers of Thomas Jefferson* initially intended to create temporary indexes during the life of the project and a single cumulative index when the project ended, but they abandoned that method. Volume 21 is a cumulative index, and each subsequent volume is indexed at the back of the book. (See Julian P. Boyd, et al., eds., *Papers of Thomas Jefferson* [Princeton: Princeton University Press, 1983], 21:vii–viii.)

Specialized Indexes

8.6　　A single index has many advantages, but editors may create multiple or specialized indexes if an edition contains distinct categories of information that readers may want to locate or if editors believe multiple indexes will provide greater access to the documents. In general, the number and type of indexes reflects the content of the documents and the needs of the edition's audience.

8.7   A separate name index can provide readers easy access to references to specific individuals. For example, the editors of the *Diary of Elizabeth Drinker* created a separate name index because of the thousands of individuals mentioned in the diary:

> The Index of Names reflects the difficulties inherent in eighteenth-century documents where the author's spelling of names is inconsistent. Thus, the following editorial policies have been adopted:
>
>   1. First names are formalized. "Sally," for example, appears as "Sarah." (See page 2098 for a list of formal names and their most commonly used nicknames.)
>
>   2. Family names with numerous spelling variations have been standardized to the spelling most frequently used by ED: "Cathral," "Catheral," and "Catherell," for example, are uniformly indexed as "Catherall." Where the potential exists for misidentification, the names are indexed by variant spellings: David Commins, David Cumming, David Cummins.
>
> Because ED created an indexing quandary by referring to people by their initials or without sufficient information to distinguish among people of the same name, some individuals are indexed in more than one form, while two different people with similar names may appear in the same entry. For example, the two Benjamin Swetts are entered as Senior and Junior, with a third, "generic" category for references that had no specific generational attribution. In such cases, subentries may also refer to more than one person.
>
> Since nurses and physicians are subjects, but the entries are names, they are listed in the Index of Names both individually and by category.

Fig. 8.7a Crane, Drinker, 3:2235

Editors of correspondence may create an index of authors or recipients of letters, such as this list of recipients produced by the editor of the *Selected Letters of Charles Sumner*:

LIST OF RECIPIENTS

Adams, Abigail Brooks
     I: 334, 513–15; II: 379–80
Adams, Charles Francis
     I: 128–29, 212–13, 238–40, 316–17, 317–18, 318–19, 343–45,
     349–52, 359–60, 362, 369–70, 377, 382–83, 395–96, 438–39,
     442–43, 444–45, 477–79, 511–12, 519–22, 529–30
Adams, John Quincy
     I: 177
Agassiz, Louis
     II: 199–200, 275–76, 620

Fig. 8.7b Palmer, Sumner, 1:xxvii

8.8   Editors of documentary editions of legislative documents may create specialized indexes to lead readers to different types of legislative documents. For example, the *State Records of South Carolina: Journals of the House of Representatives* contained three separate cross-referenced indexes: an index of reports and resolutions, an index of ratified and unratified bills, and a standard index:

REPORTS AND RESOLUTIONS

R1. Report on rules and orders of the House: committee appointed, 5; report considered, amended, and agreed to, 6–8

R2. Resolution appointing a cashier and assistant cashier of the House, agreed to, 25

R3. Resolution appointing chaplain of the House: agreed to, 26

R4. Resolution regarding eligibility of legislators to serve as presidential

R13. Report on petition (pp. 20–21) of Elias Smerdon regarding purchase of land from the commissioners of the loan office: reported, 47; considered and recommitted, 61; reported, 87

R14. Report on petition (p. 21) of Sarah Moore regarding amercement on estate of James Mackie: reported, 47; considered and postponed, 61

R15. Report on petition (pp. 17, 18) of officers of the state dragoons com-

Fig. 8.8a Stevens, *House: 1792–1794*, 595

BILLS

Unratified Legislation

1. Bill to amend the laws relative to the poor in this state: received from Senate and 1st reading, 49; 2nd reading and committed, 61–62; committee report read, 117; 2nd reading of bill and sent to Senate, 232; rejected by Senate, 232n

2. Bill to provide for the maintenance of illegitimate children and for other purposes therein mentioned: re-

4. Bill for repealing so much of "An Act" for granting licences for retailing liquors, as requires a consideration to be exacted for the retailing of malt and other fermented liquors, and for other purposes therein mentioned (based on Reports and Resolutions No. R19): 1st reading, 100; 1st reading, 274; 2nd reading and committed for further investigation, 286

Fig. 8.8b Stevens, *House: 1792–1794*, 612

Akin, Adam, 414

Ale houses. *See* Taverns

Alexander, Eleazer, 450

Alexander, Isaac: as justice of the peace, 256, 256n, 258–59; lost indent of, 358–59, 399; signs petition as warden of Camden, 83n

Alexander, Joseph, 444

Alexander, William, 157

Alkin, Martyn, 574

Anderson, Thomas, 278

* Anderson, William, 588; in attendance, 272; carries papers, 195, 215, 222, 249, 334; and claims against confiscated estates, 70, 138, 399, 465, 556–57; as commissioner for building jail in Ninety Six District, 43; as commissioner to run boundary, 121, 404, 442; as commissioner to value tracts of land, 215, 333; committee assignments, 12n, 21, 105,

Fig. 8.8c Stevens, *House: 1792–1794*, 624

8.9   For editions dealing with natural history, a special index listing flora or fauna might be useful, such as the index of plant materials created by the editors of the *Papers of Frederick Law Olmsted:*

INDEX OF
PLANT MATERIALS

Acacia, 540
Ailanthus, 86, 87, 90
Aloe, 540
Aralia, 87, 90
Aurucaria braziliensis [*Araucaria agusti-folia*, Parana pine], 281
Aurucaria imbricata [*Araucaria araucana*, monkey-puzzle tree], 281
Azalea, 540

Cedar of Lebanon [*Cedrus libani*], 281, 480, 481
Chamerops Sinensis [*Livistona chinensis*, Chinese fountain palm], 281
Chestnut, 88
Chestnut, golden-leafed [*Castanopsis chrysophylla*], 282, 540
Clematis, 88, 90
Convolvulus, 87

Fig. 8.9 McLaughlin, *Olmsted*, 5:791

8.10   Because of the frequent references to scientific works in the *Collected Papers of Albert Einstein*, the editors included a citation index to allow readers to locate passages where scientific works were mentioned:

INDEX OF CITATIONS

Aarau Programm 1904, 227n
Aargau Bericht 1892–1904, 227n
Aargau Kantonsschule 1952, 11
Aargau Lexikon 1958, 383
Aargau Programm 1895/1896, 11, 12, 21n, 335n, 359

Clausius 1889–1891, 95n
Clemenceau 1889, li n

Darmstadt Verzeichniss 1900, 267n
Dingfelder 1927, lix n
Drude 1894, 213n, 223

Fig. 8.10 Stachel, *Einstein*, 1:430

Indexing Annotation

8.11   Substantive information in the footnotes of an edition may also be indexed. The *Papers of Robert Morris* indexed footnotes but did not distinguish between references to notes and references to text, unless the notes identified an individual. The index created by the editors of *John Jay* distinguished between textual references and notes, by following the page number with a lowercase *n:*

Adams, John Quincy, 153n, 317, 640, 641n:
with father in Holland, 52, 691, 709; journeys from Russia, 569, 570; in boarding school, 589n; with father in England, 630, 631n, 646, 662
Adams, Samuel, 85n, 95n
Adams, Thomas, of New Kent County, Va., 218, 220

Fig. 8.11a Morris, *Jay*, 2:727

For index entries referring to information in footnotes, the editors of the *Papers of James Madison* gave the page number, followed by *n* and the number of the footnote containing the reference. For example, the following entry begins with a reference to footnote 1 on page 95:

> Mason, George, 95 n. 1, 173, 180, 182 and
> nn. 2, 3, 191 n. 5, 198, 199 n. 4, 201,
> 227 and n. 3, 231, 242; opposes Consti-
> tution, 189–90, 191 nn. 3, 8, 193, 194
> n. 2, 202, 215–16, 217, 221, 225, 230,
> 291, 293, 298, 312, 318, 331, 339, 346,
> 355, 418 n. 1, 520, 543–44 n. 6; views
> on Constitution criticized, 196–97, 375
> n. 2, 510 and n. 3; at Federal Conven-
> tion, 17 n. 1, 29, 74, 104, 135–36 n. 2,

Fig. 8.11b Hutchinson, *Madison,* 10:566.

8.12 Editors may provide readers with assistance in locating passages where individuals are identified in the notes or text. For example, in the *Documentary History of the Supreme Court of the United States,* index entries for individuals identified in footnotes were followed by *id.* and italicized page numbers to indicate where biographical descriptions could be found. The italicized phrase *biographical headnote* was used to indicate when individuals had been identi-fied in a headnote:

> Blair, Jean, 54; *id., 56n*
> Blair, John: *biographical headnote, 54–56;* as

Fig. 8.12a Marcus, *Supreme Court,* vol.1,2:947

The *Papers of Robert Morris* indexed the location of biographical identifications by placing those page numbers in italics:

> Adam, Robert, *150*

Fig. 8.12b Ferguson, *Morris,* 6:699

The *Papers of Andrew Jackson* listed the page number where a biographical identification occurred, followed by the italicized word *note.* If a picture was included, the editors added the word *portrait:*

> Anderson, Joseph, 78 *note;* 177 *portrait;*
> 147, 153*n,* 180, 192, 196; land pur-
> chases of, 77–78, 283*n,* 299; mentioned
> for federal judgeship, 121–22; serves as
> U.S. senator, 156, 176*n;* re-elected to
> U.S. Senate, 366; letters from, 77, 97,
> 192, 283; letters from to John Adams,

Fig. 8.12c Smith, *Jackson,* 1:507

The editors of the *Family Letters of Victor and Meta Berger* indicated pages where individuals were identified by placing those page numbers in bold type:

> Augustyn, Godfrey William, 115, **118n,** 127,
> 187–188. 190. 192n. 407

Fig. 8.12d Stevens, *Berger,* 417

8.13   Editors may include biographical data in their index entries. The editors of *Lafayette in the Age of the American Revolution: Selected Letters and Papers* provided birth and death dates and brief descriptions for important individuals:

> **Arnold, Benedict (1741–1801), American major general, defected to British Sept. 25, 1780, British brigadier general:** American dealings with, 335, 342, 364, 412, 413n, 419, 554; anticipated capture of, 336n, 388; blockade of, 344, 350, 363; British service of, 229; character of, 229, 230n; efforts to prevent escape of, 358, 361, 387, 393, 397, 399, 414; expedition

Fig. 8.13 Idzerda, *Lafayette,* 3:558

Special Problems

8.14   A problem faced by editors preparing the index for an edition that focuses on a single individual or topic is deciding how much information to place under the entry for the principal subject. The editors of the *Papers of John C. Calhoun* did not include an index entry for Calhoun himself, but instead placed information under more specific subject headings. The editors of the *Papers of Ulysses S. Grant* created an entry for Grant but specified that letters written by him would not be indexed there. The editors of the *Papers of Andrew Jackson* provided a thorough entry under Jackson's name, with entries grouped into general subheadings:

> Jackson, Andrew
> *Agent*: for Joseph Anderson, 149, 153, 180; for King, Carson & King, 25; for Anna Moore, 229; for Norton Pryor, 74–75, 296; for war department, 3, 4, 5, 19–20, 25; for Kinchen T. Wilkinson, 269, 299–300
> *Duels and Quarrels*: as issue in presidential campaigns, 104, 172–173; as second, 66–70, 408, 414–15, 416, 419–25; involvement of AJ's friends in, 8–9, 12, 14–15, 89, 90–91, 102,

109, 426; quarrels publicized, 97; with
the Bentons, 408–15, 418–28; with
Nathan Davidson, 25, 28, 30–32,
37–40; with Charles Dickinson, 24,
57, 77–109, 416; with Silas Dinsmoor,
262, 277–79, 295–96, 334–36; with
Andrew Hamilton, 170–72; with Samuel D. Hays, 161; with John C. Hen-
derson, 16; with Samuel D. Jackson,
172–74; with Nathaniel McNairy,
90–91; with William Purnell, 224–25,
253–54, 257–58; with James Sanders,
145–47; with John Sevier, 7–9, 11–
15, 78; with Thomas Swann, 77–
99; with Thomas G. Watkins, 24,
102–103, 106–109
Farms: management of in absence, 354,
362, 370, 372–73, 387, 400, 436,
437, 486, 516; overseers on, 354, 370,

Fig. 8.14a Smith, *Jackson,* 2:620

The editors of the *Adams Family Correspondence* created topical subheadings
under the names of members of the Adams family to make it easier to find
information about them:

ADAMS, JOHN (*continued*)
   FINANCES AND ACCOUNTS
   1:107, 109, 113–14, 117, 119, 123,
286, 383–84, 408; 2:27, 50, 128–29,
144–45, 251, 267, 288, 304–05, 330,
336, 340, 353–54, 375

   HEALTH AND ILLNESSES
inoculated with smallpox, 1:12–47;
2:109; rumor of his being poisoned in
New York, 2:113, 115, 121–22, 124,
128, 132; "My Eyes are somewhat
troublesome," 2:163, 243; "I cannot
pass a Spring, or fall, without an ill
Turn," 2:224; "loaded constantly with
a Cold," 2:238–40, 266; mentioned,
1:75, 107, 134, 158, 173, 195, 207–
08, 213–14, 217, 226, 243, 246, 308,
399, 420; 2:12, 44, 56, 71, 78, 81,
83–84, 94, 103, 108–09, 114, 119,
128–32, 138, 172, 216, 253, 258, 262,
272, 276, 298, 310, 323, 335, 339, 350

   LAND TRANSACTIONS
buys woodland in Braintree from Mrs.
Elihu Adams, 1:415, 418; 2:12

counsel by Col. David Henley, 2:395.
*See also under the names of JA's law
clerks and names of particular cases*

   PUBLIC LIFE
Local, Provincial, and State Politics:
role in impeachment proceedings against
Chief Justice Peter Oliver, 1:97; elected
member of Mass. Council but negatived,
1:108, 124, 193–94; Braintree delegate
to 1st Provincial Congress, 1:181; member of Mass. Council, 1:263–64, 269,
273, 342; appointed chief justice of
Superior Court of Judicature, 1:271–72,
314, 327–28, 333, 342, 351, 405; commissioned justice of peace and quorum
in Suffolk co., 1:314; rivalry with Robert Treat Paine, 1:351; resigns chief
justiceship of Superior Court, 1:406–
07, 417–19; 2:16, 27, 99–100, 113,
139, 159, 164, 185; resigns seat in
Council after complaints about plural
officeholding, 1:421
   Continental Congress: 1774: JA's
election to, 1:109, 129, 136; "I dread
the Thought of the Congress's falling
short of the Expectations of the Con-

Fig. 8.14b Butterfield, *Adams Family,* 2:414

8.15 Editors often must create index entries for people for whom they do not have full names. The editor of the *Pettigrew Papers* listed the single available names in alphabetical order, followed by identifiers in parentheses:

> **Steven (slave), 24**
> **Stevens, Mr., 14**
> **Stewart (tailor), 51**
> **Stickney, Rev. William, 16n**
> **Stone, D., 69; letter from, 97-98**
> **Strange, Robert, 371, 373n**
> **Stubbs (overseer), 126, 130**

Fig. 8.15 Lemmon, *Pettigrew,* 2:629

8.16 The editors of the *Collected Papers of Charles Willson Peale and His Family* created a special system within their index for identifying artwork included in the edition:

> **Portraits or miniatures by CWP are designated by boldface type under the sitter's name; paintings or portraits by other artists are listed by title and under the artist's name. Identification of individuals is designated by italic type. (M) indicates a miniature painting.**

Fig. 8.16 Miller, *Peale,* 1:643

8.17 Indexers may refer readers to maps included in an edition. The editors of the *Papers of General Nathanael Greene* indexed place references on maps in the edition:

> **Ft. Dreadnought, S.C., (Map 2); capture of, xiii, 292 and n, 293 and n, 309, 315–16, 325, 326, 326n, 347n, 436; convoy takes refuge at, 224 and n; stores captured at, 293, 294n, 309, 312, 328n, 335 and n, 341, 347; Lee's Legion and, 310**

Fig. 8.17 Showman, *Greene,* 8:536

Running Heads and Numbered Documents

8.18 Running heads at the top of the pages can help readers locate documents. Editors should consult with book designers to create running heads that will provide maximum assistance to readers. The editors of the *Booker T. Washington Papers* placed the title of the edition in the left-hand (verso) running head and the month and year of the most recent document on that page in the right-hand (recto) running head:

The BOOKER T. WASHINGTON *Papers*

full particulars. I think this trip South opened his eyes to a good many matters.

*   *   *   *

APRIL · 1894

  Mr. Washton I am very glade to say that I am expence time I think as much off one mumit I thought off one dollar   So Mr Washton if

Fig. 8.18a Harlan, Washington, 3:396,397

The editor of the *Journal of Samuel Curwen, Loyalist* printed the place and date of composition in the running heads:

AT SEA   *May–June 1775*   1 5

Ship Diana Daniel Clarke from New York bound to Bristol out since Saturday last who told us a 60 gun ship was arrived there from Boston.

Fig. 8.18b Oliver, Curwen, 15

The *Papers of George Catlett Marshall* placed chapter titles in the verso running head and the inclusive dates of the chapter in the recto running head:

Aide to Pershing

---

other large groups, but it is in the civil institutions that remarkable progress has been made, particularly in winning the sympathetic cooperation of the heads of colleges and their staffs of professors and instructors.
  The Citizen Military Training camps provide a channel to a commission for

*   *   *   *

May 1919–August 1924

---

fatal to the leadership of the latter force. The small number of units at our disposal and the tremendous number of tasks away from troops imposed by our

Fig. 8.18c Bland, Marshall, 1:240,241

The editor of the *Diary of Samuel Sewall* placed the year of the entry in brackets and Sewall's age preceded by ÆT, an abbreviation for the Latin word *ætas* (age), in the running head:

[1687] ÆT. 35   155

> Monday, Dec 12. Col. Mason calls here with Mr. Hutchinson; I stick at his Reservation of Masts 24 Inches Diameter.

Fig. 8.18d Thomas, *Sewall*, 1:155

8.19 Editors may number documents in order to make them easier for readers to locate. The editors of the *Papers of Dwight David Eisenhower* sequentially numbered all documents in each series of their edition:

847   *Eisenhower Mss.*

To Lester Bowles Pearson   *May 30, 1952*

Dear Mr. Minister: I am deeply touched by your letter of May 22nd,[1] which reached me this morning just prior to my relinquishment of the

Fig. 8.19 Chandler, *Eisenhower*, 13:1240

Access to Microform and Electronic Editions

8.20 Like editors publishing book editions, editors of electronic and microform editions use a variety of devices to make their documents as accessible as possible to researchers. Standard indexes may be extremely difficult and expensive to produce for microform editions, so editors of these documentary works often use different means to provide access.

8.21 Editors of microfilm editions take steps early in the project to ensure that they have provided their users with maximum access to the filmed documents. Because microfilm editions do not have pages but are a continuous series of images, editors improve access by numbering rolls of film or pages of fiche and include frame numbers for each image to help readers quickly locate desired items. Unlike book indexes that usually refer readers to specific pages, microform editions use reel and frame numbers as well as targets to mark the location of documents.

8.22 The quantity and genres of documents published by editors of microform editions lead editors to create different types of indexes from those used in book editions, providing readers with different levels of access to the documents. The editors of the *Microfilm Edition of the Papers of Elizabeth Cady Stanton and Susan B. Anthony* described their system of access in the printed guide to their edition:

Introduction to the Index

The index provides access to all three sections of the microfilm by reference to the reel number (in bold) and inclusive frame numbers of documents. Because all but the two reels in series 2 are arranged in chronological order, researchers who want to determine the time period of a document from its index citation may consult the list of dates covered in each reel.

Although not as comprehensive as the index to a book, the index offers more than an item list of documents. Designed to supplement the chronological order of documents on the film, the index uses other points of reference, providing additional ways to identify records on Stanton and Anthony and some access to people, places, and organizations documented in the collection. To help researchers understand uses of the index, this introduction describes the guidelines by which entries were created.

ENTRIES FOR PEOPLE

The index contains names of all people whose correspondence with Stanton or Anthony appears in the edition. The names are arranged alphabetically, using the form that accords with the date of the document. If a woman appears in the index under two or more names, references to other names are provided within each entry. Rarely are pen names used, but for people well known by a pseudonym, references indicate the name selected for the index.

Correspondence with Stanton or Anthony is not indexed at their names but only at the names of senders or recipients. When senders or recipients would or could not be identified, entries appear at "anonymous," "unidentified correspondents," or "unidentified members of ECS [or SBA] family."

Correspondence *between* Stanton and Anthony is entered at both their names, at the entries headed "Anthony, Susan B., and Elizabeth Cady Stanton" and "Stanton, Elizabeth Cady, and Susan B. Anthony."

Letters to editors are indexed at "Editor," followed by the paper's name. If Stanton or Anthony also corresponded with the editor by name, references identify the names.

Entries for people other than Stanton and Anthony are *not inclusive* of their representation or appearance in the edition. If a document contains what a person *wrote*, authorship is noted at their main entry. However, in an effort to simplify a complex index, no entries were made when people spoke at a meeting or on the platform with Stanton or Anthony. Thus at the entry for Matilda Joslyn Gage, for example, no reference is made to her considerable participation in meetings of the National Woman Suffrage Association. If a person was the principal subject of an article, speech, or interview by Stanton or Anthony, a subject entry appears at his or her name.

Despite efforts to confirm the identities of hundreds of correspondents and distinguish among people with similar names, errors no doubt remain. Newspapers proved to be grossly unreliable in their transcriptions of signatures to letters, the *Revolution* most of all. The editors welcome clarification and correction from researchers about the identities of people listed in this index.

For further detail about the construction of entries for individuals, see the guidelines for entries to series 1 and 2.

ENTRIES FOR INSTITUTIONS AND ORGANIZATIONS

Like the names of persons, names of organizations were standardized to the date of the document. Thus the National Woman Suffrage Association (or NWSA) is superseded by the

National-American Woman Suffrage Association (or NAWSA) in January 1890. Organizations appear as correspondents, as sponsors of meetings or events in which Stanton or Anthony participated, and as the groups through or for which documents like appeals or petitions were issued. These distinctions are described in subentries.

National associations are alphabetized by name, but most state and local groups are entered with reference to their location. A few major women's organizations with strong local units, like the Woman's Christian Temperance Union, appear at entries for both the parent organization and the local unit, whether state, county, or town. Entries for colleges and universities appear by name only.

ENTRIES FOR PLACES

Entries refer to nations, states, counties, and towns or cities. At the largest units, cross-references direct readers to counties and towns. These geographical entries serve several purposes.

First, they systematize the hundreds of names of local organizations into a geographical order.

Second, they identify units of government with which Stanton or Anthony interacted, whether by filing deeds to their property or by testifying for woman's rights.

Third, *in series 2 only,* they indicate the point of origin for nearly 2,000 letters written in support of woman suffrage.

Finally, they identify occasions when Stanton and Anthony conducted lectures, interviews, and meetings in each town or city. Their public activities are indexed by town except as follows: meetings of neither state associations nor major national organizations are indexed at the city selected for an annual meeting; interviews given in Rochester, New York; Tenafly, New Jersey; Washington, DC; or New York City appear at the city name *only* if the interview treats local events.

Fig. 8.22a Holland, *Stanton–Anthony,* 71–75

The editor of the microform edition of the *Papers of Eugene V. Debs* created an index that had headings for names, organizations, and some geographic areas:

Description of Index to Correspondence in Series I

This index includes every item of correspondence found in Series I. Letters have been indexed by the name of the correspondent, with the exception of Eugene and Theodore Debs; under their own names only the brothers' letters to each other have been listed. Letters have been cross-listed under the names of organizations in cases where the correspondence is on behalf of an organization. Unsigned letters whose authors could not be identified are indexed under the entry "Unidentified Correspondents."

The index to Series I also contains geographical entries. Letters have been cross-listed by state, only if the place of origin is indicated on the original document. The cities of New York and Chicago and all foreign countries have been given separate entries. The very large number of letters originating from Terre Haute, Indiana and Atlanta Federal Penitentiary (during Debs' second imprisonment) have been excluded from the geographical listings. Researchers should be aware that the geographical entries, while useful, are by no means complete, since many letters do not indicate the place of origin.

In the index entry for each correspondent incoming and outgoing letters are grouped separately, and listed chronologically by year, month, and day. Entries for undated letters—indicated by the abbreviation "n.d."—follow the chronological entries. All undated letters will be found at the end of Series I, on Reel 5, and are arranged alphabetically by non-Debs correspondent. Figures in parentheses in index entries indicate the number of items of that correspondent that can be found under a given date.

Researchers should note that enclosures have been filed *and indexed* under the date of their covering letter.

Fig. 8.22b Constantine, *Debs: Guide,* 50

The printed guide to the *Thomas A. Edison Papers: A Selective Microfilm Edition* provided researchers with an index to authors and recipients by name and date:

INDEX TO AUTHORS AND RECIPIENTS

ABEL (C.C.) & CO

    from Charles Batchelor

        03/27/77   28: 600

ABRAHAM BROS

    to Thomas Alva Edison

        08/29/78   18: 456

ADAMS, Ellen (Mrs James)

    to Thomas Alva Edison

        09/11/78   17: 425

Fig. 8.22c Jeffrey, *Edison,* 1:35

The *Edison* edition also provided a separate index, listing date, reel, and frame number, for technical notes and drawings:

CHRONOLOGICAL INDEX TO TECHNICAL NOTES AND DRAWINGS

1867	6: 767	01/18/72	3: 58
07/23/70	5: 131	01/20/72	3: 25
09/00/70	6: 64	01/27/72	3: 60
10/03/70	6: 809	01/29/72	3: 60
10/10/70	6: 808	01/30/72	3: 27
12/02/70	5: 120	01/30/72	3: 63
12/02/70	5: 217	01/30/72	3: 93

Fig. 8.22d Jeffrey, *Edison,* 1:123

The *Edison* edition provided a third index for financial documents:

Index to Financial Documents

	ACCOUNTS (cont'd)		
	1878	19:	381
	1878	19:	450
	1878	20:	5
	1878	20:	62
	1878	20:	102
	1878	22:	549
	1878	22:	706
	1879	16:	584
	1879	20:	102
	1880	20:	102
BILLS AND RECEIPTS			
	1869	12:	33
	1870	12:	44

Fig. 8.22e Jeffrey, *Edison,* 1:136

The printed guide to the microfilm edition of the *Jane Addams Papers* provided a modified archival container list, with corresponding reel numbers:

MICROFILM EDITION

	Reel Number(s)
CORRESPONDENCE	
n.d., 1868 May–1935 May	1–26, Addendum 1A
DOCUMENTS	
I. PERSONAL DOCUMENTS, 1873–1935	27–28, Addendum 1A
A. CHILDHOOD JOTTINGS, n.d., 1873–1876	27
B. EDUCATIONAL RECORDS AND PAPERS, 1870–1883	27
1. Cedarville, IL, School, 1870–1877	27
2. Rockford Female Seminary, IL, 1877–1882	27, Addendum 1A
3. Woman's Medical College of	
Pennsylvania, Philadelphia, 1881–1882	27
C. LEGAL RECORDS, 1883–1935	27
1. Birth Deposition, 1919	27
2. Passports and Travel Documents, 1883–1929	27
3. Real Estate Documents, 1883–1919	27

Fig. 8.22f Bryan, *Addams,* 25

The editors of the *Emma Goldman Papers: A Microfilm Edition* included six different indexes on the first reel providing access to different series—(1) drafts, publications, and speeches (*not shown*); (2) newspaper and periodical articles (*not shown*); (3) government documents by title (*not shown*); (4) government documents by subject (*top*); (5) correspondence by personal name (*not shown*); and (6) government documents by personal name (*bottom*):

The Emma Goldman Papers
Government Documents Series
Index by Subject

Subject Date	Reel
Abrams-Steimer Case	
1918 Oct. 22	62
1918 Oct. 25	62
1919 Oct. 3	63
1919 Oct. 6	63
[1919 Nov. 13]	64
1921 Nov. 16	65
ACLU—History	
[193-?]	66
Addams, Jane	
1920 April 17	65
Addresses	
1919 Dec. 21	64
[1921 Dec.]	65
[1922 March? 17?]	65

The Emma Goldman Papers
Government Documents Series
Index by Name

Correspondent Date	Reel
Abbot, Edith, et al.	
* 1934 April 5	66
* 1934 April 5	66
* [1934 April 5]	66
* [1934 April 5]	66

Abbott, Leonard D.
* 1918 June 14   61
* 1918 Dec. 27   62
* 1919 March 18   62
* 1919 July 26   62

Fig. 8.22g Falk, *Goldman*, reel 1:395,514

8.23   Unlike most book-edition indexes that refer readers to particular pages, or microfilm-edition indexes that refer readers to particular frames, electronic indexes often link the reader to codes embedded in the text, or they search for specific dates, words, or word combinations. Electronic databases can often undertake complex searches, locating documents using combinations of characteristics such as date, genre, author, recipient, and subject, and can even provide the viewer with a facsimile of the desired document that can be printed or dispatched over the Internet. As electronic editions become more common, editors will develop methods of electronic indexing that emulate book indexes in their ability to direct readers to thematic passages that might elude a keyword search. The fluid nature of an electronic edition may also provide new possibilities for readers, enabling them to search for topics that the original author or indexer never envisioned. (See also Section 7.20.)

Chapter Nine

Front and Back Matter

Front Matter

9.1   Although the documents form the heart of any edition, front matter serves an important function, offering editors an opportunity to explain the value of the project and the decisions made in producing the edition, to acknowledge those people and organizations whose skills and financial support made the edition possible, and to provide tools that will make the edition accessible to its readers. The front matter of book editions contains a number of stylistic elements not required by electronic or microform editions, some created to aid cataloging by librarians, others part of publishing tradition. Similar items in microform editions accomplish some of the same ends but appear either at the beginning of the film or in printed guides. Regardless of its form of publication, the style and substance of an edition's front matter require careful attention because it sets the tone for a work and often determines how useful an edition will be. (Many devices that serve as annotation, including calendars, item lists, lists of abbreviations, and family-history charts, can appear in an edition's front matter. These are dealt with in Chapter 7.)

Half-Title Page

9.2   The half-title page at the front of book editions is a stylistic convention retained from the era when books lacked covers and the half-title page kept the unbound book's full title page pristine. Half-title pages generally include only the title of the book, without subtitles. For example, consider the half-title page of *Writing Out My Heart: Selections from the Diary of Francis E. Willard:*

Writing Out My Heart

Fig. 9.2a Gifford, *Willard,* 3

Half-title pages from multiple-volume series can include information about the particular volume, as with the half-title page from the *Diary of Charles Francis Adams*, which contains the title of the project, the name of the project's editor in chief, the title of the series, and the title of the volume:

The Adams Papers

RICHARD ALAN RYERSON, EDITOR IN CHIEF

SERIES I

DIARIES

Diary of Charles Francis Adams

Fig. 9.2b Donald, *Adams,* 8:1

Frontispiece

9.3   Editors of book editions may include a frontispiece—that is, a photograph or illustration facing the title page of the edition.

Title Page

9.4   The title page of an edition should contain the full title of the work, its subtitle, the names of the editors, the full name and location of the publishing house, and, if relevant, the name or number of the edition, volume, and/or series. The date of publication is optional. For example, consider the title page of the *Papers of Henry Laurens:*

The Papers of

Henry Laurens

Volume One: Sept. 11, 1746—Oct. 31, 1755

———◆———

Philip M. Hamer, Editor

George C. Rogers, Jr., Associate Editor

Maude E. Lyles, Editorial Assistant

Published for the South Carolina Historical Society by the

UNIVERSITY OF SOUTH CAROLINA PRESS
COLUMBIA, S.C.

Fig. 9.4a Hamer, *Laurens,* 1:iii

The microfilm edition of the *Papers of General Friedrich Wilhelm von Steuben* included a complete title page:

THE PAPERS OF GENERAL FRIEDRICH WILHELM VON STEUBEN 1777-1794

Edited by Edith von Zemenszky
Robert J. Schulmann, Associate Editor

© 1982 by Edith von Zemenszky

Permission to copy any manuscripts included on this film must be obtained from the institution named on the header for each document.

Published By
KRAUS INTERNATIONAL PUBLICATIONS
A Division of Kraus-Thomson Organization Limited
Millwood, New York   London, England   Nendeln, Liechtenstein

1982

Fig. 9.4b von Zemenszky, *von Steuben*, reel 1

Copyright Notice

9.5 The edition's copyright notice, publishing history, ISBN number, CIP data, and publication support all generally appear on the reverse of the title page (the copyright page), as shown in this example from *Religious Philanthropy and Colonial Slavery: The American Correspondence of the Associates of Dr. Bray:*

Publication of this work was supported in part by a grant from the National Historical Publications and Records Commission.

© 1985 by the Board of Trustees of the University of Illinois
Manufactured in the United States of America
C 5 4 3 2 1

This book is printed on acid-free paper.

LIBRARY OF CONGRESS CATALOGING IN PUBLICATION DATA

Main entry under title:

Religious philanthropy and colonial slavery.

Includes bibliographical references and index.
1. Missions to Afro-Americans—History—18th century—Sources. 2. Afro-Americans—Education—History—18th century—Sources. I. Van Horne, John C. II. Associates of Dr. Bray (Organization)
BV2783.R45 1985 266 .023'41008996073 84-2766
ISBN 0-252-01142-2 (alk. paper)

Fig. 9.5a Van Horne, *Dr. Bray,* vi

The editors of the *Letters from the Front* also included on their copyright page a statement explaining how permission to reproduce passages from the edition could be obtained:

Copyright © 1992 by
THE STATE HISTORICAL SOCIETY OF WISCONSIN
***All rights reserved.* Permission to quote from or reproduce any portion of this copyrighted work may be sought from the publisher at 816 State Street, Madison, Wisconsin 53706.**

Fig. 9.5b Stevens, *Letters,* ii

The copyright and publication information for the microform edition of the *Victor L. Berger Papers* appeared at the beginning of the edition's first reel of film and in its published guide:

Publisher's Note

Distributed on microfilm by:
Scholarly Resources Inc.
104 Greenhill Avenue
Wilmington, DE 19805-1897

Distributed outside the USA

in Japan by:
Far Eastern Booksellers
P.O. Box 72
Kanda, Tokyo 101-91, JAPAN

in Taiwan by:
Transmission Books & Microforms Company, Ltd.
P.O. Box 96-337
Taipei, TAIWAN, R.O.C.

Location of original materials:
The originals of this collection are located at the State Historical Society of Wisconsin in Madison and the Milwaukee County Historical Society.

Reproduction rights:
The access, use, and dissemination of these private documents are controlled by the State Historical Society of Wisconsin and the Milwaukee County Historical Society, with the consent of the Berger family. The microfilm may not be duplicated without written permission from Scholarly Resources Inc.

Citation:
Researchers citing this microfilm edition should use the following format:

Victor L. Berger Papers, Reel [No.], Frame [No.]. (Madison: State Historical Society of Wisconsin, 1995).

Fig. 9.5c Stevens, *Berger Papers*, iv

Dedications and Epigraphs

9.6   A dedication can be placed on the recto page following the copyright and publication information, or it may appear on the copyright page. The dedication in *Mary Dodge Woodward: The Checkered Years* consisted of a centered note in capital letters on a full recto page:

DEDICATED TO THE MEMORY OF

MY MOTHER

NELLIE WOODWARD BOYNTON

Fig. 9.6 Cowdrey, *Checkered*, 5

9.7   Editors may include a pertinent phrase or passage in their front matter as an epigraph. For example, the editors of *By Force of Arms: The Journals of Don Diego de Vargas* used the quotation from which the title of the volume was drawn:

> Uprisings against his royal superiority set bad examples for those barbarous nations who do not understand it, but must be made to see it. Thus, they must be made to understand by force of arms. Your excellency will see fit to leave the way this is done to such valiant captains as serve under your superior order.

————Dr. don Benito de Noboa Salgado, fiscal

Fig. 9.7 Kessell, *Force*, 2

Acknowledgments

9.8   Editors should include a list of the patrons, sponsors, organizations, and major contributors that funded their work. Placement of the list can vary, with common locations including the copyright page, the reverse of the half-title page, and a full recto page. The editors of the *Correspondence of James K. Polk* acknowledge their principal sponsors both on the recto page facing the volume's copyright and publication information and in the acknowledgments:

Sponsored by

Vanderbilt University

The National Historical Publications Commission

The Tennessee Historical Commission

Fig. 9.8 Weaver, *Polk*, 1:v

9.9   Editions often provide listings of their advisory boards, as in this example from the *Papers of Andrew Jackson*:

Advisory Board

Robert V. Remini, Chairman

Walter Armstrong, Jr.	John Mallette
Edward J. Boling	Carol Orr
Mrs. Cawthon Bowen, Jr.	Frank L. Owsley, Jr.
Donald B. Cole	Mrs. James H. Reed III
John W. Cooke	Mrs. Fred Russell
Katheryn C. Culbertson	Mrs. Allen Steele
David Herbert Donald	Mrs. Robert W. Sturdivant
LeRoy P. Graf	Henry Lee Swint
Mrs. Harry A.J. Joyce	Eugene Upshaw
Mrs. Walter M. Morgan, Jr.	William Waller

Ann Harwell Wells

Fig. 9.9 Smith, *Jackson*, 2:v

9.10 Editors may list their editorial staff on the title page, in the acknowledgments, or separately within the front matter, as did the editors of the *Emma Goldman Papers: A Microfilm Edition:*

The Emma Goldman Papers Project

Professional Editors

Candace Falk, Ph.D	Ronald J. Zboray, Ph.D	Daniel Cornford, Ph.D
Editor and Director	*Microfilm Editor*	*Associate Editor*

Administration and Production

Sally Thomas	Ellen Ratcliffe	Jennifer Collins
Administrative Analyst	*Production Coordinator*	*Administrative Assistant*

Editors

Alice Hall	Jennifer Smith	Kurt Thompson

Editorial Assistants

Susan Grayzel	Marilynn Johnson	Sherry Katz
Joanne Newman	Julia Rechter	Rachel Rivera
Maxine Snow		Jessica Weiss

Research Associates

Sarah Crome	Robby Cohen	Barbara Loomis
	Dennis McEnnerney	

Document Search Coordinators

Brenda Butler		Karen Hansen

Research Assistants and Translators

Howard Besser	Khojesta Beverleigh	Sigrid Brauner
Leif Brown	June Brummer	Yvette Chalom
Roger Cook	Erik Ellner	Simonetta Falasca-Zamponi
Karl Fields	Salvador Garcia	Jeffrey Garrett
Rose Glickman	John Guo	Catherine Houndshell
Andrew Heinz	Rebecca Hyman	Gerd Horton
Yoshi Igarashi	Titch Jones	Susan Kahn
Vivian Kleiman	Liu Zi-Zian	Rae Lisker
Delfina Marcello	Caroline Massee	Nancy Mackay
Mary Odem	Sheila O'Neil	Caroline Pincus
Elizabeth Reis	Paola Sesia-Lewis	Daniel Soyer
Betsy Station	Jenny Terry	Lars Tragardh
	Marcia Yonemoto	

International Staff

Henrik Berggren	Furio Biagini	Maria Jose Del Rio
Paul Durden	Wolfgang Haug	Miguel Flamarich I Tarrasa
Kazuko Ohta	Barry Pateman	Susumu Yamaizumi
	Lu Zhe	

Fig. 9.10 Falk, *Goldman,* reel 2

9.11 Acknowledgments allow editors to thank the people and institutions that made the edition possible, including sponsoring institutions, archives and manuscript repositories, financial contributors, reference librarians, archivists, and the project's editorial staff. The editors of the *Selected Papers of Charles Willson Peale and His Family* produced an acknowledgment statement that concisely recognized the diverse forms of assistance the editors had received:

This edition of the selected papers of the Peale Family has been sponsored by the National Portrait Gallery of the Smithsonian Institution, with financial assistance from the National Endowment for the Humanities and the Andrew W. Mellon Foundation. We are very grateful to all these organizations for their generous support and encouragement. At the Smithsonian Institution, we especially wish to thank S. Dillon Ripley, secretary, for his interested efforts in our behalf. Jeffrey Stann, Joseph Shealy, and Robert Falconi were of great assistance in helping to raise funds, write contracts, and administer the finances of the project. The staff of the National Portrait Gallery has been most helpful and supportive. We wish especially to acknowledge the assistance of Marvin Sadik, former director; Douglas Evelyn, former deputy director; William Walker, former librarian; Eugene Mantie, senior photographer; Mona Dearborn, keeper of the Catalog of American Portraits; Robert Stewart, curator; Ellen G. Miles, associate curator; and Suzanne Jenkins, registrar.

We are grateful to the members of the editorial advisory board of the Peale Family Papers, whose names appear at the head of this volume, for their encouragement and assistance. We owe a particular debt to the late Dr. Charles Coleman Sellers, to whom we frequently turned for help at all stages of our project. His wit, intelligence, and large fund of knowledge were a source of delight and illumination. We shall sorely miss him, for the project as a whole, as well as this particular volume, profited much from his enthusiastic interest.

We are very grateful to the staffs of all the institutions listed under Location Symbols for their assistance in our research and their generosity in allowing us to publish their documents. Special mention should be made of the staff of the library of the American Philosophical Society—Dr. Whitfield J. Bell, executive officer; Murphy Smith, associate librarian; Carl F. Miller, assistant librarian; and Stephen Catlett, manuscript librarian—whose cheerfulness never wavered under the barrage of our demands. The staff of the Library Company of Philadelphia, particularly Gordon M. Marshall; the staff of the manuscript division of the Historical Society of Pennsylvania—Peter Parker, Linda Stanley, and Lucy Hrivnak; the archivist of the state of Maryland, Edward C. Papenfuse; and the staffs of the Peale Museum in Baltimore, the Maryland Historical Society, the Maryland Hall of Records, the National Portrait Gallery/National Museum of American Art Library, and the Library of Congress all responded generously to our requests for information.

We are pleased to acknowledge the generous assistance of the staff of the National Historical Publications and Records Commission—Frank Burke, director, and Mary Giunta, Sara Jackson, Richard Sheldon, Fred Shelley, and George Vogt—who provided more than moral support for our efforts by searching assiduously in their various archives for relevant materials and by providing us with the year's services of a fellow, Dr. Jeffrey L. Meikle, now of the University of Texas at Austin. Dr. Meikle's contributions to this volume were intelligent and dedicated, and this volume profited from his assistance.

The Peale Family Papers staff is particularly fortunate in having as its administrative assistant Rose S. Emerick, who has been indispensable in all aspects of work on the project; we are glad to be able to acknowledge here our gratitude for her innumerable services.

To the director and staff of the Yale University Press we are happy to express our appreciation of their fine efforts on our behalf; we are particularly grateful to Edward Tripp for his enthusiastic support, to Judy Metro and Charlotte Dihoff for skillfully seeing this volume through the press, and to Floyd Tomkins for his editorial help.

To all these institutions and individuals, and to the many who assisted in smaller but equally important ways, we extend our thanks and deep appreciation.

Fig. 9.11 Miller, *Peale*, 1:xxiii–xxiv

Tables of Contents

9.12 Editors have used different formats for tables of contents and have included varying amounts of detail. All tables of contents list the principal parts of the book, such as sections of the front matter and the index, but they differ on how much detail to provide about the location of the documents in the text. Some editions, such as the *Salmon P. Chase Papers*, note only the page on which the documents begin:

Contents

Fig. 9.12a Niven, *Chase,* 2:vii

The table of contents in the *Papers of George Catlett Marshall* directed readers to chronologically grouped chapters:

Contents

Fig. 9.12b Bland, *Marshall,* 1:vii

The table of contents of the *Political Correspondence and Public Papers of Aaron Burr* listed every document, arranged chronologically, and the page on which it began:

CONTENTS

Fig. 9.12c Kline, *Burr,* 1:v

Editors may direct readers both to chapters and to individual documents, a practice adopted by the editors of the *Papers of Thomas A. Edison*. The table of contents in the *Papers of Woodrow Wilson* served both its traditional role and also as an index; it listed the front matter and provided an additional list of correspondents, with page numbers indicating where the documents were located:

CONTENTS

Fig. 9.12d Link, *Wilson*, 23:ix

Illustrations

9.13 Editors usually provide, in front or back matter, a list of illustrations for a project, as did the *Expeditions of John Charles Frémont*:

ILLUSTRATIONS

Fig. 9.13a Jackson, *Frémont*, 1:xv

Some editors include commentary on the illustrations, such as in the listing produced by the editors of the *Papers of James Madison:*

ILLUSTRATIONS

JAMES MADISON   FRONTISPIECE

Oil portrait by Joseph Wood on paper pasted to a small wooden panel. It was painted in March 1817 and was presented by the Madisons to Mrs. Richard Bland Lee. She commented: "The likeness of your dear Husband almost breath[e]s. and expresses much of the serenity of his feelings at the moment it was taken. in short, it is, *himself.*" (Courtesy of the estate of John W. Davidge, Washington, D.C.)

AUTOBIOGRAPHICAL SKETCH   132

The first page of a three-page sketch written by Madison in 1816 for use in Joseph Delaplaine's *Repository of the Lives and Portraits of Distinguished American Characters.* (Courtesy of the Princeton University Library.)

Fig. 9.13b Hutchinson, *Madison*, 1:xiii

A concise way to lead readers to illustrations without using the space of a full listing is to provide a reference at the bottom of the table of contents, as did the *Letters of William Cullen Bryant:*

Illustrations   **between pages 232 and 233**

Fig. 9.13c Bryant, *Bryant*, 4:v

Forewords, Prefaces, and Introductions

9.14   A foreword precedes the preface of an edition and is generally a short statement written and signed by someone other than the author or editor. For example, the editors of the *Naval War of 1812: A Documentary History* included a preface written by a retired U.S. Navy officer. The first volume of the *Papers of John C. Calhoun* contains a foreword eulogizing the editor of the volume, who died before it appeared in print.

9.15 Editors may include a preface, which is generally a short statement describing the origins of the project. For example, see Warren M. Billings, ed., *Papers of Francis Howard, Baron Howard of Effingham* (Richmond: Virginia State Library and Archives, 1989), pp. xxi–xxii.

9.16 Introductions contain significant information necessary to use the volume effectively. Within this rubric, editors have used the introductions to editions in different ways. For example, the introduction to the first volume of the *Papers of Benjamin Franklin* includes sections on the history of the Franklin papers, their publication history, and Franklin's literary legacy, as well as separate sections on the edition's principles of selection, arrangement, presentation, transcription, and editorial practices. In the introduction to the first volume of the *Papers of General Nathanael Greene*, the editors describe earlier failed attempts to publish Greene's papers, the project's goals, difficulties in documenting Greene's early years, and a list of recommended reference works. The edition's criteria for selection, presentation, arrangement, and transcription appear in a separate section on editorial methods. Each volume also contains a historical introduction to the period covered. The first volume of *Documentary History of the Ratification of the Constitution* contains an introduction to the series that explains the scope and difficulties of the project. Each volume also includes a historical introduction. An introduction can be an all-encompassing piece providing background and technical information for a volume, or just one of several specialized front sections helping an edition's audience to understand the volume's contents.

Statement of Editorial Method

9.17 The editorial-methods statement for a book should be a distinct section within the front matter. For an article or pamphlet, this statement should be set off from the text of the document. An editorial-methods statement should address the major decisions made by the editors about the conception, selection, transcription, annotation, arrangement, and presentation of an edition. After consulting an editorial-methods statement, readers should be confident that they will know what portions of an original document's text were literally reproduced, altered by the editor, symbolically represented, or eliminated, and which parts of the text were supplied by the editor. Editors will need to gauge the audience's degree of interest in the editorial methods and adjust the amount of detail provided accordingly.

9.18 The length and style of editorial-methods statements will vary considerably among editions, reflecting the degree of detail the audience demands, the extent of editorial intervention in the documents, and editors' preferences. The space constraints of periodicals demand brevity, as with this footnoted editorial statement for "A Mississippian at Yale in 1849: Two Letters of H. Winbourne Drake":

> ¹The letters, in the custody of the editor, are part of a collection of family letters and papers covering the period from the 1820s to the 1890s. As transcribed here, the original spelling and capitalization have been retained. Expansions of abbreviations and conjectural completions are included in brackets.

Fig. 9.18a Drake, *Mississippi History*, 43(4):310

Because their editorial intervention was relatively limited in volumes published after 1980, the editors of the *Documentary History of the Ratification of the Constitution* required only a brief statement to describe their editorial policy:

Editorial Procedures

With a few exceptions all documents are transcribed literally. Obvious slips of the pen and errors in typesetting are silently corrected. When spelling or capitalization is unclear, modern usage is followed. Superscripts and interlineated material are lowered to the line. Crossed-out words are retained when significant.

Brackets are used for editorial insertions. Conjectural readings are enclosed in brackets with a question mark. Illegible and missing words are indicated by dashes enclosed in brackets. However, when the author's intent is obvious, illegible or missing material, up to five characters in length, has been silently provided.

All headings are supplied by the editors. Headings for letters contain the names of the writer and the recipient and the place and date of writing. Headings for newspapers contain the pseudonym, if any, and the name and date of the newspaper. Headings for broadsides and pamphlets contain the pseudonym and a shortened form of the title. Full titles of broadsides and pamphlets and information on authorship are given in editorial notes. Headings for public meetings contain the place and date of the meeting.

Salutations, closings of letters, addresses, endorsements, and docketings are deleted unless they provide important information, which is then either retained in the document or placed in editorial notes.

Contemporary footnotes and marginal notes are printed after the text of the document and immediately preceding editorial footnotes. Symbols, such as stars, asterisks, and daggers have been replaced by superscripts (a), (b), (c), etc.

Many documents, particularly letters, are excerpted when they contain material that is not directly relevant to ratification. When longer excerpts or entire documents have been printed elsewhere, or are included in the microfiche supplements, this fact is noted.

Fig. 9.18b Jensen, *Ratification*, 18:16

The editors of the *Colonial Records of North Carolina: Second Series* developed an editorial method statement that efficiently outlined the procedures used to present the edition's documents:

EDITORIAL METHOD

The method employed in transcribing documents for this volume is based on rules for the "expanded method" in Frank Freidel (ed.), *Harvard Guide to American History* (Cambridge: Belknap Press of Harvard University Press, Revised Edition, 2 volumes, 1975), I, 30-31. Most abbreviations and contractions have been expanded. Those retained include all proper names, dates, titles, and abbreviations in use at the present time. If more than one expanded form fitted the context, abbreviations were retained as written. In those few instances in which it was impossible to distinguish among abbreviations, contractions, or misspellings on the part of the contemporary scribe, no expansion has been made where the literal meaning is clear. Superior letters have been brought down to the line of text.

Spelling in the manuscript has been followed, with the exception of expansions, substitution of *th* for the symbol (resembling a *y*) indicating the archaic letter *thorn*, and substitution of modern usage with respect to *i* and *j*, and *u* and *v*, which sometimes were used interchangeably in the documents. Interpolation of *sic* has been restricted primarily to indicating words and phrases omitted in the manuscript. A few obvious slips of the pen, such as the repetition of words, have been silently corrected.

Capitalization in the manuscript has been followed, with some exceptions. Each heading, paragraph, or notation is begun with a capital letter regardless of its form in the manuscript. A capital letter likewise follows a period ending a sentence or other passage. If a proper name is not capitalized in the manuscript, it is not capitalized in this volume unless it meets one of the above conditions.

Very limited modification has been made in *punctuation*. Periods follow entries that require them as well as all retained abbreviations. Commas separate names in lists changed from vertical to horizontal form. In a few cases the editor has deleted extremely erratic punctuation, such as colons or dashes after every few words.

Square brackets enclose material supplied editorially. Inferred readings of missing and partially missing passages are printed in roman type, as are words and passages found in minutes other than those selected for the text copy. Other supplied material is in italics, including the source reference for each document and such interpolations as *torn*, *illegible*, and *blank*. Words and phrases underlined in the original are also italicized.

Boldface type is used for the title and date preceding the text of each paper.

Angle brackets enclose material that occurs in the manuscript but has been transferred to a different position on the printed page. Such items chiefly include marginal notations; they are in italic type, except that roman type is used for manuscript page numbers.

Footnotes in the documentary text have been used chiefly to indicate significant variations between the text copy of minutes and other versions, to identify papers referred to in the minutes, and to provide information about dates assigned certain documents.

The documents are divided into two sections, the first consisting of minutes and the second of papers. Each section is arranged chronologically within the volume. In several instances closely related papers have been grouped together for clarity under the date of the first document. Where no date is given in the manuscript, an approximate date, based on internal evidence, has in most instances been supplied and is enclosed within square brackets.

Fig. 9.18c Parker, *North Carolina*, 9:lxx

Projects addressing many different types of documents produced over a long period of time may require more extensive statements of method. The editors of the *Papers of Woodrow Wilson* produced a statement marked by its thoroughness and thoughtful consideration of the choices and obstacles they faced:

EDITORIAL OBJECTIVES AND METHODS

The editors hope to publish a comprehensive edition that will include all important letters, articles, speeches, interviews, and public papers by Woodrow Wilson. These volumes, when complete, should make available to readers all the materials essential to understanding Wilson's personality, his intellectual, religious, and political development, and his careers as educator, writer, orator, and statesman. The editors also hope that these volumes will be useful to scholars and others in various fields of history between the 1870's and the 1920's.

It would perhaps be ideal if the editors could set as their goal publication of every document by or relating to Wilson. They have concluded for a number of reasons that this goal is neither feasible nor desirable. There is first the fact of the huge bulk of documentary materials now available. Most of Wilson's career fell in the period when the typewriter was in general use. This technological advance combined with a rapid increase in population and governmental activities to cause a much larger volume of letters and documents to pour into the White House during Wilson's time than earlier. The editors estimate that they have photocopied about 250,000 documents, totaling considerably more than 500,000 pages. Clearly, it is not feasible to think of publishing all these documents, not even all documents by Wilson. Furthermore, it is doubtful that they would want to print all documents by Wilson even if it was possible to do so. For example, it would hardly advance the cause of scholarship to include in this series all of Wilson's perfunctory replies and form letters to well-wishers and patronage-seekers. Letters of this type will be represented by samples.

More specifically, the editors intend:

1. To publish all letters by Wilson that are essential to understanding his thought and activity. These, they think, have the highest priority. This first volume includes all of Wilson's letters thus far discovered for the period that it covers. Selection of letters for future volumes will obviously depend upon their quality and significance. The editors, when necessary, will also publish incoming letters or extracts from or digests of such letters, particularly when they provide the only indications concerning Wilson's missing replies or furnish the only information about events in Wilson's life. The first two or three volumes, which cover a hitherto sparsely documented period, will include a substantial proportion of incoming letters.

2. To print a selection of Wilson's speeches. Public speaking was for Woodrow Wilson a very important form of communication, and the editors will not neglect it. But Wilson made hundreds of speeches during his lifetime, and publication of all of them would consume disproportionate space. It seems advisable, therefore, to publish in full only the most important speeches, and to edit others by eliminating inordinate repetition.

3. To print as much as seems wise of a wide variety of Wilson manuscripts. Diaries will be published in full, but only samples of Wilson's voluminous classroom and lecture notes will be included. Additional items, such as commonplace books, memoranda, lists, accounts, records of organizations in which Wilson participated, and marginal notes in books, will be printed in whole or in part depending upon importance. However, the editors will describe the contents of all important Wilson documents (e.g., scrapbooks, notebooks, and copybooks) that they do not print in full.

4. To publish all of Wilson's important articles, because the journals in which they appeared are in many cases unavailable even in good libraries.

5. To publish from among Wilson's books only *Congressional Government* and *Constitutional Government in the United States*, on the ground that they are so central in the development of his political thought that they cannot be omitted from a comprehensive edition of his papers.

6. To publish all items in as strict chronological order as possible. The editors believe such arrangement necessary because of the intimate relationship between letters, speeches, and other writings. Documents are presented in chronological order. Enclosures are printed with the letter in which they were enclosed. Attachments appear in chronological order.

These, then, are the general objectives that the editors have in view for *The Papers of Woodrow Wilson*. They would add a further word about the specific task of clarifying and annotating documents. The editors have concluded that it is not possible for them to do all the things that a biographer and historian would ordinarily do. They conceive their most important task to be the presentation of a reliable Wilson text. In addition, they believe that this text must be accompanied by as much editorial treatment as is necessary to make it meaningful in its context. Hence they will employ the following editorial practices:

(a) Each document will be given a descriptive heading. Titles, headings, and so on that are part of the document will be printed in the type used for documentary text.

(b) Each document will be dated, either exactly or approximately.

(c) Each document will be briefly described physically and its location given. It will be apparent from these descriptive-location notes whether the document is being printed from a manuscript or from a printed source.

(d) That the reader may be assured that he is seeing the document as it stands, each document, whether manuscript or printed, will be reproduced *exactly* as it appears in the original, with the exceptions noted hereafter. The editorial *sic* will be reduced to the minimum and used only in cases where absolutely necessary for clarity. Completion of words and alterations of punctuation marks, including the use of single and double quotation marks, will likewise be resorted to (enclosed in square brackets) only for the sake of clarity. The only silent alterations employed will be in letters, where, for the sake of clarity, periods in salutations will be changed to commas, periods will be substituted for dashes when the dashes would ordinarily be read as periods, and superior letters will be lowered to the regular line.

(e) Each document will be annotated when this is necessary for identification of individuals and events. The editors, when possible, will briefly identify casual friends, subjects, and events. They will provide longer biographical notes for subjects whose relationships with Wilson stretched over a number of years and were important to him. The main purpose of these notes is to signal to the reader the importance of that relationship. It is not their function to provide full biographies of persons or definitive accounts of events involved. Fortunately, in most cases the documents speak for themselves about the character and significance of these relationships. Well-known historical personages and literary figures, as well as writings and events, will not ordinarily be identified. Except in unusual cases, the editors will not cite the standard biographical and other references used for information or attempt to provide extensive bibliographical data. They will also leave genealogical tables to biographers.

(f) Editorial notes will be supplied when the briefer and more specific footnotes would not sufficiently indicate the importance of the subject to Wilson or the context of the document.

. (g) When similar documents are grouped under a single editorial heading, such as "Two Letters from . . ." or "Three Items from . . ." there will be only one descriptive-location note. This will come after the last document in the group, and will describe all the preceding documents equally. In this case such an abbreviation as ALS will indicate a plural. But if this note does not apply identically to all the documents included under the common editorial heading, then each document so included, whose descriptive-location note differs in any respect from the final note, will carry its own descriptive-location note. This innovation is adopted by the editors in the hope that, without sacrificing accuracy, space will be saved in eliminating unnecessary repetitions of headings and notes.

(h) In order to distinguish between references to incoming letters that are printed and to those that are not included, references to letters or documents that are not printed in whole or in part will include full descriptive and location abbreviations such as ALS (WP, DLC). The abbreviations will be omitted if the item referred to appears in the series.

In all cases the editors have sought original documents for photocopying. Fortunately, the existence of the central core of the Wilson Papers and the recovery of thousands of original Wilson letters have greatly simplified the editors' task. Wherever originals have been lost and other copies are available, the copy deemed to be most similar to the original will be used. Wherever possible, photocopies have been checked against the originals by the editors, with special care being taken to indicate significant characteristics of the document.

The editors established at the outset master files consisting of control cards for every item, describing documents according to order and source of acquisition, chronology, sender and recipient, and, in the case of speeches, according to date and location.

Fig. 9.18d Link, *Wilson,* 1:xiv–xvii

9.19 Editors of multivolume editions sometimes change their editorial methods in response to new standards or practices in the field of documentary editing, to accommodate new finds in their collections, to revise their principles of selection, or to respond to changing financial conditions. The editors of the *Papers of Benjamin Franklin* announced a change in their selection policy in a special note to the reader (see Section 2.2). In volume 10 of the *Papers of Henry Laurens,* the editors announced both new selection criteria and a new method of transcription:

> This volume marks the beginning of a new format for *The Papers of Henry Laurens.* The most significant change is the selectivity which has been exercised. The earlier volumes included almost every known Laurens document; the current volume includes only 49 percent of the known documents. A second change is the rendering of the text. In previous volumes, the text was partially modernized. In this volume, the text is rendered as close to the original as possible.

Principles of Selection

The decision to adopt a selective policy is one which has long been anticipated by the editors. The repetitive nature of HL's public correspondence coupled with the rising costs of the edition dictated the shift to selective printing. At the same time, the editors' concern to make all of the documents readily accessible led to a collateral decision that comprehensiveness would be achieved through a fully indexed microform supplement to be issued after the printed edition has been completed.

Documents printed in this volume were selected on the basis of two principles. First those selected must have an intrinsic value. Second they must be representative of the whole. The first principle could be restated as simply "letting the documents speak for themselves." As Arthur Link has often remarked, documents seem to have a "will" of their own. The documents in this period reflect HL's role in organizing the revolutionary forces in South Carolina, his disagreements with the more radical patriots, his hopes for a mediated settlement with Britain, his candid views of the actions of both American and British leadership, and his personal concerns for his family and business interests. This selection gives the fullest documentation of those themes possible within the confines of this volume. The second principle of selection, to present a representative group, is not meant in a statistical sense. Rather, an effort has been made to achieve a selection which provides a sense of the breadth and the depth of the documents. To further this goal, many of the documents which are not printed were employed in the annotation.

Revision in Textual Principles

The shift to a more literal rendering of the text is the result of a change in textual principles. The textual policies adopted in 1965 were patterned after those developed by Julian P. Boyd and Samuel Eliot Morison. In the first nine volumes, a number of silent changes were made in the text of the documents. Punctuation was regularized, long blocks of text were broken into paragraphs, capitalization was supplied at the beginning of sentences, and certain abbreviations and contractions were expanded. As a rule, those changes created little difficulty for historians and others whose primary focus was on the content of the documents.

In the thirty-odd years since the first volume of Boyd's *Jefferson* appeared in 1950, a new school of textual criticism has emerged in the United States which demands a closer textual fidelity that will allow volumes of historical documents to be of greater service to those who study authorial conventions. In response to these scholars, the editors have adopted a new set of textual guidelines. These principles can be summarized succinctly. The text contains no silent editorial changes. Editorial changes which affect all documents are discussed in the paragraphs below; changes which apply to particular documents are reported in textual notes. The object of the new textual policy is to enhance the utility of this and future volumes for an audience which includes scholars from many disciplines.

Selection of Text for Publication

When multiple copies of a document are available, the editors have chosen that copy which is closest to the author as the basis for the published text in this edition. For example, a letter signed by the author carries more authority than a letterbook copy created by a clerk. Less obvious is the choice between a letterbook copy and a contemporary copy based on the recipient's copy of the original letter. In those instances where multiple texts are available, the texts are collated and an appropriate publication text has been chosen. The basis of that decision is reported in the textual annotation.

From Holographs to Print

The conversion of hand-written manuscripts into typescript or print inevitably alters certain characteristics of those manuscripts. The reader of a transcribed document cannot see a hasty scrawl or the ill-formed letters of an author who is suffering from illness. Textual notes are used to alert the reader to such characteristics. Other variations between documents and the transcriptions thereof are created by editorial decisions to use typographical conventions which include justifying the right margin as well as the left, adopting standards for indenting paragraphs and extracts, and adopting rules for vertical spacing. The document format and the conventions used in presenting the documents in this volume are listed below.

Document Format

The title of each document appears as the first line of a document. The title is in capital letters, printed in italics, and is flush with the left margin. The title of each document is supplied by the editors.

The place-date line appears as the second line of a document. Printed in roman type and in upper and lowercase letters, the place-date line is flush with the right margin. The place-date line is supplied by the editors.

If the original document has a salutation, the salutation follows the place-date line and is flush with the left margin. If the document does not have a salutation, none is supplied.

Paragraphing follows the original document. A standard indention of three ems of space is used for indented paragraphs; block paragraphs are indicated by the use of six points of vertical space.

Extracts or block quotations within the body of a document are indented three ems of space from both the left and right margins of the document.

The complimentary close of a document is printed on one or two lines depending upon its length. The signature of a document is printed on a separate line following the complimentary close.

Postscripts are printed as running text after the complimentary close or the signature as the case may be.

Lists which appear in the manuscripts will be printed as lists.

The source note for each document is printed at the end of the document. The source note contains a description of the document type, its location, the address of the document, the date of the document, endorsements and/or dockets found on the document, with comments on any special characteristics encountered in the document including the placement of the address and the date.

Textual Conventions

Capitalization, spelling, punctuation, abbreviations, and contractions are normally retained. If a word is unclear because of spelling, a note is supplied.

Dashes used as commas or periods are printed as one en dashes at the baseline of the text and are followed by normal word spacing.

Superscripts are printed as superscripts.

Special characters like the English pound sign, the per sign, etc. will be reproduced when available; substitutions are noted.

Words underlined in manuscript documents are underlined in the edition.

Text in the body of the document is set with justified left and right margins.

Textual Devices

The following devices have been used to clarify the text of the manuscripts or to represent the orthography of the writers.

[roman][1]	Text supplied from another source identified in footnotes or text set apart when editorial clarification is required.
[*italic*]	Editorial insertion.
↑text↓	Interlineations above the line in text.
↓text↑	Interlineations below the line in text.
~~text~~	Cancelled text which has been recovered.
~~illegible~~	_Cancelled text which has not been recovered.
☛	Weight symbol used for pound or pounds.
℔	Per symbol.
þ	Thorn.
~	Flourish at end of word is writer's form of abbreviation and indicates omission of characters.
–	Bar over character in word is writer's form of abbreviation and indicates omission of one or more characters.
/	Indicates line break (used only in source notes).

Fig. 9.19 Hamer, *Laurens*, 10:xxiii–xxvii

Errata, Addenda, and Appendices

9.20 Because mistakes will inevitably appear in all editions and because documents may be discovered too late for inclusion in a particular volume, editors may have to include an addenda and errata section. Because of the precision expected of documentary editions and the rarity of revised editions, it is important to correct errors that would be ignored or left to the new editions of many other types of scholarly publications. Errata may be placed on a sheet inserted into a one-volume edition or provided in a separate section in subsequent volumes of a multivolume edition. The fourth volume of the *Booker T. Washington Papers* included an errata section that identified a few minor factual errors in earlier volumes:

ERRATA

VOLUME 2, p. 262, John Massey died in 1918, not 1911.

VOLUME 2, p. 351, the Afro-American Cotton Mill Company should be the Afro-Alabama Cotton Mill Company.

VOLUME 3, p. 162, Reverend Pitt Dillingham was the brother, not the father, of Mabel Wilhelmina Dillingham.

VOLUME 3, p. 243, Livingstone College is an A.M.E. Zion school, not an A.M.E. school.

VOLUME 3, illus. 7, following p. 290, should be Daniel Alexander Payne, not Daniel Augustus Payne.

Fig. 9.20 Harlan, *Washington*, 4:xxv

9.21   At the end of a series or edition, editors commonly include additional in-scope documents discovered after the section where they should have been placed was completed.

9.22   Editors may include appendices of materials that are out of the edition's scope but may be interesting or useful for readers. Appendices generally contain documents written by authors who were not within the scope of the edition, important documents believed to be written by the subject of the edition whose authorship cannot be confirmed, documents that might be difficult to read or classify, or editorial apparatus such as biographical dictionaries, glossaries, or tables. For example, the editor of *A Plantation Mistress on the Eve of the Civil War: The Diary of Keziah Goodwyn Hopkins Brevard* included two appendices following the text of the diary: one contains Brevard's will, the other an inventory of her estate. An appendix included in series 1, volume 1 of the *Frederick Douglass Papers* included speeches delivered by persons other than Douglass referring to him or in his honor. The appendices to volume 2 of the *Papers of Thomas A. Edison* included excerpts from Edison's autobiographical writings, a reminiscence produced by one of Edison's co-workers, documents summarizing a patent dispute, and a list of Edison's patents obtained during the time span of the volume.

Bibliography and Short Titles

The following is a list of all works from which we have drawn examples in this volume. Each bibliographic entry is preceded by the short title we have used in citing facsimiles. On the page where it appears, each facsimile is followed by a short title, a volume or microfilm reel number when relevant, and a page or microfilm frame number. The example drawn from the World Wide Web is followed by a URL.

Abbot, *Washington: Colonial*
Abbot, W. W., et al., eds. *The Papers of George Washington.* Colonial Series. 10 vols. Charlottesville: Univ. Press of Virginia, 1983–1995.

Anderson, *Kerler*
Anderson, Harry H., ed. *German-American Pioneers in Wisconsin and Michigan: The Frank Kerler Letters, 1849–1864.* Milwaukee: Milwaukee County Historical Society, 1971.

Arndt, *Harmony*
Arndt, Karl J. R., ed. *A Documentary History of the Indiana Decade of the Harmony Society, 1814–1824.* 2 vols. Indianapolis: Indiana Historical Society, 1975–1978.

Barbour, *Smith*
Barbour, Philip L., ed. *The Complete Works of Captain John Smith (1580–1631).* 3 vols. Chapel Hill: Univ. of North Carolina Press, 1986.

Berlin, *Free*
Berlin, Ira, et al., eds. *Free at Last: A Documentary History of Slavery, Freedom, and the Civil War.* New York: The New Press, 1992.

Berlin, *Freedom*
Berlin, Ira, et al., eds. *Freedom: A Documentary History of Emancipation, 1861–1867.* 3 vols. to date. Cambridge: Cambridge Univ. Press, 1982–.

Berlin, *Nurse*
Berlin, Jean V., ed. *A Confederate Nurse: The Diary of Ada W. Bacot, 1860–1863.* Columbia: Univ. of South Carolina Press, 1994.

Bland, *Marshall*
Bland, Larry I., and Sharon R. Ritenour, eds. *The Papers of George Catlett Marshall.* 3 vols. to date. Baltimore: Johns Hopkins Univ. Press, 1981–.

Bland, *Marshall: Interviews*
Bland, Larry I., and Joellen K. Bland, eds. *George C. Marshall: Interviews and Reminiscences for Forrest C. Pogue.* Lexington, Va.: George C. Marshall Research Foundation, 1991.

Blassingame, *Douglass*
Blassingame, John W., et al., eds. *The Frederick Douglass Papers.* 5 vols. to date. New Haven, Conn.: Yale Univ. Press, 1979–.

Boehm, *AFL Records*
Boehm, Randolph, and Martin Schipper, eds. *American Federation of Labor Records: The Samuel Gompers Era, Part II: President's Office Files, Series A: William Green Papers, 1934–1952 (Guide).* Frederick, Md.: University Publications of America, Inc., 1986.

Boyd, *Jefferson*
Boyd, Julian P., et al., eds. *The Papers of Thomas Jefferson.* 26 vols. to date. Princeton, N.J.: Princeton Univ. Press, 1950–.

Branch, *Twain*
Branch, Edgar Marquess, et al., eds. *Mark Twain's Letters.* 4 vols. to date. Berkeley and Los Angeles: Univ. of California Press, 1987–.

Broderick, *Thoreau*
Broderick, John C., et al., eds. *Henry D. Thoreau: Journal.* 4 vols. to date. Princeton, N.J.: Princeton Univ. Press, 1981–.

Brugger, *Madison: State*
Brugger, Robert J., et al., eds. *Papers of James Madison.* Secretary of State Series. 3 vols. to date. Charlottesville: Univ. Press of Virginia, 1986–.

Bryan, *Addams*
Bryan, Mary Lynn McCree, ed. *The Jane Addams Papers.* Ann Arbor, Mich.: University Microfilms International, 1985.

Bryant, *Bryant*
Bryant, William Cullen II, and Thomas G. Voss, eds. *The Letters of William Cullen Bryant.* 6 vols. New York: Fordham Univ. Press, 1975–1992.

Burr, *Secret Eye*
Burr, Virginia Ingraham, ed. *The Secret Eye: The Journal of Ella Gertrude Clanton Thomas, 1848–1889.* Chapel Hill: Univ. of North Carolina Press, 1990.

Butterfield, *Abigail and John*
Butterfield, L. H., Marc Friedlaender, and Mary-Jo Kline, eds. *The Book of Abigail and John: Selected Letters of the Adams Family, 1762–1784.* Cambridge, Mass.: Harvard Univ. Press, 1975.

Butterfield, *Adams Family*
Butterfield, L. H., et al., eds. *Adams Family Correspondence.* 6 vols. to date. Cambridge, Mass.: Belknap Press of Harvard Univ. Press, 1963–.

Butterfield, *Diary*
Butterfield, L. H., Leonard C. Faber, and Wendell D. Garrett, eds. *Diary and Autobiography of John Adams.* 4 vols. Cambridge, Mass.: Belknap Press of Harvard Univ. Press, 1961.

Carson, *King*
Carson, Clayborne, et al., eds. *The Papers of Martin Luther King, Jr.* 2 vols. to date. Berkeley and Los Angeles: Univ. of California Press, 1992–.

Carter, *Territorial Papers*
Carter, Clarence Edwin, et al., eds. *The Territorial Papers of the United States.* 28 vols. Washington: Government Printing Office, 1934–1976.

Chandler, *Eisenhower*
Chandler, Alfred D., Jr., et al., eds. *The Papers of Dwight David Eisenhower.* 13 vols. to date. Baltimore: Johns Hopkins Univ. Press, 1970–.

Chase, *Washington: Revolutionary*
Chase, Philander D., and Frank E. Grizzard, Jr., eds. *The Papers of George Washington.* Revolutionary War Series. 7 vols. to date. Charlottesville: Univ. Press of Virginia, 1985–.

Cole, *Witness*
Cole, Donald B., and John J. McDonough, eds. *Benjamin Brown French: Witness to the Young Republic, A Yankee's Journal, 1828–1870.* Hanover, N.H.: Univ. Press of New England, 1989.

Constantine, *Debs*
Constantine, J. Robert, ed. *Letters of Eugene V. Debs.* 3 vols. Urbana: Univ. of Illinois Press, 1990.

Constantine, *Debs: Guide*
Constantine, J. Robert, ed. *Papers of Eugene V. Debs, 1834–1945: A Guide to the Microfilm Edition.* Glen Rock, N.J.: Microfilming Corp. of America, 1983.

Constantine, *Papers of Debs*
Constantine, J. Robert, ed. *Papers of Eugene V. Debs, 1834–1945.* Glen Rock, N.J.: Microfilming Corp. of America, 1983.

Cowdrey, *Checkered*
Cowdrey, Mary Boynton, ed. *The Checkered Years.* Caldwell, Idaho: The Caxton Printers, Ltd., 1937.

Crane, *Drinker*
Crane, Elaine Forman, et al., eds. *The Diary of Elizabeth Drinker.* 3 vols. Boston: Northeastern Univ. Press, 1991.

Crane, *Drinker: Life Cycle*
Crane, Elaine Forman, ed. *The Diary of Elizabeth Drinker: The Life Cycle of an Eighteenth-Century Woman.* Boston: Northeastern Univ. Press, 1994.

Cunningham, *Circular Letters*
Cunningham, Noble E., Jr., and Dorothy Hagberg Cappel, eds. *Circular Letters of Congressmen to Their Constituents, 1789–1829.* 3 vols. Chapel Hill: Univ. of North Carolina Press, 1978.

De Pauw, *Congress*
De Pauw, Linda Grant, et al., eds. *Documentary History of the First Federal Congress of the United States of America, March 4, 1789–March 3, 1791.* 14 vols. to date. Baltimore: Johns Hopkins Univ. Press, 1972–.

Donald, *Adams*
Donald, Aida DiPace, et al., eds. *Diary of Charles Francis Adams.* 8 vols. Cambridge, Mass.: Belknap Press of Harvard Univ. Press, 1964–1985.

Drake, *Mississippi History*
Drake, W. Magruder. "A Mississippian at Yale in 1849: Two Letters of H. Winbourne Drake." *Journal of Mississippi History* 43(1981):310–314.

Dudley, *1812*
Dudley, William S., and Michael J. Crawford, eds. *The Naval War of 1812: A Documentary History.* 2 vols. to date. Washington: Department of the Navy, 1985–.

Dunn, *Penn*
Dunn, Mary Maples, et al., eds. *The Papers of William Penn.* 5 vols. Philadelphia: Univ. of Pennsylvania Press, 1981–1986.

Ely, *Jackson*
Ely, James W., Jr., and Theodore Brown, Jr., eds. *Legal Papers of Andrew Jackson.* Knoxville: Univ. of Tennessee Press, 1987.

Falk, *Goldman*
Falk, Candace, et al., eds. *The Emma Goldman Papers: A Microfilm Edition.* Alexandria, Va.: Chadwyck-Healey, 1990.

Farrand, *Convention*
Farrand, Max, ed. *The Records of the Federal Convention of 1787.* 4 vols. 1937. Reprint, New Haven, Conn.: Yale Univ. Press, 1966.

Ferguson, *Morris*
Ferguson, E. James, et al., eds. *The Papers of Robert Morris.* 8 vols. to date. Pittsburgh: Univ. of Pittsburgh Press, 1973–.

Ford, *Jefferson*
Ford, Paul Leicester, ed. *The Works of Thomas Jefferson.* 12 vols. New York: G. P. Putnam's Sons, 1904–1905.

Franklin, *Writings*
Franklin, Benjamin (notes by J. A. Leo Lemay). *Writings.* New York: Library of America, 1987.

Gettleman, *Hopkins*
Gettleman, Marvin E., et al., eds. *The Johns Hopkins University Seminary of History and Politics: The Records of an American Educational Institution, 1877–1912.* 5 vols. New York: Garland, 1987–1990.

Gifford, *Willard*
Gifford, Carolyn De Swarte, ed. *Writing Out My Heart: Selections from the Diary of Francis E. Willard, 1855–96.* Urbana: Univ. of Illinois Press, 1995.

Glennon, *Foreign Relations*
Glennon, John P., et al., eds. *Foreign Relations of the United States, 1961–1963.* 24 vols. Washington: Government Printing Office, 1988.

Goldman, WWW
Emma Goldman Papers Homepage. *http://www.sunsite.berkeley.edu/Goldman*

Graf, *Johnson*
Graf, LeRoy P., et al., eds. *The Papers of Andrew Johnson.* 13 vols. to date. Knoxville: Univ. of Tennessee Press, 1967–.

Hamer, *Laurens*
Hamer, Philip M., et al., eds. *The Papers of Henry Laurens.* 14 vols. to date. Columbia: Univ. of South Carolina Press, 1968–.

Harlan, *Washington*
Harlan, Louis R., et al., eds. *The Booker T. Washington Papers.* 14 vols. Urbana: Univ. of Illinois Press, 1972–1989.

Harrison, *Jefferson*
Harrison, Maureen, and Steve Gilbert, eds. *Thomas Jefferson, Word for Word.* La Jolla, Calif.: Excellent Books, 1993.

Herr, *Frémont*
Herr, Pamela, and Mary Lee Spence, eds. *The Letters of Jessie Benton Frémont.* Urbana: Univ. of Illinois Press, 1993.

Herwig, *Carpenter*
Herwig, Miriam, and Wes Herwig, eds. *Jonathan Carpenter's Journal: Being the Diary of a Revolutionary War Soldier and Pioneer of Vermont.* Randolph Center, Vt.: Greenhill Books, 1994.

Hill, *Garvey*
Hill, Robert A., et al., eds. *The Marcus Garvey and Universal Negro Improvement Association Papers.* 7 vols. to date. Berkeley and Los Angeles: Univ. of California Press, 1983–.

Hobbs, *Dear General*
Hobbs, Joseph Patrick, ed. *Dear General: Eisenhower's Wartime Letters to Marshall.*
Baltimore: Johns Hopkins Univ. Press, 1971.

Holland, *Stanton–Anthony*
Holland, Patricia G., and Ann D. Gordon, eds. *The Papers of Elizabeth Cady Stanton and Susan B. Anthony: Guide and Index to the Microfilm Edition.* Wilmington, Del.: Scholarly Resources, Inc., 1992.

Hutchinson, *Madison*
Hutchinson, William T., et al., eds. *The Papers of James Madison.* 17 vols. Chicago: Univ. of Chicago Press (vols. 1–10) and Charlottesville: Univ. Press of Virginia (vols. 11–17), 1962–1991.

Idzerda, *Lafayette*
Idzerda, Stanley J., et al., eds. *Lafayette in the Age of the American Revolution: Selected Letters and Papers, 1776–1790.* 5 vols. Ithaca, N.Y.: Cornell Univ. Press, 1977–1983.

Jackson, *Frémont*
Jackson, Donald, and Mary Lee Spence, eds. *The Expeditions of John Charles Frémont.* 3 vols. Urbana: Univ. of Illinois Press, 1970–1984.

Jackson, *Washington*
Jackson, Donald, and Dorothy Twohig, eds. *The Diaries of George Washington.* 6 vols. Charlottesville: Univ. Press of Virginia, 1976–1979.

James, *WTUL*
James, Edward T., Robin Miller Jacoby, and Nancy Schrom Dye, eds. *Papers of the Women's Trade Union League and Its Principal Leaders: Guide to the Microfilm Edition.* Woodbridge, Conn.: Research Publications, Inc., 1981.

Jeffrey, *Edison*
Jeffrey, Thomas E., et al., eds. *A Guide to the Thomas A. Edison Papers: A Selective Microfilm Edition.* 3 vols. to date. Frederick, Md.: University Publications of America, 1985–.

Jenkins, *Edison*
Jenkins, Reese V., et al., eds. *The Papers of Thomas A. Edison.* 3 vols. to date. Baltimore: Johns Hopkins Univ. Press, 1989–.

Jensen, *Elections*
Jensen, Merrill, et al., eds. *The Documentary History of the First Federal Elections, 1788–1790.* 4 vols. Madison: Univ. of Wisconsin Press, 1976–1989.

Jensen, *Ratification*
Jensen, Merrill, et al., eds. *The Documentary History of the Ratification of the Constitution.* 13 vols. to date. Madison: State Historical Society of Wisconsin, 1976–.

Johnson, *Marshall*
Johnson, Herbert A., et al., eds. *The Papers of John Marshall.* 8 vols. to date. Chapel Hill: Univ. of North Carolina Press, 1974–.

Johnston, *Vance*
Johnston, Frontis W., and Joe A. Mobley, eds. *The Papers of Zebulon Baird Vance.* 2 vols. to date. Raleigh, N.C.: State Department of Archives and History, 1963–.

Kaminski, *Necessary Evil*
Kaminski, John P., ed. *A Necessary Evil?: Slavery and the Debate Over the Constitution.* Madison, Wis.: Madison House, 1995.

Kaufman, *Gompers*
Kaufman, Stuart B., et al., eds. *The Samuel Gompers Papers.* 4 vols. to date. Urbana: Univ. of Illinois Press, 1986–.

Kessell, *Force*
Kessell, John L., et al., eds. *By Force of Arms: The Journals of don Diego de Vargas, New Mexico, 1691–93.* Albuquerque: Univ. of New Mexico Press, 1992.

King, *Gregg*
King, Pauline, ed. *The Diaries of David Lawrence Gregg: An American Diplomat in Hawaii, 1853–1858.* Honolulu: Hawaiian Historical Society, 1982.

Kline, *Burr*
Kline, Mary-Jo, et al., eds. *Political Correspondence and Public Papers of Aaron Burr.* Princeton, N.J.: Princeton Univ. Press, 1983.

Koelling, *Nebraska*
Koelling, Jill Marie, ed. "A Thousand Mile Motor Trip through Western Nebraska, 1916." *Nebraska History* 78(1) (Spring 1997):22–27.

Konefsky, *Webster: Legal*
Konefsky, Alfred S., and Andrew J. King, eds. *The Papers of Daniel Webster.* Legal Papers. 3 vols. Hanover, N.H.: Univ. Press of New England, 1982–1989.

Labaree, *Franklin*
Labaree, Leonard W., et al., eds. *The Papers of Benjamin Franklin.* 32 vols. to date. New Haven, Conn.: Yale Univ. Press, 1959–.

LaFantasie, *Williams*
LaFantasie, Glenn W., ed. *The Correspondence of Roger Williams.* 2 vols. Hanover, N.H.: Univ. Press of New England, 1988.

Lasser, *Friends*
Lasser, Carol, and Marlene Deahl Merrill, eds. *Friends and Sisters: Letters between Lucy Stone and Antoinette Brown Blackwell, 1846–1893.* Urbana: Univ. of Illinois Press, 1987.

Lemay, *Franklin: Genetic Text*
Lemay, J. A. Leo, and P. M. Zall, eds. *The Autobiography of Benjamin Franklin: A Genetic Text.* Knoxville: Univ. of Tennessee Press, 1979.

Lemmon, *Pettigrew*
Lemmon, Sarah McCulloh, ed. *The Pettigrew Papers.* 2 vols. Raleigh, N.C.: State Department of Archives and History, 1971–1988.

Levenson, *Adams*
Levenson, J. C., et al., eds. *The Letters of Henry Adams.* 6 vols. Cambridge, Mass.: Belknap Press of Harvard Univ. Press, 1982–1988.

Limbaugh, *Muir*
Limbaugh, Ronald H., and Kirsten E. Lewis, eds. *The Guide and Index to the Microform Edition of the John Muir Papers, 1858–1957.* Alexandria, Va.: Chadwyck-Healey Inc., 1986.

Lincoln, *Speeches and Writings*
Lincoln, Abraham (notes by Don E. Fehrenbacher). *Speeches and Writings, 1832–1858.* New York: Library of America, 1989.

Link, *Wilson*
Link, Arthur S., et al., eds. *The Papers of Woodrow Wilson.* 69 vols. Princeton, N.J.: Princeton Univ. Press, 1966–1994.

LOC, *Harrison*
Library of Congress. *Benjamin Harrison Papers*. Washington: Library of Congress, 1964.

Marcus, *Supreme Court*
Marcus, Maeva, et al., eds. *The Documentary History of the Supreme Court of the United States, 1789–1800*. 5 vols. to date. New York: Columbia Univ. Press, 1985–.

Massachusetts Historical Society, *Knox*
Massachusetts Historical Society. *Index to the Henry Knox Papers*. Vol. 56. Boston: Massachusetts Historical Society, 1960.

McCausland, *Ballard*
McCausland, Robert B., and Cynthia MacAlman McCausland, eds. *The Diary of Martha Ballard, 1785–1812*. Camden, Maine: Picton Press, 1992.

McLaughlin, *Olmsted*
McLaughlin, Charles Capen, et al., eds. *The Papers of Frederick Law Olmsted*. 6 vols. to date Baltimore: Johns Hopkins Univ. Press, 1977–.

McLoughlin, *Backus*
McLoughlin, William G., ed. *The Diary of Isaac Backus*. Providence, R.I.: Brown Univ. Press, 1979.

Meltzer, *Child*
Meltzer, Milton, Patricia G. Holland, and Francine Krasno, eds. *Lydia Maria Child, Selected Letters, 1817–1880*. Amherst: Univ. of Massachusetts Press, 1982.

Meriwether, *Calhoun*
Meriwether, Robert L., et al., eds. *The Papers of John C. Calhoun*. 23 vols. to date. Columbia: Univ. of South Carolina Press, 1959–.

Mevers, *Bartlett*
Mevers, Frank C., ed. *The Papers of Josiah Bartlett*. Hanover, N.H.: Univ. Press of New England, 1979.

Miller, *Dear Master*
Miller, Randall M., ed. *"Dear Master": Letters of a Slave Family*. Ithaca, N.Y.: Cornell Univ. Press, 1978.

Miller, *Peale*
Miller, Lillian B., et al., eds. *The Collected Papers of Charles Willson Peale and His Family*. 3 vols. to date. New Haven, Conn.: Yale Univ. Press, 1983–.

Monroe, *Davis*
Monroe, Haskell M., Jr., et al., eds. *The Papers of Jefferson Davis*. 9 vols. to date. Baton Rouge: Louisiana State Univ. Press, 1971–.

Moore, *Plantation Mistress*
Moore, John Hammond, ed. *A Plantation Mistress on the Eve of the Civil War: The Diary of Keziah Goodwyn Hopkins Brevard, 1860–1861*. Columbia: Univ. of South Carolina Press, 1993.

Morris, *Jay*
Morris, Richard B., et al., eds. *John Jay*. 2 vols. to date. New York: Harper and Row, 1975–.

Moser, *Jackson*
Moser, Harold D., et al., eds. *The Papers of Andrew Jackson: Guide and Index to the Microfilm Editions*. Wilmington, Del.: Scholarly Resources, Inc., 1987.

Moulton, *Lewis and Clark*
Moulton, Gary E., ed. *The Journals of the Lewis and Clark Expedition*. 8 vols. Lincoln: Univ. of Nebraska Press, 1983–1993.

Moulton, *Ross*
Moulton, Gary E., ed. *The Papers of Chief John Ross.* 2 vols. Norman: Univ. of Oklahoma Press, 1985.

Myers, *Children*
Myers, Robert Manson, ed. *The Children of Pride: Selected Letters of the Family of Reverend Dr. Charles Colcock Jones from the Years 1860–1868, with the Addition of Several Previously Unpublished Letters.* New Haven, Conn.: Yale Univ. Press, 1984.

Nash, *Augusta*
Nash, Charles E. *The History of Augusta.* Augusta, Maine: Charles E. Nash and Son, 1961.

Nelson, *Koren*
Nelson, David T., ed. *The Diary of Elizabeth Koren, 1853–1855.* 1955. Reprint, New York: Arno Press, 1979.

Niven, *Chase*
Niven, John, et al., eds. *The Salmon P. Chase Papers.* 3 vols. to date. Kent, Ohio: Kent State Univ. Press, 1993–.

Oliver, *Curwen*
Oliver, Andrew, ed. *The Journal of Samuel Curwen, Loyalist.* Cambridge, Mass.: Harvard Univ. Press, 1972.

Olson, *Voyageur*
Olson, Kris Beisser, ed. "The Great Fire of 1871: A Nation Responds." *Voyageur* 13(1997):10–17.

Palmer, *Sumner*
Palmer, Beverly Wilson, ed. *The Selected Letters of Charles Sumner.* 2 vols. Boston: Northeastern Univ. Press, 1990.

Parker, *North Carolina*
Parker, Mattie Erma Edwards, et al., eds. *Colonial Records of North Carolina: Second Series.* Raleigh: North Carolina Tercentenary Commission and North Carolina Department of Cultural Resources, Division of Archives and History, 1963–.

Patrick, *Indiana*
Patrick, Jeffrey L. "On Convoy Duty in World War I: The Diary of Hoosier Guy Connor." *Indiana Magazine of History* 89(1993):335–352.

Prince, *Livingston*
Prince, Carl E., et al., eds. *The Papers of William Livingston.* 5 vols. Trenton: New Jersey Historical Commission, 1979–1988.

Reingold, *Henry*
Reingold, Nathan, et al., eds. *The Papers of Joseph Henry.* 6 vols. to date. Washington: Smithsonian Institution Press, 1972–.

Ripley, *Black Abolitionist*
Ripley, C. Peter, et al., eds. *The Black Abolitionist Papers.* 5 vols. Chapel Hill: Univ. of North Carolina Press, 1985–1992.

Rock County, *Recorder*
Rock County Historical Society (Wisconsin). "Dear Rock County." *The Recorder* (April 1997):10.

Rogers, *Florida*
Rogers, William Warren, Jr., ed. " 'As to the People': Thomas and Laura Randall's Observations on the Life and Labor in Early Middle Florida." *Florida Historical Quarterly* 75, no. 4 (Spring 1997):441–446.

Rothberg, *Jameson*
Rothberg, Morey, and Jacqueline Goggin, eds. *John Franklin Jameson and the Development of Humanistic Scholarship in America.* 1 vol. to date. Athens: Univ. of Georgia Press, 1993–.

Rutland, *Mason*
Rutland, Robert A., ed. *The Papers of George Mason, 1725–1792.* 3 vols. Chapel Hill: Univ. of North Carolina Press, 1970.

Shewmaker, *Webster: Diplomatic*
Shewmaker, Kenneth E., et al., eds. *The Papers of Daniel Webster.* Diplomatic Papers. 2 vols. Hanover, N.H.: Univ. Press of New England, 1983–1987.

Showman, *Greene*
Showman, Richard K., et al., eds. *The Papers of General Nathanael Greene.* 8 vols. to date. Chapel Hill: Univ. of North Carolina Press, 1976–. •

Simon, *Grant*
Simon, John Y., et al., eds. *The Papers of Ulysses S. Grant.* 20 vols. to date. Carbondale: Southern Illinois Univ. Press, 1967–.

Smith, *Delegates*
Smith, Paul H., et al., eds. *Letters of Delegates to Congress, 1774–1789.* 23 vols. to date. Washington: Library of Congress, 1976–.

Smith, *Jackson*
Smith, Sam B., et al., eds. *The Papers of Andrew Jackson.* 5 vols. to date. Knoxville: Univ. of Tennessee Press, 1980–.

Sokal, *Cattell*
Sokal, Michael M., ed. *An Education in Psychology: James McKeen Cattell's Journal and Letters from Germany and England, 1880–1888.* Cambridge, Mass.: MIT Press, 1981.

Stachel, *Einstein*
Stachel, John, et al., eds. *The Collected Papers of Albert Einstein.* 6 vols to date. Princeton, N.J.: Princeton Univ. Press, 1987–.

Steel, *Jones*
Steel, Edward M., ed. *The Correspondence of Mother Jones.* Pittsburgh: Univ. of Pittsburgh Press, 1985.

Stevens, *Berger*
Stevens, Michael E., and Ellen D. Goldlust-Gingrich, eds. *The Family Letters of Victor and Meta Berger, 1894–1929.* Madison: State Historical Society of Wisconsin, 1995.

Stevens, *Berger Papers*
Stevens, Michael E., and Myrna T. Williamson, eds. *Guide to the Microfilm Edition of the Victor L. Berger Papers.* Wilmington, Del.: Scholarly Resources, Inc., 1995.

Stevens, *House: 1791*
Stevens, Michael E., and Christine M. Allen, eds. *Journals of the House of Representatives, 1791.* The State Records of South Carolina. Columbia: Univ. of South Carolina Press, 1985.

Stevens, *House: 1792–1794*
Stevens, Michael E., ed. *Journals of the House of Representatives, 1792–1794.* The State Records of South Carolina. Columbia: Univ. of South Carolina Press, 1988.

Stevens, *Letters*
Stevens, Michael E., Sean P. Adams, and Ellen D. Goldlust, eds. *Letters from the Front, 1898–1945.* Madison: State Historical Society of Wisconsin, 1992.

Stevens, *Voices*
Stevens, Michael E., et al., eds. *Voices from Vietnam.* Madison: State Historical Society of Wisconsin, 1996.

Stevens, *Women*
Stevens, Michael E., and Ellen D. Goldlust, eds. *Women Remember the War, 1941–1945.* Madison: State Historical Society of Wisconsin, 1993.

Syrett, *Hamilton*
Syrett, Harold C., et al., eds. *The Papers of Alexander Hamilton.* 27 vols. New York: Columbia Univ. Press, 1961–1987.

Taylor, *Adams*
Taylor, Robert J., et al., eds. *Papers of John Adams.* 10 vols. to date. Cambridge, Mass.: Belknap Press of Harvard Univ. Press, 1977–.

Thomas, *Sewall*
Thomas, M. Halsey, ed. *The Diary of Samuel Sewall, 1674–1729.* 2 vols. New York: Farrar, Straus & Giroux, 1973.

Twohig, *Washington: Presidential*
Twohig, Dorothy G., et al., eds. *The Papers of George Washington.* Presidential Series. 6 vols. to date. Charlottesville: Univ. Press of Virginia, 1987–.

Urofsky, *Brandeis*
Urofsky, Melvin I., and David W. Levy, eds. *"Half Brother, Half Son": The Letters of Louis D. Brandeis to Felix Frankfurter.* Norman: Univ. of Oklahoma Press, 1991.

Van Horne, *Dr. Bray*
Van Horne, John C., ed. *Religious Philanthropy and Colonial Slavery: The American Correspondence of the Associates of Dr. Bray, 1717–1777.* Urbana: Univ. of Illinois Press, 1985.

Van Horne, *Latrobe*
Van Horne, John C., et al., eds. *The Correspondence and Miscellaneous Papers of Benjamin Henry Latrobe.* 3 vols. New Haven, Conn.: Yale Univ. Press, 1984–1988.

von Zemenszky, *von Steuben*
von Zemenszky, Edith, and Robert J. Schulmann, eds. *The Papers of General Friedrich Wilhelm von Steuben, 1777–1794.* Millwood, N.Y.: Kraus International Publications, 1982.

Weaver, *Polk*
Weaver, Herbert, et al., eds. *Correspondence of James K. Polk.* 8 vols. to date. Nashville: Vanderbilt Univ. Press, 1969–.

Wiltse, *Webster: Correspondence*
Wiltse, Charles M., and Harold D. Moser, eds. *The Papers of Daniel Webster.* Correspondence. 7 vols. Hanover, N.H.: Univ. Press of New England, 1974–1986.

Wright, *Irving*
Wright, Nathalia, ed. *The Complete Works of Washington Irving: Journals and Notebooks.* 5 vols. Madison: Univ. of Wisconsin Press, 1969–1986.

Wroth, *Adams*
Wroth, L. Kinvin, and Hiller B. Zobel, eds. *Legal Papers of John Adams.* 3 vols. Cambridge, Mass.: Belknap Press of Harvard Univ. Press, 1965.

Permissions

Figures 1.7, 1.14b(1), 1.19, 2.14c, 3.10a, 4.6b, 5.2a, 5.28c, 6.3a, and 7.23 copyright © 1993 Cambridge Univ. Press. Reprinted with the permission of Cambridge Univ. Press.

Figures 1.6, 2.14d, 3.7a, 3.7b, 5.19c, and 8.12a reprinted from *The Documentary History of the Supreme Court of the United States* edited by Maeva Marcus and James R. Perry. Copyright © 1985 by Columbia Univ. Press. Reprinted with permission of the publisher. Figures 5.5a, 5.11e, and 5.21b reprinted from *The Papers of Alexander Hamilton* edited by Harold C. Syrett, et al. Copyright © 1969, 1979 by Columbia Univ. Press. Reprinted with permission of the publisher.

Figures 5.15b and 8.13 copyright © 1980 by Cornell Univ. Figure 7.14b copyright © 1978 by Cornell Univ. Used by permission of the publisher, Cornell Univ. Press.

Figures 2.14b, 7.19d, 8.22e, and 9.10 used with the permission of the Emma Goldman Papers and Chadwyck-Healey.

Figures 4.16a and 4.16b used with the permission of the Eugene V. Debs Foundation and the Cunningham Memorial Library of Indiana State Univ.

Figure 3.13e used with the permission of Excellent Books.

Figure 6.15c used with the permission of the Florida Historical Society and E. O. Painter Printing Company.

Figure 9.13c used with permission of Fordham Univ. Press.

Figure 3.6a used with the permission of Garland Publishing, Inc.

Figure 5.20a used with the permission of Greenhill Books.

Figures 2.7c, 5.36a, 6.8a, and 8.11a from *John Jay* edited by Richard B. Morris, et al. Copyright © 1975, 1980 Harper and Row. Reprinted with permission of HarperCollins Publishers.

Figures 1.4b and 8.14b reprinted from *The Adams Family Correspondence* edited by L. H. Butterfield, et al. Cambridge, Mass.: Belknap Press of Harvard Univ. Press, copyright © 1963 by the President and Fellows of Harvard College. Reprinted by permission of the publisher. Figure 5.20b reprinted from *The Book of Abigail and John: Selected Letters of the Adams Family, 1762–1784* edited by L. H. Butterfield, Marc Friedlaender, and Mary-Jo Kline. Cambridge, Mass.: Harvard Univ. Press, copyright © 1975 by the President and Fellows of Harvard College. Reprinted by permission of the publisher. Figure 2.14a reprinted from *The Diary and Autobiography of John Adams* edited by L. H. Butterfield, Leonard C. Faber, and Wendell D. Garrett. Cambridge, Mass.: Belknap Press of Harvard Univ. Press, copyright © 1961 by the President and Fellows of Harvard College. Reprinted by permission of the publisher. Figure 9.2b reprinted from *The Diary of Charles Francis Adams* edited by Aida DiPace Donald et al. Cambridge, Mass.: Belknap Press of Harvard Univ. Press, copyright © 1986 by the President and Fellows of Harvard College. Reprinted by permission of the publisher. Figure 2.15b reprinted from *The Legal Papers of John Adams* edited by L. Kinvin Wroth and Hiller B. Zobel. Cambridge, Mass.: Belknap Press of Harvard Univ. Press, copyright © 1965 by the President and Fellows of Harvard College. Reprinted by permission of the publisher.

Figures 5.3c, 5.15c, 5.32, 6.15a, 7.10b, 7.16b, 8.7a, and 8.7b used with the permission of Northeastern Univ. Press.

Figure 8.18b used with the permission of the Peabody Essex Museum and Harvard Univ. Press.

Figure 5.13 used with the permission of Picton Press.

Figure 1.5b used with the permission of Primary Source Media, Inc. (Research Publications International), Dr. Remmel Nunn, Publisher.

Figures 2.9, 4.10b, 4.19a, 6.6e, 7.28b, and 8.10 reprinted from *The Collected Papers of Albert Einstein* edited by John Stachel et al. Copyright © 1987, 1993 by Hebrew Univ. of Jerusalem. Reprinted by permission of Princeton Univ. Press. Figures 1.3a, 2.6b, 2.20d, 4.15b, 5.16b, 5.26a, 5.37b, 7.22b, 9.12d, and 9.18d reprinted from *The Papers Of Woodrow Wilson* edited by Arthur Link et al. Copyright © 1966, 1977, 1979, 1984, 1985. Vol. 1 renewed 1994. Reprinted by permission of Princeton Univ. Press. Figures 5.7a, 5.26d, 5.28a, and 9.12c reprinted from *Political Correspondence and Public Papers of Aaron Burr* edited by Mary-Jo Kline et al. Copyright © 1983 by Princeton Univ. Press. Reprinted by permission of Princeton Univ. Press. Figures 3.13d, 5.13f, and 7.22a reprinted from *The Papers of Thomas Jefferson* edited by Julian P. Boyd et al. Copyright © 1950. Renewed 1978 by Princeton Univ. Press. Reprinted by permission of Princeton Univ. Press. Figure 3.12 reprinted from *Henry D. Thoreau: Journal* edited by John C. Broderick et al. Copyright © 1981 by Princeton Univ. Press. Reprinted by permission of Princeton Univ. Press.

Figure 1.18 used with the permission of the Rock County (Wisconsin) Historical Society.

Figures 7.19b, 8.22c, 8.22d, and 8.22e copyright © 1985 by Rutgers, The State University. Used with the permission of Rutgers Univ.

Figures 1.4a and 8.22a copyright © 1992 by Scholarly Resources, Inc. Reprinted by permission of Scholarly Resources, Inc.

Figures 4.10a, 5.9a, 7.2e, and 7.28a used with the permission of Smithsonian Institution Press.

Figures 3.10b, 5.13c, 5.22a, 6.17a, 7.2a, and 7.17 used with the permission of Southern Illinois Univ. Press. Copyright © 1967 by the Ulysses S. Grant Association.

Figures 2.5b, 2.16a, 2.20c, 3.11a, 3.11b, 4.14d, 4.15a, 4.22a, 4.31, 4.33, 4.35, 5.4c, 5.5c, 5.14a, 5.35b, 5.38, 6.6a, 6.6b, 6.6g, 6.14a, 7.5b, 7.13, 7.19a, 7.31, 8.12d, 9.5b, 9.5c, and 9.18b used with the permission of the State Historical Society of Wisconsin.

Figures 3.8b, 4.30b (text), and 5.8a excerpted with the permission of Twayne Publishers, an imprint of Simon & Schuster Macmillan, from *The Complete Works of Washington Irving*, Henry A. Pochman, General Editor: *Journals and Notebooks,* vol. 1, 1803–1806, edited by Nathalia Wright (Boston: Twayne Publishers, 1975), ISBN: 0-8057-8500-0.

Figures 5.20d and 7.2d used with the permission of the United States Naval Historical Center.

Figures 1.5a, 2.5a, 2.18d, 4.7b, 4.14b, 4.18a, 4.18b, 4.21a, 4.22b, 5.9d, 5.11d, 5.21c, 5.24b, 5.27b, 6.6c, 6.6f, 6.14b, and 7.5a used with the permission of Univ. of California Press.

Figures 2.18a, 3.11c, 4.5b, 4.21b, 5.6b, 5.12b, 5.21a, 5.36b, 8.11b, and 9.13b from *The Papers of James Madison* edited by William T. Hutchinson et al. Chicago: Univ. of Chicago Press. Excerpts from vols. 1, 8, 10 copyright © 1962, 1973, 1977 by The Univ. of Chicago. All rights reserved. Reprinted with the permission of the publisher.

Index

Unless otherwise noted, references are to section numbers, not page numbers. When page numbers are referenced, they are from the Introduction and Preface and are preceded by the abbreviation *p.*

manuscript collections, microfilming of,
2.16
maps
as annotation, 7.17
indexing of, 8.17
transcriptions of, 4.32
marginalia, transcription of, 5.10
mark for signature, 5.6
marriage certificates, 4.19
material objects. *See* artifacts
microforms
advantages and shortcomings
discussed, 1.9, 2.3
annotation in, 7.19
archival order, 2.16
calendar of documents in, 2.24
comprehensive editions as, 1.22
copyright notice for, 9.5
facsimiles of documents in, 3.6
indexing of, 8.20–8.22
provenance notes for, 6.6
publishing historical documents in,
1.9, *p. 19*
with selective book editions, 2.3
title pages and, 9.4
missing information
abstracts summarize, 2.23
annotation supplies, 6.16
date and place information, 5.3
lost document noted, 5.26
text indicated or supplied by editor,
5.21–5.23
Model Editions Partnership, 7.20
multiple copies. *See* variant drafts
multivolume editions
editorial methods statement of, 9.18
indexing, 8.5
Mumford, Lewis, 3.8
music, 4.33

N
names
index of, 8.7
indexing partial, 8.15
newsletters, for publishing documents,
1.18
newspapers
provenance notes for, 6.6
for publishing single documents,
1.18, *p. 19*
as source of documents, 1.21, 4.21
transcription of, 4.13–4.14
nineteenth-century documents, 4.6

notes, editorial. *See* annotation
numbered documents, 8.19

O
objects, three-dimensional, 4.34
obsolete words, 4.4
oral documents, 4.20–4.22
overt emendation, 3.4

P
page headers or page headings. *See*
running heads
pamphlets, publishing documents in, 1.9,
p. 19, p. 24
paragraphing, transcription of irregular,
4.4, 4.5, 4.6, 5.7
periodicals, publishing documents in,
annotation of, 7.8
benefits and drawbacks, 1.9, *p. 19*
editorial statement for, 9.18
single documents suitable for, 1.18
permissions to publish, 1.23, 2.9, 9.5,
p. 19
petitions, 5.6
photographic facsimile, 1.10, 3.6, 3.13,
4.10
photographs, 4.29. *See also* illustrations;
photographic facsimile
placelines. *See* datelines and placelines
planning a project, *p. 18*
portraits, indexing of, 8.12, 8.16
postal markings, 5.27
prefaces (front matter), 9.15
presentation
in expanded transcription, 5.1
facsimile and transcribed documents
compared, 1.10
influenced by prospective audience,
1.11
See also arrangement for publication;
transcription
printed forms, 4.17–4.19. *See also*
machine-created documents
printer's errors, 4.13, 5.16
privacy issues, 1.23, 2.9, *p. 19*
professional documents
papers of careers of as scope of
project, 1.3
transcription of, 4.8–4.11
See also architectural drawings; legal
papers
proofreading, 3.14–3.16, *p. 21*
provenance notes, 6.4–6.6, 7.2, *p. 22*